BOATS & SHIPWRECKS OF
IRELAND

COLIN BREEN
AND WES FORSYTHE

TEMPUS

For our colleagues in the Centre for Maritime Archaeology, University of Ulster, and in the Underwater Archaeology Unit (DEHLG), Dublin

Illustrations compiled under the direction of Claire Callaghan

First published 2004

Tempus Publishing Ltd
The Mill, Brimscombe Port
Stroud, Gloucestershire GL5 2QG
www.tempus-publishing.com

British Library Cataloguing in Publication Data.
A catalogue record for this book is available from the British Library.

ISBN 0 7524 3122 6

Typesetting and origination by Tempus Publishing.
Printed and bound in Great Britain.

CONTENTS

PREFACE

The archaeological study of ships and boats in Ireland is in its infancy. Constraints imposed by technology have resulted in the means to find and visit underwater sites becoming available only within the last 50 years. The attitudes of professional archaeologists to the potential and significance of underwater finds have also contributed to the marginalisation of maritime archaeology. Nevertheless from time to time finds relating to boats and shipping have been reported by antiquarians and interested individuals and have found their way into our local journals and newspapers. More recently, concerted efforts have been made to investigate individual shipwreck sites and to study our indigenous traditions of boat-building. Recognition by government and academic institutions of the importance of maritime archaeology has been gained within the last 10 years and has led to research programs aimed at assessing the maritime resource and legislation designed to protect it.

This book aims to provide a broad introduction to the archaeology of vessels in Irish waters by reviewing the types of evidence available and presenting a survey of past work in this field. It will become immediately obvious to the reader that many periods of our past are scantily represented by physical evidence. It is our hope however that this paucity of evidence will challenge archaeologists to begin to address the more thorny and exciting questions raised by the archaeological record – in particular the use of sewn planked boats and Romano-Celtic boats in Irish prehistory, the possibility of a pre-Viking clinker-built tradition, and the discovery of more consolidated medieval wrecks. After 1400, documentary sources expand and give us a fuller account of the vessels in use around our coast. These reveal the existence of both Irish and foreign vessels engaged in trade, piracy, transport and war. Although Ireland was not a major ship-builder until the nineteenth century, many of the advances in shipbuilding technology are witnessed in the vessels visiting our shores. As such the Irish wreck record is well represented by the major ship types and a broader discussion of their historical context is then possible.

As Irish maritime archaeologists working in governmental, academic and commercial fields enlarge our knowledge of ships and boats, this book will likely become out of date within a short time. In the meantime we would ask that they forgive any errors of fact or interpretation on our part. Thanks are due to our friends, family and colleagues for their support and opinions. In particular we wish to acknowledge the contribution of the Underwater Archaeology Unit formerly of *Dúchas* – The Heritage Service, now the Department of the Environment, Heritage and Local Government who funded the early research and reviewing of this book. Our thanks go specifically to Olive Alcock for her patience and hard work in editing this volume, David Sweetman, formerly chief archaeologist with *Dúchas* who initiated this project and many others; thanks also to Fionnbarr Moore, Connie Kelleher and Karl Brady of the underwater unit who are now leading this work in the Republic of Ireland. At the University of Ulster; Kilian McDaid, Lisa Rogers and Nigel McDowell for their graphics work. We also wish to thank Aidan O'Sullivan at University College Dublin for his comments on the text and support, and Dr Niall Brady and Donal Boland for their contributions. Thanks to Lar Dunne for information and please excuse us if we have forgotten anyone else.

Colin Breen and Wes Forsythe
January 2004

INTRODUCTION

It is surprising that as an island nation we have paid little attention to our maritime heritage. The popular perception of this country's heritage is of the heroic Celtic period, romantic castles and ruined monasteries while the traditions of our coast have been effectively ignored. Yet people have lived on and around our coast for over 9,000 years, exploiting its resources and using the sea as a means of transport and communication *(1)*. Until relatively recently there has been great continuity of tradition along the coast with, for example, the methods of fishing changing little over the millennia. Consequently, people still live at the landfalls and harbours that would have been known to the original settlers. It is only since the nineteenth century, with growing industrial activity, that profound changes have been witnessed in these traditions. The decline in the use of traditional boats and the decay of many local piers and quays around the coast is clear evidence of this.

Boats and ships have played a pivotal part in the lives of coastal peoples from the earliest times. They were necessary for trade and transport and provided a means of making a living. Different types of boats were evident in different parts of the country, reflecting adaptations to local environments as well as to local needs. In medieval times, ships and foreign-trading vessels were common at the larger ports where they played a central role in the maintenance of the economy as well as supporting war and conflict. Few of these wooden vessels survive today as, like all organic materials, they rapidly disintegrated once abandoned to the elements. However, if a vessel was lost underwater, and especially in estuarine muds or sands, its chances of survival and preservation into the present day, albeit in an incomplete form, are greatly enhanced. It is as a result of such losses that we have an important historical boat and ship resource preserved in our coastal and inland waters. This component of our heritage has just recently been recognised, having previously lacked the visibility which the terrestrial archaeological resource enjoys. As a result of the developments in diving and underwater survey technology, this disparity is now beginning to be addressed.

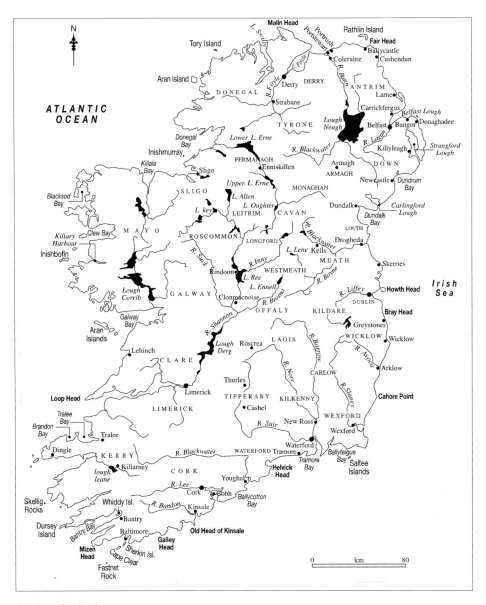

1 Map of Ireland

HISTORY OF RESEARCH

People have long been fascinated with the underwater world but up until the last 50 years it was for the most part inaccessible and unexplored. Through the centuries various ways of entering this realm have been devised, with inventions ranging from the innovative to the ridiculous. In the early seventeenth century Jacob Johnson, a Dutch salvage diver, became well known in Irish waters for his salvage work on a number of important wreck sites off the

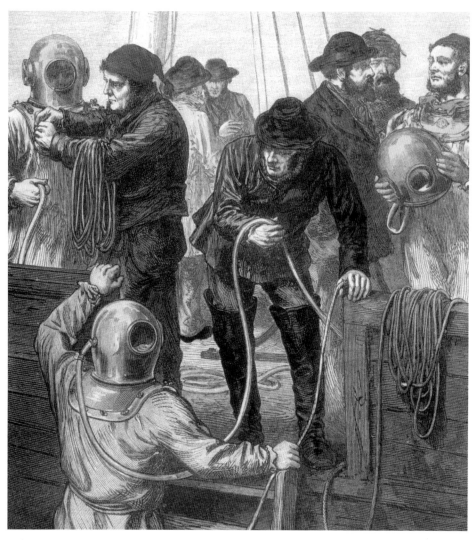

2 Nineteenth-century illustration of divers at work. *Museum of Diving and Underwater Exploration*

western seaboard.[1] By the early nineteenth century, divers such as the Dean brothers achieved fame through their underwater work on the historic sites of the *Royal George* and the *Mary Rose* off the south coast of England.[2] Antiquarian interest in sites under water developed, especially in relation to lake sites, when W.G. Wood-Martin, a captain in the English army, carried out extensive research on Irish lake habitation sites.[3] However, underwater exploration was severely limited by the nature of the diving equipment that was available at this time *(2)*. Standard dress, consisting of a large brass helmet, heavy lead boots, a canvas suit and air pumped from the surface, limited the amount of work that could be carried out and the depth to which a diver could descend.

It was only with the development of Self-Contained Underwater Breathing Apparatus (SCUBA) by French engineers during the Second World War that underwater exploration by scientists and interested non-professionals became viable. For the first time, divers could move about freely underwater, with fins and light-weight gear. The development of the aqualung led to an upsurge in people taking up the sport of diving and, in turn, various scientific disciplines such as marine biology and seabed geology were transformed. This development of underwater science also saw the emergence of underwater archaeological investigations. Many of the techniques of this new discipline were pioneered in the 1960s on sites in the Mediterranean and the Caribbean by individuals like George Bass from the Institute of Nautical Archaeology at Texas A&M University and Peter Throckmorton.[4] Techniques from land excavations were simply adapted by these early pioneers to the underwater environment, ensuring that underwater sites were investigated to the same standard as those on land. As a consequence of the success and proven viability of investigations on these sites, underwater archaeological investigations quickly spread to other regions.

Sub-aqua clubs (SACs) were first established in Ireland in the early 1960s and were responsible, in their early years, for the discovery of many of the wrecks around our coast. Some were found on the advice of fishermen who knew the wreck locations as areas of foul ground, while others were located after many hours of research and through a process of trial and error. The emergence of diving as a sport coincided with the beginnings of the Archaeological Survey of Ireland under the auspices of the Office of Public Works (OPW) in 1963. The initial priority of the survey was to record and survey earthworks and prehistoric monuments; medieval monuments were included from the 1970s. Sites on the seabed and below the marine high-water mark were excluded for a number of reasons. There was a common perception at the time that underwater sites simply did not survive in the harsh and dynamic waters which surround this island. The few known sites, like the Spanish Armada wrecks, were not considered part of our national heritage and were excluded on these grounds. The feeling was that the material from these wrecks had accidentally ended up in our waters and, therefore, played no part in the material culture of the State. However, while the State professed no interest in underwater sites, a number of individuals and clubs initiated exciting and archaeologically important projects. Des Brannigan, Colin Martin, Robert Stenuit and the City of Derry SAC were all involved with investigations on various Spanish Armada wrecks. The results of their work highlighted the rewards that underwater investigations could yield.

In 1980 the Archaeological Survey of Ireland began a crannóg (ancient lake dwelling) survey in an attempt to list all such sites in the country. The survey, while extensive, was limited to observations made above water and did not involve diving or the examination of the sites underwater. In 1983 the

National Museum of Ireland (NMI) and the National Monuments Service (NMS) of the OPW, along with Robert Farrell of Cornel University in the United States, undertook a survey of Cró-inish on Lough Ennel, Co. Westmeath. This survey was supported by underwater investigations and led to the creation of the Crannóg Archaeology Project (CAP) in 1987.[5] Many non-professional Irish divers became involved with the project, which investigated other archaeological sites, including the find sites of a number of logboats and that of the Lough Lene boat in Co. Westmeath. The project also assisted in underwater surveys at a number of excavations, including an OPW excavation at Clough Oughter Castle, Co. Cavan, and a NMI excavation of an Iron Age burial at Lough Lene.[6] Personnel from these surveys were also involved with excavations on the sites of a number of fording points in the midlands under the direction of Eamonn Kelly and Niall Brady from the NMI. An excavation in advance of a bridge development on the River Boyne, Co. Meath, was also carried out at this time. These excavations produced an assortment of artefactual material highlighting the importance of river-crossing points as areas of trade, conflict and possible settlement.

Staff from the NMI were also involved in the investigation of a number of marine sites. Trained diving staff began working in close co-operation with *Comhairle Fó-Thuinn* (CFT), the largest sport-diving body in Ireland, affiliated to the *Confederation Mondiale des Activities Subaquatiques* (CMAS), the international governing body for sport diving. A number of projects were undertaken on nineteenth-century wreck sites, including the *John Tayleur* off Lambay Island, the *Victoria* off Dublin and the *Aid* off Wicklow. These were investigated by divers from Trinity College Dublin.[7] Survey work was also undertaken on a Spanish Armada site, *La Trinidad Valencera*, in 1989 following the exposure of a gun carriage, and some in-situ conservation work was undertaken.[8] New wreck sites were continually being brought to the attention of the authorities. For example, the French frigate *La Surveillante*, wrecked in 1797, was found during sonar sweeps in Bantry Bay following the *Betelgeuse* disaster in 1981.[9] In 1988-'90, the Leinster Divers Group recovered artefacts from the wreck of a possible Dutch West Indiaman, as well as another Spanish Armada site in Broadhaven Bay, Co. Mayo. Throughout this period the NMI was also involved in the recovery and investigation of a number of anchors and cannon retrieved by fishermen and divers.

In 1987 the Maritime Institute, an independent and voluntary research body based in the Maritime Museum in Dún Laoghaire, and CFT set up committees on underwater archaeology. Both committees amalgamated in 1989 to form the Irish Underwater Archaeological Research Team (IUART). This was an island-wide organisation made up primarily of sports divers, with representatives from the State bodies with responsibility for underwater archaeology sitting on its committee in an advisory capacity. The primary purpose of IUART was to develop the discipline of underwater archaeology in Ireland through education and project-based research. Its educational drive has been most successful through its training programme, which was adopted from that of the Nautical Archaeology Society in the United Kingdom. The team has carried out many projects ranging from wreck surveys at Derrynane, Co. Kerry, to crannóg surveys on a number of inland lake sites.

One of the defining moments in the development of underwater archae-ology in this country came with the introduction of the National Monuments (Amendment) Act in 1987. This act placed blanket protection on all sites and artefacts over 100 years old that are covered by water, and it made it illegal to dive on these sites without a licence. Mandatory reporting of artefacts from a site, or of an individual find, was also introduced as the State sought to address the serious emerging problem of underwater treasure hunting. The 1994 National Monuments (Amendment) Act further strengthened the legislation, ensuring that Ireland has one of the most powerful pieces of underwater-heritage legislation in Europe. However, while strong protective legislation was now in place, a number of problems still existed. There was no inventory of underwater marine sites and the State lacked trained personnel who could work underwater and manage the submerged cultural resource effectively. In order to address this problem, the Maritime Sites and Monuments Record (MSMR) was established in February 1997 within the NMS of the then Department of Arts, Culture and the *Gaeltacht*. Its primary aim was to compile an inventory of wreck sites around the coast and to quantify the nature and extent of the underwater resource. It was also set up with the capability to operate as an archaeological diving unit in order to inspect and survey sites as required. The establishment of this unit marked a milestone in the State's rela-tionship with underwater archaeology as, for the first time, there was a dedicated professional unit dealing with the underwater cultural resource (*3*). The establishment of the MSMR came about as a result of a growing awareness within the State's archaeological service of the value and potential of under-water archaeology, something which IUART and the diving bodies have been highlighting over the last few years. Its emergence comes at an opportune time when our coastal waters are witnessing an increase in commercial development and fishing, as both processes will have a negative impact on underwater sites.

In Northern Ireland, government became concerned about maritime archaeology in 1990 with the publication of *This Common Inheritance*, a White Paper on the environment and archaeology.[10] The paper announced proposals for dealing with historic wrecks, which resulted in an Agency Agreement being signed with the Department of National Heritage in 1992. Under the terms of the agreement, the Department of the Environment, Northern Ireland, accepted responsibility for wrecks in its territorial waters under the Protection of Wrecks Act (1973). To date, only one wreck, *La Girona*, has been designated under this Act. In 1993, the then Environment Service: Historic Monuments and Buildings (ES:HMB), now the Environment and Heritage

Service (EHS), initiated the Maritime Archaeology Project (MAP), based at the Institute of Irish Studies at the Queen's University of Belfast. Its initial task was to develop a computerised database of all known underwater wreck sites in Northern Ireland's coastal waters *(4)*. In September 1997 the EHS established the Coastal Research Unit (CRU), staffed by three archaeologists, to provide a maritime archaeological service for the organisation. Its primary role was to expand the MSMR and develop the research of coastal archaeology in the North. A final development was the establishment in the University of Ulster of the Centre for Maritime Archaeology in 1999. The Centre comprises the CRU and university lecturers (in archaeology and geophysics) combining the tasks of survey, protection and research. A detailed programme of near-shore marine geophysics has been developed to compliment and expand the shipwreck record.

THE MARITIME SITES AND MONUMENT RECORD

The establishment of a comprehensive database of all wreck sites in Irish waters was considered a primary task for government in both jurisdictions in Ireland. Both bodies chose the year 1945 as the cut-off date for research. This date may be perceived by some as late for archaeological research but the

3 An archaeologist excavating underwater

continuity of some boat-building traditions in Ireland from the earliest to modern times necessitated it. The date also recognises the revolutionary advances in boat- and ship-building that occurred in the nineteenth century and which continued at an incredible pace throughout both the First and Second World Wars. The large number of vessels which were sunk during this period, either accidentally or deliberately as the result of conflict, is unprecedented in maritime history. Many of these wrecks serve as a physical monument of the terrible consequences of war and its associated loss of life. They are reminders of this nation's proximity to past conflicts and its role in them, whether as an active participant or as a neutral observer. The Maritime Units of the governments regarded the desk-based compilation of references to shipwrecks as the first step in the establishment of the Maritime Record before a full 'field' survey could take place. The preliminary results of these surveys yielded some 7,000 references to shipwrecks in the Republic's waters, and around 3,000 in Northern Ireland.[11] Early statistical analysis of the databases has established a basic pattern of wreckage in Irish waters, with new references being added on an ongoing basis.[12] The development of the databases has also been utilised in a number of regional surveys of shipwreck.[13]

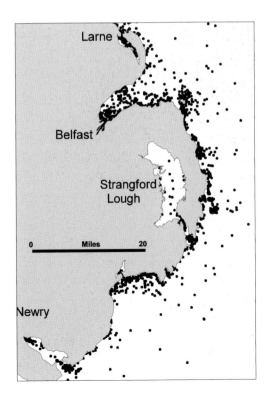

4 Wreck distribution map of east Ulster.
CMA, UUC

15

DOCUMENTARY SOURCES

Documentary sources were of primary importance to the surveys, although cartographic and illustrative material was also examined. The majority of sources relate to post-medieval wrecks and include the papers of the High Courts of the British and Irish Admiralties, *Lloyd's List*, national and local newspapers and British Parliamentary papers. Some of the wrecks noted in these sources had already been collected by Edward Bourke, Ian Wilson and Charles Hocking.[14]

Researching medieval and earlier wrecks was more difficult. The various annalistical sources contain some brief references to wrecks, mainly the result of military skirmishes.[15] The extent of the Viking influence on the maritime traditions of this country is reflected in the chroniclers' writings after AD 800, when numerous accounts of voyages and marine incidents are noted, and occasional references are made to wrecks. The records must be approached with caution as many appear to be exaggerated or fanciful accounts of wreckage, for example the 'fleet' lost in AD 923 in Dundrum Bay, Co. Down.[16] This is true of annalistical writings throughout the medieval period with only a handful of vague but important shipwreck accounts, for example the sea battle between 'the foreigners of Ath-cliath' and Niall, son of the King of Ulster.[17] The foreigners (Vikings) were defeated and their ships 'carried away', implying that the Irish fleet had gained superiority at sea in vessels capable of challenging the Norsemen.

Other medieval texts similarly contain limited information relating to shipwrecks. The *Calendar of State Papers relating to Ireland* is an invaluable source of information for medieval history, which notes a few instances of wrecking. Even the wrecking of over 25 Spanish vessels off the north and western coasts in 1588 warrants little attention and is mentioned merely in passing. When a wreck is mentioned it is generally as an aside and is usually related to arguments over salvage rights for goods or for vessels washed up or brought ashore.

The High Court of the British Admiralty was probably set up sometime in the middle of the fourteenth century in England. It operated on a limited basis over the following 150 years before it was re-established in the early 1500s. It was primarily concerned with dealing with cases of piracy and with problems arising from maritime transactions. An Irish Admiralty court was set up in Dublin in the 1570s and vice-admirals were appointed to oversee the four provinces. Extensive records for the court survive for the later medieval period and are an invaluable source for the study of maritime history. References to wrecks are common, as are records of salvage and ownership rights to the same. [18]

In the late seventeenth century Edward Lloyd began a short news-sheet called *Lloyd's News* which provided general intelligence on current affairs and the news of the day. Lloyd died in 1713 but another news-sheet inspired by his publication appeared in the 1730s which specifically wrote on shipping news and affairs, including shipwrecks. It was entitled *Lloyd's List*. This news-sheet, which was published twice a week, detailed instances of shipping loss around the world, but was particularly useful for information on wrecking around Britain and Ireland. The news-sheet continued to be produced throughout the eighteenth and nineteenth centuries and is still published today. It has had a number of competitors throughout its existence including the similarly titled *New Lloyd's List*. However, it remains one of the primary sources of up-to-date shipping information and is an invaluable source of contemporary wreck information. The entries in the paper tend to be brief and very general and include the ship's name, its master, voyage and cargo details, and its place of loss, generally given as the bay or stretch of coast where it floundered. More detailed information on wrecks of the last three centuries can be found in local newspapers' archives. Many of these newspapers are simply political pamphlets dealing with the main issues of the day but they often contain references to wrecks and provide more detailed information than the daily national papers. The local newspapers are particularly good for relating information on nineteenth-century wrecks, when they often carry the story through from the wrecking incident to any subsequent salvage or rescue attempts.

In the early nineteenth century the British Parliament became very concerned about the extent of ship loss, as the number of vessels and amount of cargo being lost was having an adverse effect on the economy. There was some concern too over the large loss of life associated with wrecking incidents but it appears that the economic impact was of primary importance. Parliament established a number of Committees of Inquiry to investigate the cause of these losses, the first of which reported back in 1834. The information regarding ship loss in this report was presented in statistical graph form and does not contain information on individual vessels *(5)*. It does confirm that the extent of wrecking in the second half of the nineteenth century matched that of the first half. In the 1850s annual lists of wrecks began to appear in the House of Commons Sessional Papers. These figures were initially provided by the Admiralty, but were supplied by the Board of Trade from 1855 onwards. The wreck lists are extensive and contain information on wrecking worldwide but with an obvious concentration on Britain and Ireland. The individual entries are, however, short, usually detailing the ship's name, its date of loss, place of loss, cargo, crew details and cause of loss. As with *Lloyd's List*, the place of loss is given only in general terms and does not include a latitude/longitude position or localised details. Later in the century the entries became more comprehensive including voyage details and, in many cases, abbreviated details of the official inquiry into the loss of the vessel. Information on strandings was also included whereby a vessel was not a total loss and this information was supplied in list form on a geographical basis. Extensive lists continued to be published up until the start of the First World War. Little was published during the war as it was felt that such information would undermine the war effort

5 British Parliamentary Papers chart showing shipwrecks off the coast of Britain and Ireland between 1852-1856

and general morale, as well as boosting the enemies' confidence. A similar strategy was adopted during the Second World War but detailed war losses were published in the House of Commons Papers after both wars. Two institutions formed primarily to preserve life at sea, the Royal National Lifeboat Institution (RNLI) and Trinity House, have also kept details on wrecking and casualties at sea but their records date primarily from the twentieth century.

In more recent times there has been a great upsurge of interest in wreck sites and underwater exploration. Diving is now a very popular pastime in this country and a wide range of publications are being produced in connection with the sport. The Irish Underwater Council (CFT), the governing body for the largest group of sports divers in the country, produces a quarterly magazine, *Subsea*, which frequently contains articles on wrecks off the coast and on underwater exploration in general. Articles dealing with wreck sites continue to appear in newspapers, academic papers and journals as fascination with the subject continues to grow.

HYDROGRAPHIC/CARTOGRAPHIC SOURCES

The primary source for data on the actual location of wreck sites is the British Admiralty's wreck office based at Taunton in Somerset. The British Admiralty has been carrying out hydrographic surveys of the coast of Ireland since the early nineteenth century and it has extensive records on wrecks encountered during the course of these surveys *(6)*. The Admiralty has details on 950 wrecks in Irish waters with 494 currently charted and 456 uncharted. The wreck section has maintained a wreck index since 1913 and continually updates hydrographic charts with the information it has stored on file. The need to record the position of wrecks as accurately as possible was recognised at an early stage as they constitute a hazard to shipping. Once a wreck has ceased being a hazard, having either disintegrated naturally or been cleared away, it becomes a 'dead' wreck and is no longer included in chart updates. However, even if a wreck is no longer standing proud of the seabed, it may have collapsed onto itself or have become buried in the sediment and so is still of interest to the archaeologist. Wrecks on old charts are, therefore, a valuable addition to the MSMR.

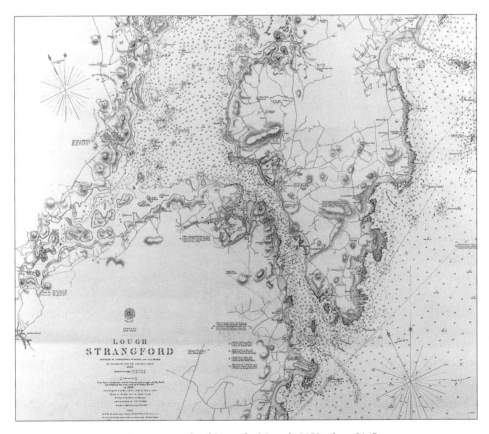

6 Hydrographic map showing mouth of Strangford Lough 1859, chart 2165

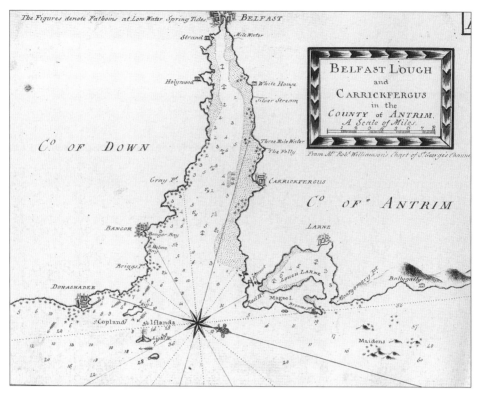

7 Chart of Belfast Lough and Carrickfergus, Co. Antrim from Robert Williamson's Chart of St George's Channel dating to 1774

The first comprehensive hydrographic survey of Ireland was carried out by Murdoch McKenzie in the latter part of the eighteenth century. Although the charts produced contain little if anything relating to wreck sites, they do contain valuable bathymetric and current information. British Admiralty surveys of the Irish coastline have been ongoing since the early part of the nineteenth century. The bathymetric data on these charts is one of the primary 'field' sources of information for the maritime archaeologist, supplying information on seabed topography and the nature of the coast. The older charts, in particular, can be used to trace coastal erosion and features of interest to mariners of the day, including navigation marks and anchorages (7).

Ordnance Survey maps were checked as they record coastal monuments such as weirs, landing places, beacons and details of port evolution. A number of the maps mark the location of wreck sites such as the site of the *Thetis*, which stranded in 1834 and was marked on sheet 1 of the six-inch to one-mile maps for Co. Kerry. Place names such as Galley Head, Co. Cork, can also be used as indicators of the location of a wreck site. The name *Port-na-Spaniagh*, or Port of the Spaniards, was instrumental in locating the Spanish Armada site *La Girona* in Co. Antrim. Large-scale maps accompany the wreck lists in the

8 Salvage operations on a schooner lost at Strangford, Co. Down, *c.*1885. *Courtesy of Ulster Folk and Transport Museum*

Commons Sessional Papers. Black dots are used to indicate the position of wrecks mentioned in the text but the large scale of the maps invalidates precise locational information.

Illustrative and pictorial sources were also consulted with the National library's nineteenth- and twentieth-century photographic collections being especially useful *(8)*. These include a range of depictions of shipwrecks on manuscripts such as Burghley's 1589 map of Sligo, which clearly shows three Armada ships breaking up on Streedagh Strand.[19] Photographic material, such as the Lawrence Collection, contains many images of ports and harbours at the turn of the twentieth century, including abandoned or stricken vessels.

CHARACTER OF THE COAST

The shipwreck resource can be better assessed with an understanding of Ireland's varied 6,331km coastline. Most wreck sites in these waters will quickly disintegrate to a fraction of their original form through the processes of erosion and chemical and biological breakdown. The majority of wrecks

9 Wreck of the *Pintail*, lost in 1949. *Photograph: W. Forsythe*

10 Wreck of the *Trafalgar*, lost mid-nineteenth century. *Photograph: W. Forsythe*

will eventually reach a state of equilibrium with the underwater environment, which can range from a cannon and anchor spread in a rocky gully to a partially preserved hull buried in muddy sediments. The site's environment is an important predictive factor in what the diving archaeologist should expect when investigating a site. The breakdown of any vessel is accelerated by high-energy marine environments, for example a site lying on a rocky bed below an exposed western cliff *(9)*. Low-energy environments, for example within a sheltered muddy bay, will slow deterioration and may even have a preservative effect on buried components *(10)*. Both processes mean that many early wrecks have not been found during the charting and mapping of the coast. The survey equipment would not be capable of detecting or recognising them, either because they were buried or were fragmented on the seabed, having blended into their surroundings. It is possible to identify a number of typical site-types for the state of wrecks around Ireland and a cautious categorisation is listed below. These types are very general and can only be properly defined when local environmental conditions and topographical factors have been taken into account.

A   Recent wrecks, iron or wooden, lost within 50 years of the present, which are almost wholly complete and beginning the process of disintegration.

B   Iron or composite wrecks lost within the last 100 years with the hull partially or wholly collapsed.

C1 Iron or composite wrecks lost within the last 100-200 years; wholly collapsed and represented by a barely definable tangle of metal on the seabed.

C2 Iron or composite wrecks lost within the last 200 years and represented by recognisable bu broken wreckage on the seabed.

C3 Iron or composite wrecks lost within the last 200 years represented by a number of isolated structural features like beams or plates etc.

D1 Wooden wrecks lost within the last 200 years sitting on the seabed and in good condition.

D2 Wooden wrecks lying exposed on the seabed and broken down to the lowermost hull.

E1 Historic wooden wrecks lying wholly or partially buried in sediment with much of the hull preserved.

E2 Historic wooden wrecks wholly or partially buried in sediment with little preserved.

F1 Artefactual spreads of material in a low-energy seabed, e.g. within a sheltered bay.

F2 Artefactual spreads in a high-energy environment, e.g. shallow exposed rock gully.

G1 Hulks lying abandoned on the foreshore either wholly or partially intact.

G2 Hulks lying on the foreshore and eroded to the lowermost hull.

G3 Hulks lying on the foreshore and exposed occasionally.

Table 1: Wreck types in Irish coastal waters

A wreck lost off the Skelligs Rock, Co. Kerry, for example, will undergo very different site formation processes than a wreck lost in Wexford Harbour.

The variation of factors affecting our shipwrecks can be highlighted by a brief summary of the morphology of the Irish coast. The east coast from Co. Antrim's Fair Head to Larne is predominantly rocky with high cliffs occasionally interspersed with shallow bays. Larne Lough and Belfast Lough are both sheltered sea loughs with mud bottoms and large areas of intertidal mudflats. The coastline of north Down is rocky and borders Strangford Lough which is almost land-locked. The Lough opens through a deep, narrow entrance to the Irish Sea. Its inner shore is rocky with large tracts of mudflats and it has a deep shingle and mud bottom. Dundrum Bay, south of Strangford, is a large, open sandy bay backed by extensive dune systems while a low-lying rocky coastline leads from Dundrum to Carlingford Lough. The coast from Carlingford to Wicklow is generally low-lying. Dundalk Bay is a large, sheltered, shallow bay with extensive salt marshes adjacent to the entrance of its port. Its bottom type is predominantly sandy mud, becoming more muddy in the inshore area. Moving southwards, tidal strengths increase approaching the mouth of the River Boyne, Co. Meath, which features extensive intertidal areas, both within and to the north and south of the estuary. There are extensive sandy beaches and areas of salt marsh north of Dublin Bay and this is paralleled offshore where the bottom type is predominantly sand. Large sand flats dominate the shallow southern half of Dublin Bay, while the coastline from Greystones to Wicklow consists largely of a shingle beach. This is a sheltered coast with strong tides, sand banks and deposits of gravel lying offshore. The offshore banks include the Burford and Codling Banks off Dublin and the Arklow, Blackwater and Long Banks further south. Wexford is the major port of the south-east. The town is situated in a large, low energy, tidal inlet with extensive mudflats and intertidal zones. Much of the coastline is soft and under threat of erosion from very strong tides which race past the country's south-eastern tip, marked by Tuskar Rock. Here the seabed is predominately made up of gravelly sand.

The morphology of the south coast is similar to the low-lying eastern seaboard through south Wexford, however, it soon becomes a much harsher coastal environment. Extensive sand-dune systems at Ballyteigue lead to Bannow Bay, which is a large tidal inlet similar to Wexford. The shore and seabed become increasingly rocky after the Saltees and the sea cliffs west of Waterford can be over 60m high. The rocky coastline continues into Cork with high cliffs at the Old Head of Kinsale and Old Helvick Head. Cork Harbour is a wide, natural harbour with areas of intertidal muds and salt marsh with a seabed of gravelly mud. The west Cork and Kerry coast is made up of mountainous peninsulas with wide, open bays and numerous islands. The shoreline is mostly rocky with areas of salt marsh at Courtmacsherry, Co. Cork. Extensive dune systems, salt marsh and intertidal flats are also present at Tralee Bay and Brandon Bay, Co. Kerry. Currents and tide strengths are predominantly variable, though strong tides are evident at Mizen Head and around Dursey Island, Co. Cork, particularly through the Sound. The deep waters off the south coast contrast sharply with the shallow, gently sloping seabed of the east coast and depths in excess of 50m are reached very quickly.

Moving up the west coast, the Shannon tidal estuary stretches 80km inland and has the largest areas of intertidal mudflats in Ireland.[20] By contrast the west Clare coast is predominantly rocky with high cliffs at Loop Head and Moher. Extensive sand dunes are also evident at both Lahinch and at Fanore. Galway Bay is a sheltered, shallow bay protected from the full force of the Atlantic by the Aran Islands. Its coastline is largely low-lying with some areas of salt marsh and intertidal muds. The coast of Connemara and Mayo is heavily indented with rocky bays and inlets while Clew Bay's numerous islands indicate that it is a drowned glacial landscape. The deep fjord at Killary is bordered by a rocky shoreline and has a muddy, silty bottom. Killala Bay on the other hand has extensive areas of mudflats and is bordered in places by sand dune systems. Most of the seabed off this region is dominated by rock and sand deposits. Donegal's coastline is rocky and indented with large sand deposits offshore. Donegal Bay is relatively shallow and sheltered but high cliffs are present in a number of areas northwards from Malin Bay which bear the full brunt of Atlantic storms. Large storm shingle beaches near Bloody Foreland testify to the strength of these events.

North of Bloody Foreland the coast of Donegal features cliffs interspersed with beach systems and bays. Both Lough Swilly and Lough Foyle are large sea loughs and both are sheltered with large areas of intertidal muds and sands. Long beaches backed by low dune systems stretch from Magillan Point to Portstewart and Portrush where they meet the high cliffs of the Antrim coast. The seabed is deeper off the northern coast and retains a rocky and sandy character.

Ireland's wet climate creates a profusion of freshwater systems that have long been recognised as archaeologically important elements of the landscape. The country has over 4,000 lakes of varying sizes (most less than 100ha) and over 13,500km of main river channels. The environments of these freshwater bodies vary from fast-flowing mountain streams, to still, peaty lakes. Evidence for settlement in proximity to these systems is found from early prehistory to the present day in a variety of monuments, while the association of these places with ritual and the otherworld is recognised through the many votive offerings that have been recovered from these contexts. These bodies of water also offered a means of communication and many vessels that would have disintegrated on the coast have survived in gentler freshwater environments.

The boats and ships that have travelled, traded, fished, fought and ultimately been lost in our waters are rich aspects of our heritage. The efforts of a small number of interested and persistent individuals have demonstrated that our seas, rivers and loughs are capable of preserving prehistoric craft, medieval planked vessels and Armada treasures. Secondary evidence points to a vigorous and evolving shipping tradition expressed in art, documentary sources and sculpture. Recognition of this resource has in recent years led to an appreciation of the potential of underwater archaeology and, accordingly, legislation has been introduced to protect and preserve these sites despite intense commercial pressures. For all the work that has taken place, we are only beginning to understand the range and importance of our shipwrecks and the extent to which they can inform our knowledge of our ancestors' activities, beliefs and aspirations. It is to be hoped that the initial excitement and enthusiasm generated by the discoveries of pioneers in this field can be maintained and that the study of our underwater archaeology is consolidated by the research and interest of professionals and amateurs alike. The success of these measures, and the small number of underwater archaeology specialists at work in the country remains to be seen.

ONE

THE PREHISTORIC PERIOD
c.7000 BC - AD 400

MESOLITHIC (*c.*7000–4000 BC)

Ireland does not appear to have been inhabited by humans until after the last Ice Age, around 9,000 years ago. This initial phase of occupation occurred in the Mesolithic period, which has been divided into two phases in Ireland, based on a change in artefact type. The main evidence for Mesolithic settlement takes the form of scatters of stone tools and middens of domestic debris such as shells. The first inhabitants were hunter-gathers, living primarily on fish, fruit, nuts and meat. They produced a variety of stone tools, from small microliths in the early Mesolithic, to larger blades later in the period. Many of their sites have been located along riverbanks, lake shores and the coast, which would have allowed the full exploitation of local resources. An important example of such a site is our earliest, Mount Sandel in Co. Derry, located on the eastern bank of the River Bann and dating to around 7000–6500 BC.[1]

Due to our island status, the most obvious and immediate questions that arise concern the means by which the first colonists arrived and where they came from. The early Mesolithic colonists must have travelled across water as it appears that around 10,000 years ago there was no longer a land-bridge connecting Ireland to Britain.[2] Although this date is not uniformly accepted by all scholars, there is little evidence for a post-glacial land-bridge that lasted for any significant length of time.[3] While sea levels were lower than present, our first inhabitants would have had to cross a stretch of open water. What actually drove these early peoples to set out in their boats remains a speculative question. There may have been a number of reasons, such as population or resource pressure and the opportunity to exploit new territory. Ireland would have been clearly visible from Britain, notably from north Wales towards the south Leinster area and from south-west Scotland or northern England and the Isle of Man to east Ulster. The latter is the entry route favoured by Woodman, being the shorter crossing and featuring prominent landmarks. In addition the two regions display some artefactual parallels, albeit limited.[4] Indeed a conspicuous difficulty with this period is the lack of material comparisons with British sites implying that once colonisation was complete there was little contact across the Irish Sea. Nevertheless the initial crossings could have been achieved in a matter of hours in a small rowed or paddled craft. It is likely that they would only have taken place in the most favourable conditions, and so were probably infrequent. Suggestions as to what types of boats were used for crossing remains conjectural, but some ideas may be gleaned by examining the evidence available from other parts of Northern Europe, where dugout boats, bark- and skin-covered craft appear to have been in use. Although the Irish currach is one of the few European survivals of skin-covered craft, they are the

11 Currach. *Photograph: R. McConkey*

12 Lough Eskragh dugout boat. *After Collins and Seaby 1960*

most difficult to address *(11)*. While making superb sea-going craft, skin boats melt away rather quickly once abandoned, leaving a notable bias in the archaeological record. In Ireland, the vessels are constructed upside down, the gunwale is formed first, then the frames (laths or withies) and stringers are inserted. Finally, the vessel is covered in hides, which would have originally been secured by thongs.[5] McGrail has noted that by the Mesolithic period the tools and techniques for making skin boats of reasonable size would have been in place – nevertheless, evidence for them before the Iron Age remains slight.[6] Dugouts or logboats survive more successfully in the European Mesolithic record, that from Pesse in the Netherlands being the oldest at around 6315 BC.[7] Dugout boats are essentially hollowed logs or half-logs *(12)*. The timber is felled, reduced to size and stripped of branches and bark. It is then roughly shaped and the exterior of the boat is formed, or in other cases the vessel is hollowed out first. Holes may be bored into the vessel from the exterior to gauge the thickness of the finished vessel – these will later be plugged by treenails. The vessel may be hollowed-out using tools or fire, the latter method being favoured in Scandinavia. In this case a fire is lit on top of the log and limited by soaking the wood with water, and the charred element is then adzed out. Finally the boat's shape is refined and any further elements are fitted.[8] Ethnographic studies have shown that bark has been employed to cover boats and it has tentatively been suggested that the rolls of bark stored at the 8,000-year-old site of Star Carr in England could have been used to create such vessels.[9] The lakeside settlement produced a birch-wood paddle indicating that boats were in use; however, no evidence of any craft were found and it has been noted that by recent standards the size of the Star Carr rolls would have been inadequate for boat-building.[10]

Skin-covered boats and dugouts have been argued as the more likely form of transport in Irish waters. Although communities using skin-working tools and living in huts supported by lashed saplings would have not have had to take great conceptual leaps to produce skin-covered craft, there is as yet no clear evidence of them in the Irish Mesolithic record. Indeed there is little evidence even for suitable skins in early prehistory – red deer are absent from the faunal assemblages of major Mesolithic sites such as Lough Boora and Mount Sandel.[11] A possible substitute could have been seal skins, which are similar to deer in texture and size and have been used for boat-building in the Arctic.[12] The use of seal skins to construct boats in Ireland is strengthened by the fact that they were used in west Donegal currachs into the eighteenth century.[13] Johnstone has argued that skin boats were in use in Ireland in the late Mesolithic, based on their suitability for sea-going conditions and the subsequent emergence of a powerful skin boat tradition on the island.[14] In addition he cites evidence of deep-sea fishing. Finds of cod from Cushendun, Co. Antrim, imply that appropriate vessels would have been required to catch them.[15] Deep-sea species have also been recovered from Obanian sites in western Scotland, along with a proliferation of skin-working tools as opposed to wood-working implements, both factors arguing against the likelihood of using dugouts. Some European Mesolithic societies, such as the *Ertebølle* culture of Denmark present extensive evidence of marine fishing, as well as the exploitation of inshore resources such as marine molluscs. However, there is little definite evidence of an open sea economy in the Irish Mesolithic. The nature of the fish bones recovered from a number of sites implies the exploitation of inshore areas, rivers and estuaries. Species of marine fish such as cod are known to come inshore when young, and others such as bass are regularly found in freshwater or estuarine environments. At Mount Sandel, faunal evidence suggested that fishing was most common in estuarine and riverine waters.[16] The most common species were migratory fish such as salmon and eel, with sea fish capable of penetrating estuarine waters making up only 1 per cent of the overall bone assemblage. If offshore fishing did take place from a boat, it was of limited importance to a people who for the most part depended on the plentiful fish stocks of the River Bann. At Ferriters Cove in Co. Kerry, 15 species of fish were recovered from a late Mesolithic site. Their size indicated that they were probably a summer resource, caught when inshore, although the larger tope and conger eel made the use of a boat plausible.[17] Boats would, of course, have remained advantageous to fishing in inshore, estuarine or riverine environments, but apart from the colonisation event, there is no real evidence to support the need for long-range sea-going craft during this period. In terms of the Irish lithic assemblage, the presence of Mesolithic core and flake axes for chopping and planing demonstrate that coastal dwellers were working with wood, while tools for skin-working such as burins and scrapers are notably scarce towards the end of the period. The excavations at Mount Sandel produced axes with wear patterns consistent with being mounted transversely in the manner of an adze, a useful tool for shaping dugouts as confirmed by the adze marks on the late Mesolithic logboat from Brookend townland on the shores of Lough Neagh in Co. Tyrone.[18] It has been radiocarbon dated to 5490-5246 BC.[19]

There is a perception that early boats such as dugouts would have been unable to cope with maritime conditions, but in fine weather this would certainly have been feasible. Dugouts were certainly used on large inland lakes such as Lough Neagh and the Fermanagh lakes throughout the prehistoric and historic periods. These are stretches of water that, due to a long fetch, can become very choppy when the wind increases. There are around 350 known examples of logboats in Ireland, of these a small number (about 28) have been dated to the prehistoric period.[20] Most have been recovered from inland loughs and rivers.

NEOLITHIC (*c*.4000-2500 BC)

The Neolithic period saw the introduction of farming techniques and the appearance of a new range of artefacts and burial practices. New techniques were employed to produce stone tools such as pressure-flaked arrowheads, scrapers and high-quality polished stone axes. These tools were used in the clearance of forests where field systems were established for new farms. Cereals such as wheat and barley were introduced and cultivated, while domestic animals such as cattle and sheep were kept for meat and hides. Transporting the new species of animals to Ireland would have involved a sea crossing. The practice of towing animals in the water behind, for example, a currach, is well known around our inshore islands, however for such long and arduous journeys it is more realistic to envisage young, tethered animals lying in the floor of the boat. Also associated with this period are the large burial monuments known as megalithic tombs. Megalithic art, characterised by a

13 Scandinavian rock art of
a boat at Bjornstad,
Skjeberg, Norway. *After
Johnstone 1980*

series of abstract geometric designs and symbols, is a feature of many of the
tombs. This contrasts sharply with the rock carvings of northern Europe where
images of boats are very common and are one of the most recognisable features
of this early 'arctic art' *(13)*. At the Norwegian site of Evenhus and on the
banks of the River Vyg in Russia, fishing communities depicted vessels that
have been variously interpreted as skin-covered boats or dugouts.[21] Hooked or
looped ends have been interpreted as lifting handles, vertical strokes as ribs
viewed through a transparent hide and a protruding forefoot has been regarded
as a protective feature for beaching. These features suggest that the carvings are
skin boats, although planked boats are also known to have featured forefoots.
The vertical strokes have also been interpreted as crew members. Other simpler
forms, which appear to feature crews in a single line hull with an elk head at
the prow, are regarded as logboats.[22] The depiction of so many boats is hardly
surprising given the maritime context of their locations, on open coastline or
in the fjords where arctic fauna was exploited. Boats would have played a
central and important role in the everyday lives of these hunter-fisher communities, facilitating both transport and hunting, the latter clearly demonstrated
by scenes of harpooning marine animals. Irish megalithic art has more in
common with the kind of abstract art emanating from further south along the
Atlantic fringes of Europe, e.g. Brittany. Importantly this more abstract
artwork is located on funerary monuments, thus fulfilling an entirely different
function than that in the arctic circle.

Leaving aside the difficulties of interpreting rock art, the Neolithic period
provides abundant circumstantial evidence of sea-faring. The development of
foreign contact is evident through the exchanges of material goods. During
this period Tievebulliagh, Co. Antrim, Brockley on Rathlin Island off Co.
Antrim and Lambay Island off Co. Dublin were major areas of axe production.
Axes from these sites have been found throughout Ireland as well as in
Scotland, England and Wales. Conversely, British axes including Arran pitch-
stone, Welsh dolerite and Cumbria tuff have been recovered from Irish sites,

illustrating the nature of this trade in kind. Importantly, Cornish gabbro axes in Ireland demonstrate early contact with an area with crucial resources for later metallurgists and a stepping stone to the continent. This trade across the Irish and Celtic seas could only have been carried out by the movement of peoples on varying scales – movements facilitated by the use of boats.

Actual physical evidence for boats during this period is sparse and like the Mesolithic era it is confined to logboats. The finds themselves are not without significance, however, as examples appear in overtly marine locations for the first time. In Ulster, two examples from Ballylig in Larne Lough, Co. Antrim, found in peat overlain by marine mud have been radiocarbon dated to 3641-3378cal. BC and 3700-3382cal. BC (calibrated).[23] The fact that no navigable

14 Greyabbey
Neolithic logboat.
Courtesy of EHS, Belfast

rivers exist in the vicinity confirms beyond doubt the use of logboats in a marine environment.[24] Another sea lough, Strangford in Co. Down, produced a logboat found partially exposed on the sandy intertidal zone of Greyabbey Bay – it has been radiocarbon dated to cal.3499-3032 BC *(14)*.[25] Other coastal logboats include one from Cahore, Co. Wexford found in a marsh between sand dunes and hinterland, which was liable to flooding by both fresh and salt water.[26] It is notable that these surviving examples are all located within sheltered marine areas hinting at an unsurprising bias against more exposed coasts. None of the above examples show evidence of modifications, such as outriggers or a keel, to adapt them for marine use. More recently however, a logboat buried in 2m of sand was recovered during pipeline construction work within 1km of the shore at Gormanstown, Co. Meath. Not only does this find demonstrate that offshore finds may be made, but initial inspection revealed that it may have been modified for offshore use – holes in the gunwales implying outrigger attachments.[27] Inland examples of Neolithic logboats are still the most common finds; these include the vessel found in the River Bann at Ballynagowan, Co. Armagh, which has been dated to 4660±40 BP.[28]

THE BRONZE AGE (*c.*2500-600 BC)

From a maritime perspective the Bronze Age in Ireland presents a picture of essential continuity in the growing developments of contact and trade with the Atlantic fringes of Europe. The introduction of metal working, closely associated with the so-called Beaker culture, appears to have been embraced enthusiastically, judging by the early date (*c.*2400-1800 BC) detected for copper mining at Ross Island, Co. Kerry.[29] Indeed Ireland's role in trade appears to have been particularly vigorous in the early Bronze Age. Copper was soon eclipsed by more durable bronze, requiring the importation of tin, probably from Cornwall or Iberia. In exchange a variety of bronze items such as axes and weaponry were exported, a well-known example being the Irish-British type spears found in the River Huelva in Spain.[30] As well as copper and bronze, items of gold were manufactured, e.g. lunulae. Gold production culminated in the late Bronze Age with an unparalleled profusion of gold jewellery.

Apart from the circumstantial indications of sea-faring, further evidence for boats in this period is derived from iconography and the remains of vessels themselves. In Scandinavia, representations of boats continued to be carved on rock. In Bjornstad in Norway, a 4.4m-long carving of a boat featuring an extended bow, deep hull and crew members once again has been interpreted as a skin boat.[31] With the introduction of metal, images of boats were transferred to the new media, e.g. the high-prowed vessel etched on a bronze sword dated to 1600 BC from Rørby, Denmark.[32] So central were boats to Scandinavian life that by the later period (*c.*1300 BC) cremated remains were even being placed within boat-shaped settings of stone. In Britain, the Roos Carr boat model and crew from Yorkshire have been dated to the Bronze Age, based on the shape of the warriors' shields.[33] Standing on a flat wooden platform with what was probably a zoomorphic prow, the boat draws immediate comparisons with the logboat depictions seen in Scandinavian rock art. An alternative type of vessel is seen in the rounded shale bowl from Caergwrle, Clwyd, which features wave-like decoration on its lower sides, as well as elongated triangles along its base that have been interpreted as part of an internal skeleton. On this basis the artefact has been postulated as a skin boat.[34] There is a sliver of physical evidence for the use of skin boats from an early Bronze Age cemetery in Dalgety, Fife. One of the burials (and a number of fish bones) was recovered from what appeared to be a coracle – evidenced by the profile in excavation and a possible piece of hide.[35]

A further alternative to the dugout and skin boat forms has emerged in Britain with the excavation of a number of boats constructed of planks sewn together with withies. Planked boats dating to the Bronze Age have been found at North Ferriby on the Humber Estuary, Yorkshire, Dover, Kent and Brigg, Lincolnshire.[36] The three Ferriby boats were found in 1937, at what appeared to be a landing place or boat-building area, or indeed, a combination of both.[37] Structures made of wattle and alder poles, which have been interpreted as hards and holding areas for boats, were found in association with the craft. *Ferriby 1* was the best-preserved vessel and consists of an almost complete bottom section of a hull. A large keel survived, 13.32m long and 1.67m wide, which was made up of two planks joined with a box scarf amidships. A series of curved side planks with bevelled edges were joined to the keel and were stitched together with withies made of yew. Clumps of moss were forced between the planks as caulking material to provide a water-tight sealant for the boat. Four pairs of cleats were incorporated into the bottom plank of the hull through which ash battens were inserted transversely to add structural strength to the boat. These battens functioned along the same lines as ribs, which were added to boats in later centuries. Radiocarbon samples from the boat provided a date of 1880-1680 cal BC, while the earliest vessel (*Ferriby 3*) was dated to 2030-1780 cal BC.[38] Other artefacts recovered from this hugely important site included a boat patch made from oak, and a forked timber which has been interpreted as a side frame from an early beach capstan.[39] Two paddles were also found one of which was made of ash and consists of a near complete blade 0.85cm long.

The Brigg boat was made up of six flattened planks, edge joined by stitching.[40] Again the boat featured a series of cleats along the inboard of the timbers with transverse battens running through them, held in place by wedges. Various interpretations for the original shape of the vessel have been put forward but it probably represents a flat-bottomed barge. The boat has been dated to around 600 BC. In 1992 a further stitched boat was found at

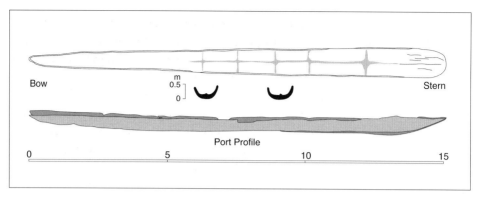

15 Line drawing of Lurgan logboat. *After Robinson, Shimwell & Cribbin 1999*

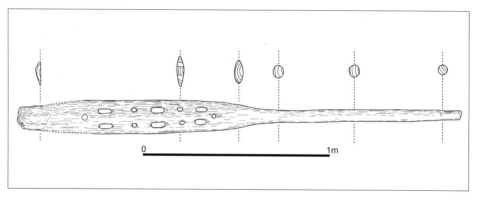

16 Paddle from Clonfinlough, Co. Offaly. *After Moloney et al. 1993*

Dover, in silts originally laid down by fresh water.[41] The boat differed from *Ferriby 1* in that it was broader and more flat-bottomed, however many of the constructional details were similar, such as the withie stitching, moss caulking, cleats and transverse strengthening members. It has been speculated that cross-Channel trade in these types of wooden stitched craft could have taken place. It certainly would have been possible during calm weather and an artefactual seabed assemblage consisting of 350 pieces of Bronze Age metalwork, excavated off Dover Harbour by Martin Dean, has been interpreted as the cargo from an ill-fated trading voyage. Similar finds, albeit on a smaller scale have been found off Salcombe, Folkestone and Bournemouth.[42]

No sewn-planked boats have been found to date in Ireland. All the boat finds from this period consist exclusively of logboats. One of the most impressive boat finds from the late Bronze Age was by workmen in a raised bog at Lurgan, Co. Galway *(15)*. It was hollowed from a single tree and measured over 15.24m in length. It has been dated to 3940±25 BP. The logboat was tranferred to the NMI where it is currently on display. Various interpretations have been offered on the basis of structural and naval architectural analysis as to whether the vessel was ever completed.[43] The features include an internal spine and tranverse ridges and a series of paired holes along the upturn of the vessel which may have been outriggers allowing the vessel to operate at sea.[44] A number of other logboats scientifically dated to this era have also been recovered. One from Inch Abbey, Co. Down, has been dated to 2771 BC by dendrochronology, while part of a logboat, found re-used as a trough in a *fulacht fiadh* at Currachtarsna, Co. Tipperary, was radiocarbon dated to 3120±35BP.[45] The excavations at Clonfinlough, Co. Offaly, uncovered what has been interpreted as a late Bronze Age settlement in the centre of a large midlands' bog. Among the many finds on the site were two ash paddles found lying parallel to each other. One paddle was broken at its blade but the surviving shaft, measuring 1.5m in length, is U-shaped where the boatman would have held it when using it to 'pole' or punt the boat.[46] Evidence for two perforations survived on the shaft. They closely resemble a series of deliber-ately-pierced holes running along both sides of the blade of the second paddle *(16)*. The perforation of oar or paddle blades in this manner actually regularises the movement of blades through the water. In this case their purpose may have been to keep the blade movements to the surface as the craft moved over shallow water.

IRON AGE, *c.*600 BC – AD 400

The Iron Age in Ireland has often been regarded as a rather contradictory period. The rise of a hierarchical, martial society first seen in the late Bronze Age seems to reach its zenith in the prestigious Iron Age royal centres, which have left both archaeological and mythological legacies. On the other hand there is remarkably little evidence of everyday life in the Iron Age. Influences of continental cultures such as Halstatt and La Tène seem limited yet this is the period when Ireland first appears in documentary sources from the ancient world. These reveal that trading contacts were in place, the extent of which is sometimes dramatically borne out by archaeological finds such as the skull of a North-African Barbary ape from Navan Fort, Co. Armagh.[47] The prehistoric archaeology of Irish boats has thus far been dominated by the logboat and while other forms have been postulated, direct evidence has been lacking, leading to an undesirable degree of conjecture. In the Iron Age, however, we glimpse the first evidence of other boat forms, both native and foreign.

Documentary evidence points to the use of skin-covered boats around Ireland and Britain in the Iron Age, however other European traditions indicate the evolution of plank-built vessels. The emerging north European tradition was to build craft using the clinker technique of overlapping hull planks, as seen in Scandinavia, e.g. the Nydam boat (AD 310-320). The carvel building method is that where hull planks are flush-laid *(17)*. This method

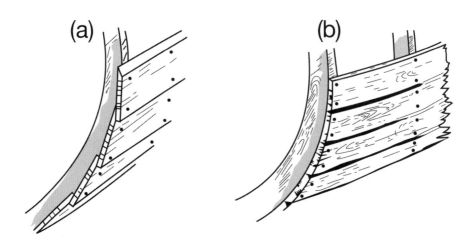

17 Two methods of wooden boat construction (a) clinker, (b) carvel. After MacPolin 1999

probably originally developed well before 2000 BC as it is known to have been used by the Egyptians. It was formerly regarded as being adopted in northern Europe only after around AD 1500. However, a third building tradition using the carvel technique and dating to the Iron Age has been detected across northern Europe. Termed 'Romano-Celtic', it has been linked to the Veneti tribe from north-west Gaul.[48] Caesar described their vessels in 56 BC as solidly built of oak with high bows and sterns. They had large ribs fastened by iron bolts to the outer planking and carried square sails of hides or leather. The tradition was first recognised in 1962 by Peter Marsden on excavating a ship from Blackfriars in London.[49] Since this discovery, further examples have been uncovered, from the Netherlands and Germany to northern France and south Wales. McGrail summarises the characteristics of this tradition, which include building with flush-laid, non-edge fastened planking, massive closely spaced framing, the use of large nails driven through treenails and hooked to fasten frames and planking, and a mast step well forward of amidships.[50] Given the distribution of these vessels, and notably the most western example from Gwent, Wales, it is not inconceivable that they were familiar to Irish mariners. [51]

References to Ireland by classical historians and geographers appear to date back as far as 500 BC, although the surviving accounts were written down many centuries later. The island is described by Avienus' *Ora Maritima* as being a 'two-day voyage from Oestrymnides islands [Brittany?] to the *sacra insula*, rich in turf, near Albion, and thickly populated by the Hierni'.[52] The boats in use around the island of Britain are also noted:

They know not to fit with pine, Their keels, nor with fir, as use is, They shape their boats; but strange to say, They fit their vessels with united skins, And often traverse the deep in a hide.[53]

Skin boats are also evident in references to Ireland. Solinus, in the third century AD, records that:

the sea which separates Ireland from Britain is rough and stormy throughout the year; it is navigable for a few days only, they voyage in small boats of pliant twigs, covered with skins of oxen. During the time they are at sea, the voyagers abstain from food.[54]

Roman contact with Ireland is asserted in both historical and archaeological sources, and a number of artefacts and sites bearing witness to this contact have been found around the country.[55] Pliny the Elder, writing in AD 77, records that

Hibernia [is the] same width as Britain but less in length; shortest crossing from Silures tribe in Britain; islands between Hibernia and Britain.[56]

Later, at the beginning of the second century AD, Tacitus records that Hibernia is in the Gallic Sea between Britain and Spain, and is smaller than Britain but has a similar climate. He also records that Agricola fortified the western coast of Britain in the hope of invading Ireland, but there is still much debate on whether or not the Romans ever carried out military incursions into the country.[57] In an intriguing reference dating from around AD 116 Juvenal refers to 'Roman arms carried beyond the shores of Iuverna' suggesting that some form of military force entered the country.[58] Importantly, Tacitus also writes that

the interior parts [of Ireland] are little known, but through commercial intercourse and the merchants there is a better knowledge of the harbours and approaches.[59]

The second century also saw the compilation of Ptolemy's *Geography*, which included a gazetteer of information on Ireland. A number of tribal groupings appear as well as physical features such as headlands and rivers. The 15 rivers in particular have been most successfully reconciled with modern names, the *Senos* – Shannon, *Buvinda* – Boyne and *Logia* – Lagan, hinting at well-known points of contact that provided trading routes inland.[60] In the voyage tale *Argonautica* (late fourth century), Orpheus narrates that 'the ship Argo fears passing Ierne… but sails pass safely'.[61] It seems that not all classical vessels may have passed safely – a fragment of a Roman *olla*, or storage jar, was trawled up by the Welsh trawler *Muroto* near the Porcupine Bank in 1934. The jar is unlikely to be later than the second century AD and the quality of the ware suggests a Romano-British origin.[62] The recovery of the artefact 150 miles off the west coast in 274m of water suggests it must have been lost overboard from a vessel or have come from a wreck. The most common explanation of this extraordinary find is that it came from the cargo of a merchant vessel, which was blown off course.[63] Another Iron Age artefact of note is the bronze sword hilt recovered by fishermen, about 1916 from Ballyshannon harbour, Co. Donegal. Cast in the form of a human figure with Celtic traits, this unique find is thought to be an import from Gaul, and the presence of a shipwreck in the area has been suggested.[64]

While no hide-covered or larger wooden ship survives in the Irish archaeological record, two important finds indicate the different concepts and technologies employed in boat-building in the Iron Age. The Broighter boat model is probably an example of the emerging native form, while the carvel-built Lough Lene boat shows unmistakable Mediterranean influences.

THE BROIGHTER BOAT

In 1896 James Morrow and Thomas Nickle uncovered a remarkable hoard of gold objects while ploughing a field at Broighter, Co. Derry. The hoard consisted of a model boat with a number of accessories and also a hanging bowl, a tubular torc, two gold chains and two looped, terminal-twisted torcs. All of the objects have been dated to the first century BC, on the basis of the La Tène decoration on the tubular torc.[65] The boat had been damaged by the plough and was subsequently sent to Dublin, to a goldsmith, for repair. It is of particular importance, as it is the earliest representation of a boat in Ireland as well as one of the earliest certain indicators of the use of a sail in northern Europe *(colour plate 1)*. The tub-shaped hull is made from a single sheet of gold, 0.18m long, which was split and rejoined at the prow and stern. The vessel has a single, central mast. The top of the mast is hook-shaped; however, this may not be an original feature but rather the result of damage. When found it was originally interpreted as a boat hook. The yard, which is secured to the mast, indicates that the boat had a single, small, square sail. The vessel originally had nine thwarts (one is now missing having been sold to a jeweller), each of which is secured to the hull by small gold rivets or pins attached through the hull. Each thwart is associated with an oar station on both the starboard and port side of the vessel. The central thwart, placed amidships, is slightly wider than the others and has a centrally placed perforation, which holds the mast. Fifteen of the oars survive – (there would originally have been eighteen) – these are fastened to the gunwale through grommets made up of wire rings. A large steering oar is attached to the port side in a similar manner. It was usual to mount the steering oar on the starboard side of early vessels although examples of port-mounted steering oars are known. A tiny corresponding hole on the starboard stern has been interpreted as another fastening position for the steering oar, suggesting that the helmsman had an option of mounting the oar on either side of the vessel.[66] In addition to these accessories, other pieces were also found which have been interpreted as a grappling iron and three forked poles, which were used for punting. The poles are similar to one of the paddles found at Clonfinlough, Co. Offaly, suggesting that the use of such propulsion aids was common over a long period of time.

There has been much debate within archaeological circles as to whether the Broighter boat model represents a skin-covered or a wooden boat. Cochrane saw faint marks on the sides of the vessel and suggested that they were ribs, indicating the framework of a wooden skeleton covered with hides.[67] Likewise, Bowen suggested that the 'straight rim of the gunwale and the short, curved stem' of the boat were indicative of a skin-covered craft.[68] However, the pinning of thwarts through a skin-covered hull would have caused problems in keeping the boat dry. Farrell and Penny, while not ruling out the possibility that it represents a skin-covered vessel, voice a number of concerns regarding such a conclusion.[69] They note that the lack of any internal framing, the unusual tub-shaped hull and the large size of the vessel are unlike any skin-covered craft known to them. They also cite the lack of resemblance to the modern-day currach. The comparison is perhaps unfair, for while currachs seem to retain some elements of their ancient form they nevertheless have undergone hundreds of years of development and are known to have changed over time. The goldsmith who originally fashioned the model has neglected to include any exterior or interior details of the hull; no planking, stitching, framing or any other feature which would firmly demonstrate the nature of the vessel. It may be that while some elements of the boat are well represented, the model maker had little real experience or knowledge of the craft on which the model was based.[70] The nineteenth-century repair work also resulted in some remodelling. It may be that the hull in its present form bears no relation to its original shape. The general consensus remains that the featureless exterior is a hide and that the model represents the earliest depiction of a skin-covered boat in Ireland.

THE LOUGH LENE BOAT

In the summer of 1968 an extraordinary boat find was made in the shallow waters of Lough Lene in Co. Westmeath. The boat, which was discovered by divers from the Mullingar SAC, was recorded at the time by Paddy Ó hEailidhe on behalf of the NMI, before being returned to the lake *(colour plate 3)*.[71] The vessel was later re-excavated in the late 1980s by CAP.[72] The small boat was originally found lying on the lake bottom in 5m of water. It was constructed

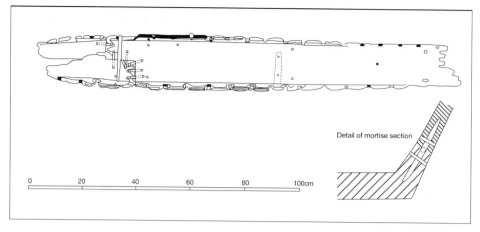

18 Line drawing of Lough Lene boat. *After Waddell, 2000*

in the Mediterranean fashion of ship- and boat-building, being of carvel construction and fastened with mortise and tenon joints. The Lough Lene vessel, as a far-western example of a Mediterranean method of boat-building, is the only boat of its kind found in Ireland and is one of less than ten such craft found in north-west Europe, all of which date to the general Roman period. Radiocarbon dating has produced a date of not later than the first century AD for the felling of the timber used in the craft (400 cal. BC – 100 cal. BC, allowing 100-200 years for old-wood effect).[73] The Lough Lene boat only partially survived and is similar in size to a dugout boat. The remains consist of the bottom of the boat, which is made up of two scarf joined planks as well as a single, side strake *(18)*. The planks measure 7.9m long by 1m wide and have withie stitching. The side strake, which was 6.5m long, would have been secured to the bottom planking by mortise and tenon joints. A total of eighteen mortises were visible on the bottom after its initial recovery and seven tenons survived. There was also evidence that the strake had been stitched to the lower timbers. A single rowlock, which survived on the strake when the divers first recovered the boat, was subsequently lost and its authenticity can not be fully attested. Other fragments of planking were found in the vicinity of the boat as well as two fragments of willow oar blades, one of which was over 0.68m long. A wood resin was used as a caulking material between the planking, although little of this survived. The date and constructional type of this boat could lead to the interpretation that it was a boat carried by a merchant or group of merchants travelling through the country from Roman-occupied territory. Some authors have used the Lough Lene find to imply a native plank building industry.[74] An Irish shipwright who was familiar with Mediterranean building techniques, perhaps through contact with merchants or travel to Roman Britain may have constructed the vessel.

While the uniqueness of this boat in the Irish archaeological record strongly argues against it being part of a local tradition of boat-building, the find does demonstrate external contact of the kind mentioned in sources such as Tacitus.

TWO

THE EARLY MEDIEVAL PERIOD C.AD 400 - 1169

The early medieval period witnessed profound and rapid changes in Irish life, most notably with the introduction of Christianity in the early fifth century. The establishment of the Church had implications for the country's overseas contacts. This was an organisation that was active in maintaining the flow of ideas and individuals to and from the continent. In addition, the arrival of the monastic way of life introduced literacy to Ireland, and with it, our first historical sources. These early sources provide tantalising glimpses of a society that was in the process of change. The old orders were fragmenting into smaller kingdoms with their own systems of rents and law. A second major development in this era was the arrival of the Vikings. These maritime raiders from Scandinavia eventually settled here and established many of Ireland's most important coastal towns and ports.

Although documentary sources provide evidence for the use of wooden boats, there are no detailed indications of their form. Large, clinker-built vessels are known to have been used in the Saxon kingdoms of England before the coming of the Vikings.[1] Excavations at the Sutton Hoo cemetery site in Suffolk have uncovered the remains of a number of large, wooden-ship burials.[2] One such burial (Mound 1), thought to be the grave of Raedwald (c. AD 596-626), was excavated in the years immediately preceding the Second World War and later between 1965 and 1967. None of the actual planking of the vessel survived but careful excavation revealed stains and residues that had been left by the iron and wood, which enabled an accurate reconstruction of the original to be made. It was a large, double-ended, clinker-built vessel some 27m long, constructed from oak and held together with iron rivets. It appears that the vessel was originally oared, since a number of rowing positions survived. There was no evidence for a mast or rigging. However, it is possible that any such fittings were displaced during, or removed before burial. A second burial (Mound 2), originally opened in the mid-nineteenth century and later re-excavated in 1938 and again between 1983 and 1991, revealed another, structurally identical but slightly smaller vessel, just over 20m long. A third vessel was found in a mound at Snape, 14km west of Sutton Hoo.[3] It was excavated in 1862-'63. It too was about 20m long and built in the same early Saxon tradition as those from Sutton Hoo. Together these three vessels are proof that there was a pre-Viking, clinker tradition in Britain, which the Irish were presumably aware of through trading and raiding, prior to the coming of the Vikings at the end of the eighth century AD. The Irish evidence for boats during this period rests, however, with documentary and iconography sources, as well as the various finds of logboats from around the country.

THE INTRODUCTION OF CHRISTIANITY

As noted above, our first documentary sources date to this period, the earliest of which survive from the seventh century AD. Some caution is needed when dealing with these early sources as many of the events recorded were transmitted orally for generations before being written down and are, therefore, likely to have become distorted, exaggerated or embellished. Nevertheless, the early Irish law texts, the Lives of Saints and associated voyage tales, and the later annals provide invaluable insights on many aspects of life. Incidental references to nautical activity also shed light on the various types of vessels in use and provide occasional details of their components. An examination of the various sources follows.

The early Irish law texts, which date from the seventh to the ninth centuries AD, are mainly concerned with farming, but they also deal with everyday issues such as contracts, injury, theft and marriage as well as ecclesiastical matters.[4] They include references to skin-covered boats, fishing and weirs mainly associated with the inland waterways and coastal estuaries. The most commonly mentioned vessel is the coracle, a small, wickerwork boat covered with an animal hide *(19)*. In the 'Law of Sunday', *Cáin Domnaig*, a fisherman had to surrender his nets, coracle and hide if he was caught fishing on the holy day.[5] The hide presumably refers to the covering on the wickerwork hull of the boat. The law text *Di Chetharslicht Athgabálae* differentiates between a small wickerwork coracle (*clíab*) and a larger boat (*náu*). The penalty for the destruction

19 Boyne coracle. *Hornell, 1938*

of a coracle amounted to five séts, payable to the owner of the vessel, while ten séts were payable in lieu of the destruction of a larger boat.[6] The larger vessel may have been the *náu trechodlide*, covered with three hides as opposed to the *curach óenseichi*, covered by a single hide.[7] The *Uraicecht Becc* text indicates the status held by a boat-builder in society, giving him an honour price of seven séts, the same as a blacksmith or silversmith.[8] This price would place the wright (*sáer*) slightly above the average honour price for a craftsman (three séts) and would suggest that he enjoyed a relatively prestigious place in society.

Some deep-sea fishing undoubtedly took place during the period as bones from deep-water species have been found on early historic excavations. For example, bones of cod and wrasse have been found at Church Island and Illaunloughan, both off Co. Kerry.[9] Finds of seal bones on Church Island imply that hunting or the opportunistic exploitation of marine mammals was also practised.[10] It is unclear whether the seals were actually hunted at sea, were killed while they rested on rocks, or were caught with the use of nets. The lost text *Muirbretha* ('Sea Judgements') may have contained more information relating to sea fishing but the only sections that survive from it deal with the ownership of flotsam and jetsam.[11] Finally, the *Bretha Étgid* refers to the risk of accidental harm when travelling by ferryboat. The owner of the vessel was liable and would be fined if he set out with an overloaded boat or during rough weather. A passenger, however, accepted personal responsibility by boarding the vessel in the first place.[12]

The *Lives of the Saints* consist of eulogies in honour of particular saints. The earliest date to the seventh century AD and relate to the lives of Colum Cille (or Columba), Patrick and Bridgit; however, the majority date to the twelfth century AD. Adomnán's *Life of Colum Cille* is amongst the more important and reliable insights into early ecclesiastical life in Ireland and Scotland.[13] It is particularly important from a maritime perspective as numerous marine voyages and episodes at sea are recounted. There are also references to both skin-covered and wooden boats. Different names are used for the various kinds of boats and ships. *Navis*, *longa navis* and *barca* seem to refer to sea-going vessels.[14] *Navis* appears to be a generic term for a ship, whether skin-built or wooden – *longa navis* is literally 'long ship'. While it is not absolutely clear that long ships were made solely of wood, the implication is that they were. On one occasion, dressed timbers of pine and oak for building long ships, were carried overland and then by sea in a fleet of currachs (*curucis*) and skiffs (*scafis*) to Iona.[15] *Barca* is used only to refer to a ship of Gallic sailors visiting Iona, implying that it was not familiar to the monastic community.[16] However, the seventh-century *Uraicecht Becc* notes the legal position of 'a builder of *ler long*, and *bairca*, and *curach*', implying that the shipbuilder was resident in Ireland.[17] Furthermore the *Dinnsenchus* notes that Crimthann Nianar was interred in his barc at Brú na Bóinne.[18] It has been suggested that *barca* was a name applied to wooden trading ships and that they may have been descendants of the types of later Iron-Age ships employed by the Veneti; however this remain speculative.[19] Another vessel mentioned with regard to cargo is the *oneraria navis*, which has been translated as 'freight-ship' – in this case it was carrying wattles for building a guest house.[20] A number of vessels are mentioned on inland waterways – both *alnus* and *caupallus* are mentioned in an incident concerning an amphibious creature in the River Ness in Scotland – supposedly the oldest account of the infamous monster.[21] In Latin *alnus* ('alder') was a wooden boat and *caupallus* has also been interpreted as such. *Cimbul* is another term used for a vessel on Loch Ness and *ratis* also appears in a lake context. Although the above terms give the impression of a plethora of different types of vessels in this period, Anderson and Anderson note that many of the terms are synoymous.[22] The skin-covered boat (*curucus*) remains the most common vessel in the lives of the saints, fulfilling both the functions of transportation and having special significance as the chosen vessel of penitential voyagers.[23] In the *Life of Colum Cille* it is recorded that some monks, during the course of a voyage, came under attack from sea creatures, which struck the keel, sides, prow and stern of the vessel. The creatures also swarmed around the handles of the oars and the boat only escaped thanks to a change in the wind. During their ordeal the crew was afraid that the creatures would pierce the 'leather covering' of the boat. There are some differences concerning the translation of the phrase *pellicum tectis* – 'skin-covering'; 'leathern covering'.[24] However, *tectis* may also mean 'deck' and this has led to a skin canopy interpretation and has even been cited to support a wooden boat argument.[25] There are also numerous references to the use of sails on-board these vessels. In one instance the crew of a boat encountered a whale during the course of their journey and immediately hauled in their sail to avoid colliding with it. They then took to their oars and pulled away from the mammal.[26] In another case twelve vessels were transporting timber across the sea to repair the monastery at Iona when they were forced to take shelter from an approaching storm. Fortunately a more suitable wind was encouraged through prayer and the crews hoisted the sail yards in the form of a cross, spread their sails out upon them and proceeded safely on their way.[27]

The presence of a leading cleric or local lord sitting in the prow of a boat is a repeated phenomenon in the document and must be taken as a position of importance in a vessel at this time. One example of this is the story in which Colum Cille managed to reverse the course of the wind by standing in the prow, raising his arms to the heavens and praying for favourable conditions.[28] A number of these vessels had crews with a defined hierarchical structure or particular roles. The crews are referred to as *nautae* and are captained by the *nauclerus*. There is also a reference to a pilot, living on either Rathlin Island off Co. Antrim or Lambay Island off Co. Dublin, who was presumably employed to guide boats safely to shore.[29] It seems that many vessels were simply beached when they came ashore. There were recognised landing places, but these may have been little more than sheltered bays with a soft beach. There is an interesting reference to an aided landing when a number of people came forward from the beach and seized the prow of the vessel presumably to drag it ashore.[30]

Accessories that would have been carried on-board include a hook, used to recover a body from the water, a leather vessel for holding milk, and containers to bale out the vessel.[31] Anchors are mentioned in an extract from the *Life of St Bridgit*, which notes that members of her community were on passage to Rome when their boat got caught in a storm and they were forced to anchor. The anchor snagged and the crew had to draw lots to decide who would swim down and loosen it. The seventh-century *Life of St Brenainn* notes that during one of his voyages an iron anchor was let go on reaching an island harbour. It became snagged, and its line had to be cut to release it. The smith on-board had died so one of the monks was pressed into making a new anchor, even though he had no formal training in smithy work.[32] As noted above, it appears that seals were hunted. The *Life of St Brigit* records that when a certain man of her household went to sea to catch fish, he came across a seal and speared it using a harpoon and line.[33] It is also interesting to note the following incident from the *Life of Colum Cille*. Erc Mocudruidi was a thief who lived on an island near Iona. He used to sail to the monastery's seal colony during the night where he would kill and steal young seals. During the day he hid under his boat, which was covered with straw and concealed among nearby sand hills, before making his escape.[34]

Other boats are mentioned in later accounts of the *Lives of the Saints*. The *Life of St Senán* records that on one occasion, St Ciáran was travelling overseas to meet Senán. When Ciáran arrived at the harbour there was no boat readily available to carry him so he was forced to travel in a boat without a hide.[35] The *Life of St Brenainn* records the use of larger, wooden vessels. Brenainn's mother encouraged him to build boats of wood in order to go voyaging. In response he built 'a great marvellous vessel' in Connacht and subsequently departed with his household and followers totalling sixty people in all. A poem in the *Life* records a previous expedition carried out by Brenainn[36]:

> Three vessels, the sage sailed
> Over the wave voice of the flowing sea
> Thirty men in each vessel he had
> Over the storm of the crested sea
>
> Three ranks of oars had they
> For every vessel, fair the decision
> A sail of hides with a powerful knowledge
> In the three vessels which sailed

A number of references in the Saint's lives allude to trading ships sailing between Ireland and the continent. The *Life of St Ciáran* records that merchants

20 St Brendan and his crew aboard a boat. *After O'Meara 1991*

from Gaul brought wine to the saint at his monastery in Clonmacnoise, while the eighth-century *Life of St Filibert*, the Abbott of Jumieges, documents an Irish ship trading shoes and leather in the Loire region.[37] There are also numerous references to Gaulish ships known as *Barca* (differentiating them from local vessels) arriving at Iona.[38]

A further source of information on seafaring in this early period is the voyage tales, or *immrama*, undertaken by certain clerics and high-status individuals. The earliest is probably the voyage of Bran, in which a skin-boat (*churchán*) was used.[39] In *The voyage of Máel Dúin*, the warrior-hero consults the druid Nuca for advice on the day he should build his boat, the number of crew he should employ, and the day he should put to sea. Máel Dúin proceeded to build a three-skinned boat equipped with a sail and oars.[40] Although the tales contain many fantastic accounts of mythical places and persons, there are occasional glimpses of the reality of life at sea. Towards the end of 'The voyage of Úi Corra' there is a reference to shipworm when it was discovered that one of the lower hides of the boat had been pierced by sea-dwelling worms.[41] The most famous voyage tale is the *Navigatio Sancti Brendani Abbatis*, or 'the voyage tales of St Brendan the navigator' *(20)*. The actual date as to when the first text was written is a subject of much debate. A date in the tenth century is generally accepted, but some scholars have dated it as early as the eighth century.[42] The tales contain a number of voyages undertaken by the saint around the waters of the north-western Atlantic, during which time the crew experienced many adventures including encounters with whales and icebergs. Elements of realism in many of the stories would suggest that they were based on actual experiences and eye-witness accounts. The monks may have sailed as far as the Faroe Islands, Iceland and even Greenland. The Brendan tales are likely to be an amalgamation of a number of stories recounted by the monks on their return.

There are similarities between these tales and those of *Adomnán's Life of Colum Cille*.[43] As with Colum Cille, Brendan is described as sitting and standing in the bow of a vessel while praying, further demonstrating the importance of this position within the vessel. Landing the boat was also carried out in a similar way. In one case Brendan's boat arrived at an island but grounded before it could reach the landing place.[44] The crew was ordered to disembark and on entering the sea they held the boat on both sides with ropes and hauled it onto the beach. Later this procedure was repeated when the crew had to haul the boat for almost a mile up a narrow stream.[45]

This text is also important in that it contains quite specific details relating to the construction of the boat.[46] It is recorded that Brendan gathered a crew of 14 monks, in Kerry, who proceeded to build a light boat with a wooden frame and ribs. This was covered with oak–bark and tanned ox–hides, the joints of which were smeared with fat to make them watertight.[47] The boat was then equipped with a mast, placed amidships, a sail and steering gear as well as spare hides and fat for the leather in case of damage. Other hides for use in the construction of two smaller boats were also placed in the vessel along with supplies for 40 days. Before they departed, three more monks joined the compliment, bringing the total to 18 including the saint himself. As soon as the boat was launched the crew sailed westwards. Initially they had no need to navigate apart from holding the sail with the wind and using the steering oar to guide the boat. Once the wind had calmed they took to the oars and rowed until their strength gave in.[48]

It seems rather incredible that a small currach-style vessel could undertake a transatlantic voyage. However, in 1976 Tim Severin reconstructed a craft based on those described in the tales. Following Brendan's route he sailed from Kerry to Newfoundland via the Hebrides, the Faroe Islands and Iceland.[49] Although some of Severin's decisions, such as the inclusion of a second mast, have been subsequently criticised, the expedition proved that early skin-boat technology was indeed capable of withstanding such a trip. This is perhaps best illustrated by the fact that during the voyage not one stitch or lashing gave way.[50]

References to travel by boats and ships begin to appear in the various annal-istical sources from the sixth century onwards. These annals are chronicles of events in Ireland that were compiled between the fourteenth and seventeenth centuries. The early annalistic references refer to boats in relation to travel, warfare and wreckage both on the sea and the inland waterways. The *Annals of the Four Masters* refer to what appears to be an assembled fleet of the Dál-Riada travelling to the islands of Coll and Islay off Scotland in AD 564. The same source contains a reference to the devastation of Tory Island, off Co. Donegal, by an unidentified marine fleet in the year AD 612. Attacks on the inland waterways are also mentioned; for example a fleet of English ships raided the territory between the Rivers Boyne and Liffey in AD 683 and carried away hostages and booty. Both the *Annals of the Four Masters* and the *Annals of*

21 (above) Drawing of Kilnaruane Pillar Stone, Bantry, Co. Cork. *After Wallace 1940-41*

22 (left) Early Medieval paddle from Nendrum, Co. Down. *T. McErlean, forthcoming*

Clonmacnoise refer to the wrecking of vessels of the Dealbna-Nuadhat on Lough Ree in AD 751-52. An unlocated wreck is mentioned 20 years earlier when Failbhe, son of Guaire, successor of Maelrubha, was drowned along with a crew of twenty-two in his ship. Transport on inland waterways was undoubtedly common at this time as attested to by the frequent finds of dugout boats associated with laucustrine and riverine sites.

THE BANTRY BOAT

An important early depiction of a boat is carved on the Kilnaruane pillar stone overlooking Bantry Harbour in Co. Cork *(colour plate 4)*.[51] The pillar stone has a number of decorated panels illustrating ecclesiastical scenes and the panel on the lowermost south-east face of the stone contains the boat. As with documentary sources, some caution is necessary when dealing with the interpretation of ships depicted on panels of stone as the vessel's shape may be distorted to fit the panel. In addition, the sculptor or mason may be unfamiliar with the true lines of ships and may be reproducing the vessel from memory or copying from another source. In this case the carving is so realistic that there can be no doubt the sculptor witnessed the actual passage of such a boat over water, even if he never actually travelled in one. The vessel is depicted being rowed and steered amongst a number of crosses *(21)*. There are five figures on-board, including a helmsman at the stern and four oarsmen. A steering oar is held on the port side of the vessel. This is interesting given the similar position of the steering oar on the Broighter boat. Once again it is possible that such steering oars were interchangeable between both sides of the craft. The four oarsmen are shown rowing the craft in a realistic manner. The aft oarsman, in particular, adopts a strong pulling pose while the figure directly behind him also appears to be pulling. The two forward oarsmen have adopted a more stationary pose even though the oarsman in the bow would usually lead the crew in modern currachs. It may be that the vessel is shown while undergoing a turning motion, being led by the two aft crew members and instructed by the helmsman. The oars are also realistically depicted and their position and form indicate that they were attached to the hull by thole pins or grommets. A possible sixth and seventh figure may be seen sitting in the bow but they are difficult to make out due to the eroded state of the carving. Harbison has suggested that one of these figures is actually facing aft with his right hand raised.[52] A gunwale, which leads from the sharp stern to the high pointed bow, is clearly visible on the vessel. One unusual feature is the apparent inclusion of a keel-type timber. This may be a form of artistic licence, particularly if the sculptor was unfamiliar with the characteristics of a boat underwater. Alternatively, its inclusion may simply be to give more shape to the vessel.

The appearance of a keel would suggest that the depiction represents a predominantly wooden boat, as skin-covered currachs lack such a feature. Indeed some authors have vigorously argued that the Bantry boat is closer in form to Icelandic wooden boats.[53] However, in light of the realism of the carving – the helmsman leaning strenuously forward, the angle of the steering oar, the position of the crew in mid-stroke and the bend and heave of the oars, it would be reasonable to expect the strakes of a clinker hull to be shown.[54] There is no suggestion of a clinker-built hull and its lines are crudely reminiscent of a currach. Johnstone sees a further indication that this is a currach by making a rather tenuous comparison with an element of drawing made by Captain Thomas Phillips in 1670 (see chapter 4).[55] This drawing of a 'Portable Vessel of Wicker ordinarily used by the Wild Irish' features a hide boat with a small cross, located in its stern, similar to that on the Bantry boat *(colour plate 2)*. The general consensus remains that the boat is more likely to represent a skin-covered craft and is an early example of a currach.

Henry dated the pillar to the eighth century, a date which was supported by Roe in her study of the iconography of high cross motifs, while Harbison favours a ninth century date.[56] This date has been employed to argue that it supports the interpretation of the vessel as an indigenous Irish boat, since the first Viking raids, and, therefore, the introduction of timber-built longships to the native Irish only occurred after AD 795.[57] Following this, depictions of boats on monastic sculptures and high crosses in the ninth and tenth century take the form of Viking-style clinker-built ships. This argument fails to take account of the fact that the Bantry stone is the sole surviving example of a hide boat carving from the period and its relatively isolated position on the south-west seaboard does not preclude the possibility that timber-built clinker vessels were used or at least encountered in other parts of the country. It is not surprising, given the documentary evidence, that a skin-covered boat should be employed by a monastic community in the south-west during the eighth century *(22)*, indeed the Bantry representation may be interpreted as an expression of the most evolved example of boat-building in the region at the time. However, early historic sources do contain indications that wooden boats in some form were known to the Irish and it would have been desirable that those fulfilling a more military function be constructed of timber. In addition Irish clerics in Britain and the continent must have encountered planked vessels and it may well be that Irish boat-builders in the east of the country imitated these previous to the first Viking raids.

Various interpretations have been made regarding the iconography of the panel. Harbison has suggested that the figure with the raised hand may be Christ stilling the tempest.[58] However, the raised hand is extremely difficult to make out and the figures in the boat certainly do not seem to be engulfed in stormy water and therefore this interpretation remains speculative. Hourihane and Hourihane believe that the boat may represent the ship of the Church and note the following passage attributed to the Book of Homilies:

> The body of the church as a whole is like a great ship carrying men of many different origins through a violent storm.[59]

The theme of the carving is undoubtedly religious although the ship of the Church again does not seem to be engulfed in a violent storm. Wallace has proposed that the panel represents a voyage tale undertaken by a navigating saint such as Brendan.[60] This saint is believed to have travelled in a large, seagoing currach-like craft and the Bantry stone may be an interpretation of this tale. The representation of the boat is far from a great ship in modern terms but it could be that it was the largest, sea-going vessel known to these early ecclesiastics.

THE COMING OF THE VIKINGS

In AD 795 the *Annals of Ulster* records the 'burning of Rechru by the pagans'. Rechru may have been a monastic foundation on either Rathlin Island, off the coast of Antrim, or Lambay Island off the coast of Dublin. This event marked the first in a series of raids, which were eventually carried out all over the country by Viking marauders. The initial raids were hit and run affairs confined to coastal areas, but by the AD 830s the Vikings moved further inland via the major rivers and became active on the inland lakes. Churches and monasteries were targeted for their precious gold and silver relics, and monks and lay people were also taken captive as slaves. By this stage the Vikings were over-wintering in temporary encampments around the coast. In the AD 840s more permanent bases known as *longphorts* – defended ship ports – were established. Some of these bases such as the possible site at Annagassan, Co. Louth, faded into obscurity, while others such as Dublin, Waterford, Wexford, Cork and Limerick had developed into commercial trading towns by AD 920. Initially these settlements were Norse speaking but with expansion, development and intermarriage, the Vikings integrated with the local Irish communities.

The extent of Viking impact in Ireland can be seen in the number of Norse place-names around the coast, indicating former settlements or landmarks used as navigational points. Along the southern and south-western coasts, Norse names include Smerwick, Dursey, Fastnet, Fota, Helvick, Waterford, Saltees, Selskar and Tuskar, while on the eastern coast they include Wexford, Arklow, Wicklow, Howth, Ireland's Eye, Lambay, Skerries, Carlingford and Strangford.[61] The assimilation of boat-building skills and techniques introduced by the Vikings is implied by the number of Irish words relating to ships that are borrowed from old Norse. These include ancaire – *akkeri* (anchor), *bád* – *bátr* (boat), *scód* (sheet), and *cnarr* – *knorr* (ship).[62] However, a number of words contained in the old Irish voyage tales or the religious 'Navigations' were in use prior to the arrival of the Vikings. *Longas* from the old Irish 'long' or ship came to mean exile in the old writings while the old Irish word *séol* for sail probably came from old English, as, according to Greene, did *bát* (boat).[63]

The success of the Viking voyages is attributable to the design of their ships.[64] These boats had been evolving over hundreds of years in Scandinavia and their emergence as ocean-going, sailing craft enabled the early Vikings, escaping from political turmoil or in search of wealth, to travel and find new conquests abroad. The Vikings travelled in double-ended, clinker-built vessels propelled by both sail and oar. The use of sail is interesting as it appears that the sail was only adopted in Scandinavia in around AD 800. It was apparently in use in Ireland since at least the last centuries BC, as evidenced by the Broighter boat.

Although the Viking boats were built to the same basic design, they varied in function and this had repercussions on their form. The best-known vessels are the warships, or longships, which were used for raiding purposes. These vessels were narrow in relation to their length and had a shallow draught. They were fully decked and had a full outfit of oars as well as a mast that was easily unstepped.[65] Longships were fast and manoeuvrable and their inherent flexibility made them very seaworthy. They could carry a large complement of men – the largest warships were able to carry in excess of 100 men and trials have shown that they could reach speeds of 20 knots in very favourable conditions, allowing them to out run any enemies. In addition the light and sturdy ships could be beached and hauled ashore if the weather turned or the crew was intent on attacking a nearby site. One example of this type of ship is from Roskilde, Denmark – *Skuldelev 5*.[66] The Vikings also developed deeper, wider-beamed traders, built for cargo capacity rather than speed. The cargo was placed amidships and the fore and aft parts of the vessel were decked and fitted with oar ports. They could carry loads of up to 30 tons with a crew of 10 men and reach speeds in excess of 10 knots. The masts of these ships were more firmly seated and designed to be unstepped only rarely.[67] An example of this type is *Skuldelev 1*, again from Roskilde.

The crews on-board these vessels navigated by known landmarks along the coast and when possible went ashore at night. Longer voyages required overnight sailing and the crews probably used the pole star as a guide – a celestial body well known to early medieval mariners. Viking ships are known to have crossed the Atlantic and to have reached the coast of Greenland and Newfoundland, where they set up colonies. These feats highlight the advanced capability of these 'dragon boats' and the crews who manned them. Apart from the vessels noted above, a great variety of smaller vessels were also in use in Scandinavian waters. These included smaller coastal traders crewed by five or six men, fishing boats, ferries and tenders.

Evidence regarding the nature of Viking ships and boats is derived from a number of sources. These include the histories and chronicles of the Vikings, representations of the vessels in stone, such as the Gotland picture stones, and graffito on wood. However, the most useful source is the boat finds themselves. Ships and boats played a central role in the lives of the Vikings and it was customary among the high-status social classes to be buried in them. The burials were then often covered with great mounds of earth. The best-known examples of such ship burials are those of Oseberg and Gokstad in Norway. These vessels reveal the state of Viking technology within a short time frame. The Oseberg vessel (*c.*AD 800) features a shallow freeboard and is the first Viking ship known to have a mast. The Gokstad ship (*c.*AD 850) was a stronger ocean-going vessel with a fully developed keel and well-supported mast.[68]

Finds of wrecked ships are another rich source of information. Between 1957 and 1962 the remarkable archaeological site at Roskilde Fjord, off western Denmark, was excavated. Five Viking ships had been deliberately sunk in the late eleventh century to provide an underwater blockade protecting the commercial town of Roskilde. The sunken vessels included two warships – *Skuldelev 2* and *5*, two merchant vessels – the ocean-going trader *Skuldelev 1*, and the coastal trader *Skuldelev 3*, as well as a smaller vessel, possibly a ferry or fishing boat, *Skuldelev 6*. Initially it was thought that six ships were involved but subsequent research revealed that *Skuldelev 4* was a piece of the warship *Skuldelev 2* that had broken away.[69] The larger of the warships, *Skuldelev 2*, is

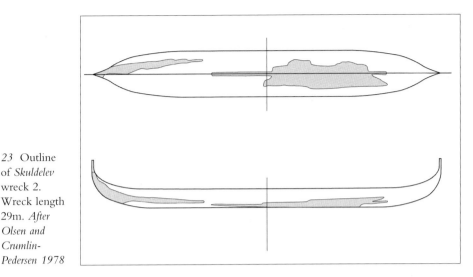

23 Outline of *Skuldelev* wreck 2. Wreck length 29m. *After Olsen and Crumlin-Pedersen 1978*

of particular interest in an Irish context as dendrochronological analysis shows that its timbers match the master Irish oak chronology, indicating that the vessel was probably built in Dublin around AD 1060-70 *(23)*.[70] Only around 10 per cent of the vessel survives, but a reconstruction of the remains indicates that it is the largest Viking ship yet found. It has an overall length of 30m, a width of 4.5m and a draught of just over 1m. The ship was propelled by between 50 and 60 oars and would have carried a crew of 60 to 100 men. It carried a large central mast with a sail area calculated at 150m sq. The vessel is estimated to have reached an average speed of 5 knots, achieving better speeds in more favourable weather conditions. *Skuldelev 5* was smaller, about 17m long and 2.5m wide, and would have been powered by 26 oars. It carried a crew of about 30 men and could achieve estimated speeds of up to 15 knots in very favourable conditions. *Skuldelev 1*, the merchant vessel, was around 16.5m long, 4.6m wide, and probably carried a crew of 12. The smaller trading and transport vessel, *Skuldelev 3*, measured around 13.3m in length and was 3.3m wide. It would have carried a crew of 5-6 men and would have had a single mast with a sail area of 45m sq. The smallest of the five vessels was *Skuldelev 6*, an open pine boat. It measured some 12m in length and 2.5m in width and was likely to have been used primarily for fishing.[71]

As in Scandinavia, numerous sources provide information relating to Viking boats in Ireland. Apart from documentary evidence and iconographical representations, the main body of material consists of numerous boat and ship timbers, graffito and boat models which have been recovered during the course of excavations in former Viking towns. There are some indications that ship burials may have taken place but the evidence is unreliable (see below), and to date no complete Viking ship or wreck site has been found. However, the annals do record the loss of a number of Viking ships. In AD 919 the *Annals*

24 Noah's Ark on east face of Killary Cross, Co. Meath. *After Harbison, 1992*

of the Four Masters refer to a fleet of 32 Viking vessels arriving in Lough Foyle, where they met with 'straits and rocks'. They proceeded to plunder Inishowen before being repelled by Fearghal, son of Domhnall, one of the local Irish lords. Ferghal captured and killed the crew of one of the vessels before destroying their ship. There is also a reference to the destruction of ships in AD 935 when Amhlaeibh, son of Godfrey, lord of the foreigners at Dublin, came to Lough Ree and destroyed ships belonging to Vikings who had formed an alliance with a local lord. In AD 922 the same source records the loss of 1,200 Vikings in their vessels at the mouth of the River Erne in south-west Donegal. There may be a certain amount of confusion relating to this incident, as the *Annals of Clonmacnoise* refers to a large number of Vikings being drowned in AD 920, while the *Annals of Ulster* claim that 900 or more Vikings from a fleet in Strangford Lough were drowned in the inner part of Dundrum Bay in AD 923. The three sources may be referring to the same event, highlighting the need for caution when dealing with these documents. As noted previously, the events were not committed to paper until many years after they occurred when memories were strained or versions of an event had changed. Nevertheless, there is no need to doubt that wrecking incidents occurred and the recording of such events into the various annalistical sources may be considered as a useful guide toward developing a general account of the episode.

The emerging dominance of the Scandinavian boat-building tradition is evident on the iconographic depictions of ships on a number of the Irish High Crosses. These crosses, which generally date to the ninth century, are decorated with panels that display scenes associated with the Bible. The east face usually depicts episodes from the Old Testament such as Adam and Eve, Noah's Ark and the Sacrifice of Isaac. On the other hand, the west face is usually associated with the New Testament and includes events such as the Miracles, the Passion, and the Death and Resurrection of Christ.[72] Ships appear on ten of the High Crosses around the country, a number of which represent Noah's Ark. These include the cross in the city of Armagh, Camus Co. Derry, Clonlea Co. Down, Donaghmore Co. Down, the West Cross in Galloon Co. Fermanagh, Killamery Co. Kilkenny, Killary Co. Meath *(24)*, and Kells Co. Meath *(25)*. The Tall Cross or West Cross in Monasterboice Co. Louth depicts Jesus saving Peter from the waves and the Bantry example in Co. Cork has been discussed. A number of general points can be made regarding the vessels on the High Crosses. All of the ships are regarded as vessels of Nordic type.

25 Noah's Ark on west face of Kells Cross, Co. Meath. *After Harbison, 1992*

They are double-ended with rounded hulls and have high stems and sterns. Harbison notes that all the arks depicted on continental Europe are shown with box-shaped hulls and are unlike the rounded Irish examples. This rounded hull may be an insular adoption by the Irish masons. A number of slight variations do occur, such as the ship on the West Cross in Galloon, which has a more rectangular shape. There is some evidence for the use of steering oars, but there are no details regarding masts or rigging on the vessels. The Irish ships are also shown with rectangular windows in the hull. These inclusions must have been adopted from the depictions in conventional European iconography, as no Viking vessel or indeed any early type of vessel would have had such features. The continental examples clearly show hut or cabin-like structures contained either on or within the hull structure and the windows on the Irish examples must be an attempt to copy this or portray similar structures. A number of the vessels display zoomorphic figures, while others depict a large bird with claws sitting on the deck or gunwale of the vessel, representing the dove returning to the ark with the olive leaf after the floodwaters had receded. Other creatures sometimes appear on the stem pieces. Finally, some of the ships are also shown resting on three triangular peaks, which represent the mountains of Ararat.[73]

The depictions of the ark on the crosses in Armagh and Camus are very similar. Both include symbols representing the mountains of Ararat and both stems are decorated with zoomorphic motifs. The stern of the Camus vessel is also decorated with a spiral motif. Rectangular windows are visible in the hull of the Armagh ark, while three are evident in that at Camus where a head is visible in each one of them. As noted above the hull of the ark on the much eroded Galloon cross is more rectangular in shape than the others and features a bird sitting on the vessel. A starboard-mounted steering oar is evident on the ark at Killamery. There are no windows visible but a deck is shown and there are three figures in the hull. The ark on the Kells cross in Co. Meath has two linear supports visible at each end of the boat. That at the stern could be interpreted as a steering oar, but it is more likely that these are support struts, which would have been used during the construction of the vessel. A number of the arks on Sicilian depictions show similar constructional phases and the Kells ark may be portraying the development of the ship from the time of its construction through to the arrival of the dove back on-board after the flood. A small protrusion on the hull below the second window may be a mounted support for a steering oar.

A further maritime scene is shown on the east face of the Tall Cross at Monasterboice. An unusual feature of this cross is that the Biblical scenes are not in scriptural order and events from the Old and New Testaments appear on both faces. The panel represents the miracle of Christ saving St Peter from drowning. Five figures are shown in a double-ended, clinker-built boat while a sixth person is foundering in the water. Three of the figures are shown holding long, straight oars while the fifth person faces forward with what could be a steering oar. The second person aft appears to be Jesus leaning over the vessel catching the drowning figure who is shown 'crouched like' in the water. Like the arks there is no mast on the vessel or any other form of rigging detail. [74]

A final depiction in stone comes not from a High Cross but the Round Tower at Roscrea, Co. Tipperary. The carving of a ship (0.3 x 0.25m) and cross appears in a second-floor window jamb of the tower. The ship is a single-masted, double-ended vessel with two stays running fore and aft, and is shown in association with a cross. The image has been carved in relief with the surrounding stone set flush with the adjoining structure implying that it is contemporary with the tower, or came from an earlier building. [75] The monastic site in the town dates from St Cronán in the seventh century, but the tower is more likely to be ninth century – the earliest reference to it is when it was struck by lightening in 1131 or 1135. [76] The depiction has no parallel in any of the country's other round towers and the presence of a wooden boat carving in the tower of a landlocked county is intriguing. The nearest major waterway to the site is the River Shannon (about 20 miles) and both the founder of Roscrea and subsequent abbots had connections with the major monastic settlement of Clonmacnoise (about 25 miles) situated upstream on the river. The association of the cross with the boat has led some commentators to see an artistic convention in Irish vessels of the period (compare with the Bantry boat) implying a missionary journey. [77] The extensive missionary contacts of Clonmacnoise with the continent are well known and the foundation's links with Roscrea were active in the ninth century leaving the prospect of a missionary connection a real possibility. [78]

Numerous fragments of boats and ships have been recovered from a series of excavations in the former Viking towns of Dublin, Waterford and Wexford. The redevelopment of inner-city Dublin, in particular, has generated extensive archaeological investigations around the area of the original Viking and Anglo-Norman town. The results of these excavations have greatly enhanced our knowledge of the archaeology and development of the capital. Numerous timbers, both in structurally articulated groups and individual pieces were found, often re-used in the building of waterfront revetments, houses, incorporated with drains or structures, or used as fill behind foreshore revetments. The recovery and systematic recording of these timbers has enabled a clearer picture to emerge of the type of craft that worked and travelled to and from the Irish Viking ports. The excavations of Brendan Ó Ríordáin and Pat Wallace at High Street, Christchurch Place, Winetavern Street, Fishamble Street and Wood Quay from the 1960s through to the early 1980s have produced the largest quantity of ships' timbers in the country. These timbers have been comprehensively studied by Seán McGrail, then of the National Maritime Museum in London, and have been published in a Royal Irish Academy Monograph. [79] The timbers represent boat and ship finds dating from the tenth through to the thirteenth century AD. All of the timbers are from

26 Paddle from Viking timbers from Fishamble Street, Dublin. *After McGrail 1993*

vessels of the Scandinavian double-ended, clinker-built tradition with the exception of one (T225), which may be a floor timber from a flat-bottomed vessel. No fastenings were evident on the timber so it is possible that it had a non-nautical function.

In his study of the recovered timbers McGrail examined over 250 oak planks and ship components such as keels, stems, knees, stringers, bulkheads, breasthooks, parrels and numerous dome-headed fastening nails, as well as one oar and two paddles *(26)*. By comparing the size of the fastenings and scantlings of the Dublin timbers with similar timbers from known sizes of boats and ships in Scandinavia, he was able to suggest the estimated size of the parent vessel. He then classified these into categories based on the overall length of the vessels (see table 2). Regarding the distinction between a large boat and a small ship, the structure of the hull and the operational role of the vessel were taken into account when classifying these vessels.

LENGTH OVERALL (M) McGRAIL'S DEFINITION	DESCRIPTION
<7	Small Boat
7-12	Boat
12-20	Large Boat Small Ship
20-24	Ship
>24	Large Ship

Table 2. *After McGrail 1993, 21*
Table 3 (opposite). *After McGrail, 1993, 96*

TE IN USE	SITE	VESSEL	TIMBERS
ly to mid-tenth tury	High Street	Boat	Floor 368
	Fishamble Street	Small Boat	Floor 372
	Fishamble Street	Boat	Keel 383
	Fishamble Street	Large Boat(s)	Keel 361; plank 384
	Fishamble Street	Small Ship	Keel 382
th/eleventh tury (955-1040)	Fishamble Street	Small Boat	Keel 378
	Fishamble Street	Boat(s)	Floor 379; planks 388-92
	Fishamble Street	Large Boat	Keel 381
	Fishamble Street	Small Ship	Knees 352, 380
venth/twelfth tury (1055-1125)	Fishamble Street	Small Boat	Stem 357
	Fishamble Street	Boat(s)	Planks TG10 (350-50); plank 387; breasthook/knee 366
	Fishamble Street	Large Boat	Bulkhead 351; oar 377
	WQ.TG7	Boat(s)	Planks 255-6; 264-6; 279
	WQ.TG7	Large Boat(s) or Small Ship(s)	Framing 245, 252, 263, 274-8, 280, 289, 290, 292, 293
	WQ.TG7	Ship	Planks 282-8
	John's Lane	Ship	Planks 353, 359
elfth/thirteenth century 60-1255)	WQ.TG1	Boat	Planks TG1 (1-30)
	WQ.TG4	Large Boat	Bulkhead 187
	WQ.TG2	Large Boat(s) or Small Ship	Side Timber 57; mast step (?) 54; stems 52 and 53
	WQ.TG2	Large Boat(s) or Small Ship	Planks TG2 (31-50)
	WQ.TG4	Small Ship(s)	Planks 147, 167, 217, 219; Floors 222 and 223
	WQ.TG4	Ship(s)	Knee 218; Parrel 220A; Parrel rib 220
	WQ.TG2	Ship(s) or Large Ship(s)	Keel 56; mykes 51 and 58
	WQ.TG1	Ship/Large Ship	Stringer 30A
	WQ.TG2	Large Ship	Floor 55
	WQ.TG6 and 9	Large Ship	Planks TG6 and 9 (226-39 and 297-329)
rteenth century 30-75)	WQ.TG3		Planks TG3 (59-146)

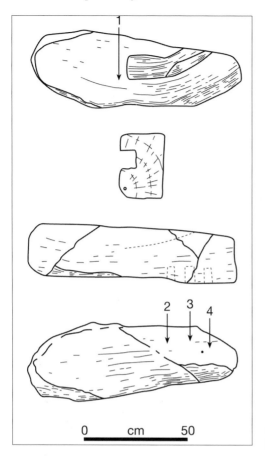

27 Possible mast step from Dublin Viking boat *After McGrail, 1993*

Timbers representing all the categories of vessels were found among the Dublin material (see table 3). McGrail was able to draw parallels between the remains of the Dublin vessels and those found in Scandinavia, thus two boats from the 1055-1125 levels were likened to the ninth-century Gokstad boat. Another large boat from similar levels drew comparisons with *Skuldelev 3*. Constructional details also emerged including evidence of nails driven from outboard and clenched inboard. The fastening nails were dome-headed with shanks that were both rounded and square in section. Evidence of caulking with the use of tar and hair was also produced. One of the most interesting boat finds was a possible mast step, T54, from a large boat perhaps used for fishing or ferrying *(27)*.

Andy Halpin's excavations at Winetavern Street in the early 1990s uncovered more boat and ship timbers. These timbers, including two stems, planking, knees and other structural elements, were re-used on four different waterfront structures *(28)*.[80] The timbers were from vessels ranging in size, from a small boat to a large boat or small ship. They dated predominately to the late twelfth century AD. One group of planking (from revetment F166)

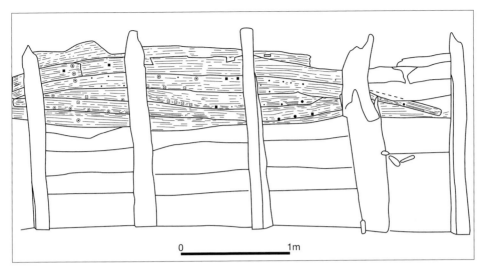

0   1m

28 Drawing of Viking ship timbers as part of waterfront structure. *After Halpin, 2000*

was from a boat which had an original length of around 8m and would have been comparable in size to the ship's boats from Gokstad (2 and 3), it may have been used for transport and fishing. All the timbers were of oak, although willow and ash were used for treenails. In addition, a large, narrow-bladed oar found with the timbers was fashioned from ash. Its form suggested that it was associated with a sea-going vessel and its similarity with earlier eighth and ninth-century Scandinavian examples demonstrated the longevity of Norse traditions.[81]

Extensive excavations which took place in Waterford between 1986 and 1992 have also uncovered a number of boat timbers.[82] All of the timbers recovered, with the exception of one, were fashioned in the Viking tradition. The finds, which were also studied by McGrail, consisted of a stem, three floor timbers, a knee, two bulkheads, a crossbeam and a possible fragment of a mast.[83] The ash mast was the only non-oak timber found, and the only evidence for rigging and the use of sail. It was dated to the early twelfth century AD. Most of the other timbers dated to the Viking period but the stem and crossbeam were later – see chapter 3. Two of the floor timbers were excavated from the same context, suggesting that they were from the same boat. Likewise one bulkhead and the possible mast fragment were found together, as were the second bulkhead and another floor timber. A comparison of the timbers with known Viking ships indicated that various sizes and types of vessels were represented.[84]

The study of the Waterford material revealed that the timbers came from hulls which had more but narrower strakes than known Viking Age vessels of a similar size. This might indicate that the supply of oak was not as good in the twelfth or thirteenth centuries, or more interestingly, that local boat-building

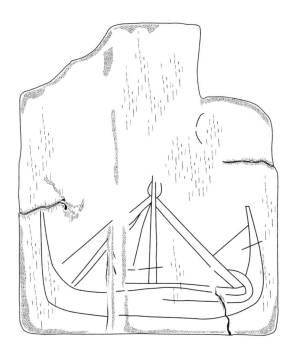

29 Viking ship sketches from Winetavern Street, Dublin. *After Wallace, 1988*

techniques were evolving, resulting in regional variations. Local shipwrights may have been refining the overall shape of the vessels in order to enhance their speed, cargo capacity or seaworthiness.[85] An assortment of boat timbers were also found in Viking levels at Wexford, including four planks from a clinker boat which had been re-used as a pathway.[86]

The remains of Viking boats and ships from the urban excavations in Dublin, Waterford and Wexford are fragmentary and heavily biased towards the lower hull structure. Little evidence regarding the nature of the rigging or sails used on the vessels survives, but graffiti and models of boats and ships are of some use in gleaning information about them. In Dublin sketches of two ships were found on some planking during the excavations carried out on Winetavern Street from 1969-71.[87] The planking was re-used as a drain cover, which dated to the eleventh century AD. The larger of the two sketches shows the port side of a Nordic-type craft *(29)*. A high, curved stern is clearly shown with a steering oar hanging on its starboard side. The vessel has a single mast with a partially lowered yard and its sails are furled. Three rigging lines run on either side of the mast to the forward and aft, while an arrow-type feature on top of the masthead may represent a weather vane. A small, double-ended boat lies off the stern of the vessel and may be a tender either belonging to the boat or servicing it, as it lies alongside. There is a second boat-like feature depicted near the masthead, which appears to be a small, flat-bottomed boat lying off the starboard. The smaller sketch shows a double-ended ship with a high stem

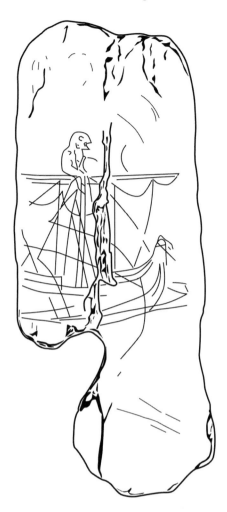

30 Viking ship sketch from
Christchurch Place, Dublin. *After
Wallace 1988*

and stern. A large, central mast has rigging lines running forward and aft while
a 'swelling' at the mast-head has been taken by Christensen to represent a hole
for the halyard.[88] This feature is quite large to classify as a hole-type fitting and
it could actually represent a parrel, an example of which was found during the
Dublin excavations at Wood Quay. A further example of ship graffito, found
in Christchurch Place, depicts one end of a clinker-built vessel *(30)*.[89] The
vessel has a short, blunt-ended post, which is unlike the other, more-rounded,
continental depictions of Viking end timbers. There is a central mast and a
yard, with a figure on top of the yard furling the sail. Stay lines run from the
yard to the gunwale of the vessel. An example of a ship carved in stone was
found in Castle Street in 1996. The vessel is double-ended and clinker-built
with a possible zoomorphic head on the prow and a curved stem.

Three boat models were also found in Dublin, one in Fishamble Street and
two in Winetavern Street *(31)*.[90] These models were probably used as toys and

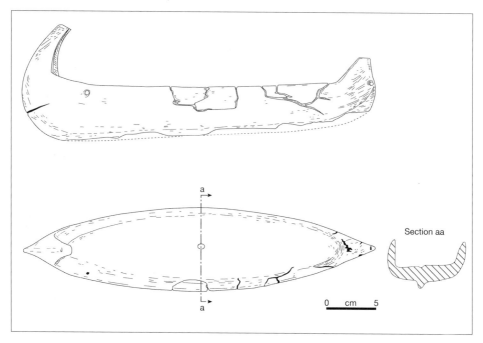

31 Viking boat model from Winetavern Street, Dublin. After Wallace, 1988

are paralleled elsewhere in Scandinavia. The earliest was uncovered in a mid-tenth century context at Fishamble Street, while the two Winetavern Street examples date to around AD 1200. The latter examples were clearly Scandinavian in character. The larger of the two was almost complete and is double-ended with a rounded stem and stern. In both vessels a hole, which is visible on the amidships floor, would have held a mast. A number of small holes in the hull are also evident. The rigging would have been fixed to these.

Two possible Viking boat-burials are recorded in the Northern Ireland SMR. There are a number of indications that such burials took place in Ireland, but the evidence remains unreliable. One of the possible burials was found in 1820 during turf cutting at Ballywillin bog near Portrush in Co. Antrim. The oak vessel, about 13m long and 2m high and made up of stone, clay and moss was found in the mound. There are differing versions regarding what was uncovered. One account states that the keel of a ship, fastened with treenails, was found, but there is no reference to metal nails associated with it. A second account recalls that neither the keel or mast survived, but large ribs over 2m long and a number of thick strakes were recovered. A third account states that a quantity of white limestone gravel, used as ballast, was in place in the bottom of the boat. In addition, a large, flat hearthstone with ashes was said to have been found at one end of the vessel. All accounts, published by Briggs, agree that a number of silver coins were found with the craft.[91] The ship was

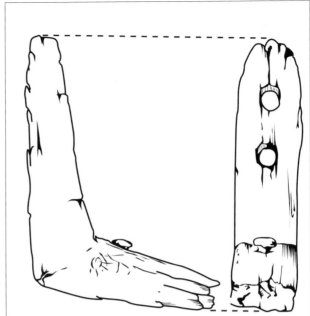

32 Right: Rib with treenail from Ballinderry 1. *After Hencken, 1936*

33 Below: Oar from Ballinderry 2. *After Hencken, 1942*

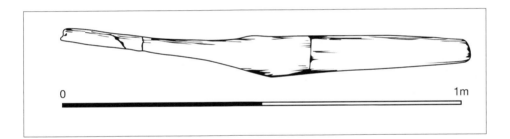

0   1m

undoubtedly a sea-going vessel and the original interpretation that it was a boat-burial is probably accurate. The absence of nails from such a vessel – if she was of Viking age – is unusual although these may have eroded within the mound. The other possible boat-burial was uncovered during field-clearance operations in the early nineteenth century on Rathlin Island, off Co. Antrim. Timbers, described as being from a Viking-type boat, were found in a field overlooking Church Bay, which had produced other burials of Viking character.[92] As noted above, boat-burials are common throughout the Viking regions and a burial of this nature would not be out of place in this country.

Although the early historic period provides evidence of skin-boats and planked craft in Ireland, the humble logboat is still represented in the archaeological record. A number of boat timbers have been found during the crannóg excavations at Ballinderry, Co. Westmeath, and Lagore, Co. Meath.

While these have previously been referred to as Viking boat timbers, they are almost certainly associated with the use of logboats on the lakes. A small knee recorded by Hencken from the tenth-century site of Ballinderry 1 appears to be a floor timber from a logboat.[93] The rib is over 0.15m long and has three wooden treenails, which attached it to the hull *(32)*. Various paddles also found on the site would have been used to propel such a boat (33). Three logboats have been dated by dendrochronology to the Early Historic period including the boat from Summerville, Co. Galway to AD 1001, Oxford Island, Co. Armagh to AD 492 and Strabane, Co. Tyrone to AD 431.[94] The continued usage of this simple vessel throughout the Irish prehistoric and historic periods indicates that it was the most enduring boat type used on this island. Its relative ease of construction and the low level of technology involved in building it, coupled with a ready source of building materials, must account for its success. As already noted, the logboat also proved itself as a safe and very functional craft to use for ferrying, transport and fishing purposes.

THREE

MEDIEVAL SHIPPING
1169 - 1600

THE HIGH MEDIEVAL PERIOD, c.1169–1400

The coming of the Anglo-Normans to Ireland in 1169 led to profound economic and social changes throughout the country. They used their skills of warfare and organisation to consolidate their newly-seized territory and within a short period had overpowered the Hiberno-Norse cities of Waterford and Dublin. The Normans claimed lordship over the whole of Ireland, but in reality they could not complete the conquest, and many northern and western areas remained free. Choosing Dublin as the capital of their lordship, they established a central government, courts of justice and an exchequer. The newcomers were keen to see a return on their military investment and so mercantile activity greatly increased under their administration. The urban centres became successful ports and important links were forged with English ports, notably Bristol and Chester. In addition, merchants from France, Iberia and Italy were trading in Irish ports, bringing wine, salt and luxury goods and receiving in return, hides, wool, fish, flax and furs. Trading networks expanded across Europe in the twelfth century as agricultural output increased. Important trading confederations such as the Hanseatic League emerged in the thirteenth century and this in turn led to a huge increase in merchant shipping in northern Europe. The increase in trade had a bearing on the development

34 Cog from
northern European
port seal. *After
Marsden, 1997*

of ships – larger merchant vessels were needed to accommodate bigger cargoes.
In the thirteenth and fourteenth centuries, these larger hulls gave rise to the
development of the end-mounted rudder, as the traditional steering oar was no
longer able to provide sufficient steerage on the larger craft.

The military function of ships became more obvious with the addition of
fore- and after-castles to the larger vessels during the twelfth century. These
castles were raised areas at the front and back of vessels to accommodate both
archers and swordsmen during conflict at sea. The raised nature of these
platforms would have given the vessel an obvious strategic advantage over
smaller craft in much the same way as a parapet on a traditional castle gives the
defenders of the site a distinct advantage over foot soldiers below.

During this period, three main types of vessel developed in Northern
Europe: the cog, the hulc and the keel. The emergence of these larger,
mercantile vessels is typified by the type known as a cog. These ships appear to
have evolved in the Baltic by the eleventh century and by AD 1200 were
reaching the shores of Britain. Cogs had a flat, flush-laid bottom with a sharp
bilge turn and they were clinker-built with hooked, iron nails attaching the
planking to the frame *(34)*. Straight, raked stem and stern posts were the most
distinctive features of this new type of craft as opposed to the rounded ends of
earlier vessels. Cogs were fitted with one central mast with a large, square sail.

Large after-castles were built on the vessels to provide security for goods carried in an open cargo space in the centre of the hull. A number of these vessels also featured a fore-castle but this was much more limited in scale than the after-castle, and usually consisted of little more than an archery platform. Cogs were substantially bigger than the earlier Viking sea-going, trading ships. The Bremen Cog, which was discovered in the River Weser in Germany in 1962 and was subsequently excavated, is the main source of information for this vessel type. This ship was just over 24m long, nearly 8m longer than *Skuldelev 1*, the Viking ocean-going trader, and had a carrying capacity of 80 tons – twice that of the Viking ship. There are medieval references to bigger cogs than that from Bremen, but it may be regarded as a large-sized vessel for the period.[1]

The second type of mercantile vessel, the hulc, is well attested to in the written sources and representations of it survive on a number of European town seals and church fonts.[2] Like the cog the hulc retained its clinker

35 Hulc from northern European port seal. *After Marsden, 1997*

36 Keel-type vessel.
After Hutchinson, 1997

character but had a more rounded profile from end to end *(35)*. The origins of the vessel may lie in northern France or the Low Countries, but the earliest historical reference to the type dates to around AD 1000, when a hulc was lying at berth at London.[3] Unlike cogs no examples of this vessel have been found.

A third type of mercantile vessel was based essentially on the Scandinavian and Anglo-Saxon traditions of boat-building. These vessels have been described as 'keels' (from the Anglo-Saxon *ceol*, meaning ship), or 'nefs' a vessel type repeatedly referred to in north-west European medieval texts, although again the term is not much more specific than 'ship' *(36)*.[4] These vessels were larger and heavier than their predecessors, and featured castles and improvements in their rigging. The differences between the three types of vessels lie in the different regions of their origin. However, common to all was the clinker form of construction that continued in use until nearly three centuries later.

Merchant vessels with defensive capabilities could be employed in conflict and were also more able to resist the attack of pirates; for example, cogs were known to have been used for defence in northern Europe.[5] At the same time there were vessels retained specifically for security – galleys. These naval vessels were prominent in the thirteenth and fourteenth centuries, patrolling inshore waters in the direct vicinity of ports and harbours. Like keels, galleys were of Scandinavian ancestry – double-ended, clinker-built vessels with a shallow draught of probably not more than 1m *(37)*. They were propelled by oars as well as by sail, and so were fast and highly manoeuvrable. The vessels were improved by the transition to stern rudders in the late thirteenth century and accounts of English galleys also mention windlasses, awning over part of the

37 Reproduction of a galley
as illustrated on Francis
Jobson's Map of Ulster, 1590
After Hayes McCoy 1949-53

deck, and fore- and after-castles.[6] The vessels fell out of favour in England in the fourteenth century but remained popular in western and northern Ireland and Scotland into the sixteenth century. These western survivals were the favoured vessels of the Gaelic world and reveal the conservatism of that society. They also adopted the stern rudder but in all other respects retained essentially Viking characteristics.

In Ireland a variety of ship names appear in documentary sources, including some of the more important European types. A number of cogs were owned by Irish merchants and operated out of Irish ports. In 1338 Maurice, son of the Earl of Desmond hired *La Rode cogge*, which was based at Limerick, for a journey to Gascony.[7] In 1335 a Cork-based merchant was transporting wool and other goods to Normandy in the *Rudecog* of Howth, when it was driven ashore in Cornwall. The hulc is first represented in an Irish context by the Waterford vessel, the *Blessed Mary*, which brought a cargo of corn to the English army in Gascony in 1297. Other vessels include the crayer, which appears to have been a small cargo and fishing vessel of over 12 tons. It is first mentioned in the mid-fourteenth century. In the 1380s James Butler, Earl of Ormond, hired the Waterford crayer *Gabriel*, to take him to England. Several references to these vessels also appear in business dealings with the port of Bristol.[8] On many occasions documentary sources refer to vessels in general as galleys. This has led to an under-estimation of boat types in Ireland during the period.

It is sometimes possible to see a clear differentiation between military and commercial vessels. The protection of ports, and the safe passage of shipping to and from them, was essential. Enemies of the king continually harassed shipping around Ireland and this began to have a major economic effect on the treasury. In response to such attacks, from as early as 1205, King John had a fleet of five galleys based in Ireland.[9] Two galleys under the command of Henry Fitz Earl and in the King's service arrived at Carlingford on 9 July 1210.[10] There is evidence later the same month (on the 28th) that these vessels were being commissioned in Ireland, when the King ordered two galleys to be built at Antrim to service Lough Neagh.[11] On 18 July 1222 the King commanded the men of Dublin, Waterford, Drogheda, Limerick and the other ports of Ireland to build galleys in each of their ports for the defence of the King's realm in Ireland.[12] In 1234, two galleys with 60 oars and four galleys with 40 oars were ordered to be built in Irish ports. Seven years later the men of Drogheda were ordered to build a second galley to accompany their existing one, while Waterford was to build two and Cork and Limerick one each.[13] The men of Dublin were ordered to build and maintain a 'great galley' for the King's service in both 1233 and 1241.[14] In 1244, Dungarvan may have taken delivery of one of the King's galleys from the Justiciar for help with trade.[15] In 1319, five ships built in Devon were delivered to the constable of Carrickfergus for the protection of the town against the Scottish warships.[16]

The use of galleys was not just confined to coastal waters. They were also employed to protect some settlements along the inland waterways. A military settlement was established in the middle of the thirteenth century at Rindoon on Lough Ree, Co. Roscommon. Its waterfront was developed in tandem with the settlement. The safest and quickest way to travel on large expanses of water such as Lough Ree and the River Shannon was by boat and so water transport played a vital part in the success of Anglo-Norman river and lake-side settlements. Sources refer to a ferry operating at Rindoon between 1302–'03 and 1315–'16. The ferry linked Co. Roscommon and Co. Westmeath and highlights the importance of Rindoon as a crossing and focal point on the lough, matched only by the bridgehead at Athlone.[17] However, the local Irish, particularly 'the Offergyles and their followers', were a constant threat. 'They make from day to day a great multitude of boats' with which they plundered the lands surrounding Rindoon. To counter this local threat the:

> Justiciar and whole Council of the King in this land, ordered that a galley be made of at least 32 oars which shall constantly remain at Randon, for the defence of the castles of Athlon and Randon if it shall be necessary.[18]

The use of 32 oars indicates an internal layout of 16 oars on either side, each manned by a solider. Few of these inland galleys would have used sails but it would not have been unusual for the vessel to be equipped with one. This type of craft would have been used for linear patrol duties on the loughs and rivers.

With regard to the commissioning of galleys, specialised boat yards must have existed at the main ports to enable these construction projects to take place.

The raw materials required for ship construction were readily at hand in the hinterland of the ports and native shipbuilders must have enjoyed successful trades. Some of the sources indicate that shipbuilding was practised; for example, payments were made to shipwrights in the years 1212 and 1213 for the repair of ships and galleys at Irish ports.[19] Native expertise is again recognised in 1225 when Earl William Marshall, or a bailiff of the Justiciary of Ireland, was ordered to have 200 ashen oars made of varying lengths and sent to the king. In addition, two ship loads of planking for use in the construction of galleys and 'long vessels' were also ordered.[20] It is interesting to note that the early sources distinguish between merchant sailors and galley crew, indicating the existence of formal naval personnel in Irish ports. Payments of over £700 were made to 'mariners and galleymen' in the summer of 1210.[21] The existence of such a specialised crew of men was important to counter the continual threat of piracy. Piracy was a common occurrence in Irish waters and each port required its own naval capability to protect against such action. For example, in 1258 a Hebridian fleet plundered a merchant ship of her cargo of wine, copper, cloth and iron off the Galway coast. The pirates were later pursued by the Sheriff of Connacht, Jordan d'Exter, as well as a fleet of local vessels.[22] Between 1307 and the Battle of Bannockburn in 1314, the Scots increased their naval strength and were ever-keen to disrupt English trade. The sea between the Isle of Man, Ireland and the North Channel was described in 1322 as being infested with the 'enemies' of the King who were intent on plundering merchant ships'.[23] European pirates were also common in Irish waters. In 1380 Thomas of Walsingham refers to a number of French and Spanish 'gallies' which took shelter in 'Kinsale haven' after a fleet of vessels from south-west England disrupted their plundering activities.[24]

Like the early historic period, the medieval period also provides us with iconographic evidence for the types of ships plying our waters *(38)*. Town charters and seals are useful sources of evidence, though as with previously mentioned iconography, caution is needed when dealing with them. The ship represented on the thirteenth-century seal of Dublin can be interpreted as indicating a transitory phase between the use of the earlier Viking vessels and the development of the later, larger mercantile vessels *(39)*. The ship retains a Viking character being double-ended and clinker-built.[25] It carries a single mast, set amidship, with one large sail. Of particular interest is the presence of fore- and after-castles set on the stem and stern posts. The positioning of the castles on the posts must be a form of artistic licence as such castles would have actually been set back from the bow and stern as indicated on the Winchelsea town seal from England.[26] The vessel also carries an anchor on its starboard forward section. Unlike the galleys, this ship could have fulfilled both military and commercial roles. A stone carving of a ship found in the graveyard of St Selskar in Wexford depicts a double-ended craft with single-mast and stays to the fore and aft. A steering oar is depicted at the stern, while a protrusion at

38 Ship carvings from a tomb-slab, Selskar Abbey (left) and the door-jamb of Roscrea round tower (right). *After O'Reilly, 1901*

39 Thirteenth-century Seal of Dublin. *After Blackwell 1992*

the bow is unclear. The vessel is associated with a carving of a man's head, leading some sources to speculate that this individual was connected with the ship. The church was founded as a priory for the Augustinian Canons Regular and was in existence by 1240 – the carving is thought to date to the twelfth century.[27] The form of the vessel can be regarded as a late example of the Viking type ship with steering oar, before the transition to stern rudder.

The co-existence of the earlier Viking-type vessels with the more modern, emerging mercantile vessels is demonstrated in an illustration from a Charter Roll for Waterford City dating to around 1370 *(colour plate 5)*. Four clinker-built, wooden vessels lie at anchor in the river by the city.[28] The two most prominent vessels, lying near the western bank, are shown with fore- and after-castles, high sweeping bows and large, central masts with castellated mast tops. They are most likely representations of hulcs. Both have end-mounted rudders and one is clearly anchored at its bow. This vessel has a bowsprit running from inside its fore-castle and a white flag flutters from it. A third, masted vessel lies closer to the city but one end of it is lost from the drawing. No castle-type structure is apparent on the end, which is probably the bow given the absence of a rudder, but the vessel has a central mast and a crow's nest. The mast has two stays running fore and aft and is more Scandinavian in character than the other vessels, retaining the slender lines of earlier Viking craft and a prominent keel. A fourth, unmasted vessel lies at anchor below the city walls. It is clinker-built with an end-mounted rudder and a high, curved bow. The lack of a mast on this vessel may indicate that it was a river boat, which was rowed or drawn up and down the river with its cargo. Another probable representation of a hulc takes the form of an ampulla discovered behind a thirteenth-century waterfront revetment at Wood Quay in Dublin.[29] This pilgrim souvenir originated in Canterbury and takes the form of a decorated pewter flask featuring the ship with St Thomas standing amidships. The hulc is typically crescent-shaped and double-ended, the strakes at stem and stern terminating in animal head carvings. A prominent keel is depicted and divisions in the upper strake have been interpreted as oar ports.[30] Rigging takes the form of stays running fore and aft, though the mast has been omitted to accommodate the neck of the ampulla and its depiction of the saint. The form of a knight's armour on the reverse side of the artefact, and the lack of a stern rudder has dated the ampulla to the end of the twelfth or early thirteenth century.[31]

The Book of Ballymote dating to around 1400, and now in the Royal Irish Academy, Dublin, contains a sketch of a boat which represents Noah's Ark *(40)*. The vessel has all the appearance of a cog, featuring clinker planking fastened with lozenge-shaped nail heads, and a single straight prow slightly curved at its head. Characteristically, the vessel has an end-mounted rudder, secured by two rudder pintles, presumably made of iron. The vessel also carries a single, central, sturdy mast.

The more well-known ship and boat types, such as the cog and hulc, have overshadowed the undoubted existence of smaller, more localised boats, which would have been owned and used by Irish coastal communities. These vessels, as with today, probably displayed a great variety of form. Some evidence for the local vessels in use may be gleaned from a number of iconographic depictions. A circular, silver matrix seal of Donough O'Brien, dated to the fourteenth century, shows a double-ended, wooden vessel with a single, central mast rigged fore and aft.[32] Two large fish are shown beneath the boat implying that the vessel and the O'Briens were primarily engaged in fishing.

Archaeological evidence for the development of Irish medieval ships is slight but some conclusions may be drawn from the timbers recovered during

40 Noah's Ark, Book of
Ballymote. *After O'Neill, 1987.*

the excavations in Dublin and Waterford. Few changes appear to have occurred
in the boats and ships using the port of Dublin in the period directly following
the arrival of the Anglo-Normans. The timbers from the excavations show
little change in technology and retain the Viking character of the earlier levels.
The numerous timbers recovered from the excavation levels dating from 1160–
1275 (see table 3) were from vessels of various sizes, ranging from boats to large
ships.[33] Overall, the trend was towards larger ships, seemingly reflecting the
expansion of mercantile growth at this time. McGrail found no evidence for
rowing in any of the timbers from the larger ships found at the twelfth- and
thirteenth-century levels, although Hutchison has speculated that they may
have come from an oared galley.[34] The vessels may represent craft in a transi-
tional phase of development from Norse vessels to larger medieval cargo ships;
however, it remains difficult to recognise this phase as many of the initial
changes were occurring in the superstructure. The excavations in Viking
Waterford also succeeded in locating a number of medieval boat timbers. A
single stem was found and dated to the late twelfth or early thirteenth century.
Four or five strakes would have run into it and a small hole for a mooring rope
was evident. The stem probably originally came from a small, four-oared boat.[35]
A possible floor timber, which was of non-Viking character was dated to the
late twelfth century and may have come from a flat-bottomed, barge-like boat.[36]
Barges appear in written sources from the thirteenth century and from the
mid-fourteenth century the term was increasingly applied to galleys.[37] In 1392

the King's council ordered the re-arrest of a barge that had left Waterford to supply Irish enemies.[38]

Apart from the material that was recovered from the Dublin and Waterford excavations, finds of timbers from medieval boats or ships are extremely rare in Ireland. Only two other examples are known. These include a possible medieval ship's timber that was trawled up from a low mound on the seabed of Dublin Bay in the late 1980s.[39] The timber appears to be a plank from a clinker-built boat and features moss caulking as a watertight sealant. A large, curved oak timber was taken up from shallow water by fishermen from the Suir estuary near Waterford.[40] It appears to be the stern post of a galley or nef. A second timber was taken up by the fishermen but this was lost as it was being towed back to shore. Underwater investigations at both sites have failed to identify further remains to date but survey work is continuing.

Outside the major ports, local, traditional types of boats continued in use. These vessels may have been increasingly restricted to westerly parts of the country, or in the case of coracles to inland rivers and lakes. Many of these vessels have a direct ancestry to the skin-covered craft of pre-Viking times. Giraldus Cambrensis, writing in the early thirteenth century, recounts a story told to him by a sailor from an English ship which had sought shelter from heavy weather among islands off the Galway coast.[41] After the vessel had anchored, the crew spotted a small boat coming towards them, being rowed by two sparsely-dressed Irish men. Their small craft was described as being narrow and oblong in shape and made of wattled boughs, covered with the hides of beasts. The two men were brought on-board and, speaking in Irish, confessed that they had never seen a vessel built of timber or of such magnitude before. There can be little doubt that their small vessel was a traditional currach-type boat. In 1203, Mellifont Abbey was granted the fishing rights along the River Boyne, adjacent to its monastic lands. Throughout the medieval period the monks developed this resource by controlling the water flow and installing fishing weirs on the river. The erection of one of these weirs got the monastic authorities into trouble in 1366 when they were penalised for obstructing the free passage of coracles on the river between Drogheda and Trim.[42]

Dugout boats were also extensively used, especially on the inland lakes and rivers, including Strabane, Co. Tyrone.[43] A recent discovery made in the Boyne estuary at Drogheda, Co. Louth uncovered a dugout associated with medieval pottery, flint flakes, large quantities of animal bone, leather shoes and a pouch. The vessel itself was oak with a pointed prow, flat-bottom and transom stern.[44] The material for the construction of rafts would have been readily available and there is limited evidence that such vessels were in use in medieval Ireland. In 1235 the *Annals of Connacht* record how the English, while attacking a stronghold on Lough Key, Co. Roscommon, built rafts from the wood taken from the houses of the district. Barrels were attached to the rafts to give them buoyancy while a large boat was used to tow them to their destination. The ease of construction of this type of floating craft and the lack of technical knowledge required to make it must have meant that they were commonly used as ferries and platforms around the country.

THE LATE MEDIEVAL PERIOD, (*c*.1400–1600)

The late medieval period in Ireland presents the archaeologist with differing theories on the social, political and economic climate of the time. These ideas are based largely on how one views the apparent stagnation of the fourteenth century in the wake of climatic deterioration, warfare and the Black Death. Commentators have argued over the extent and nature of this decline. As the population shrank, the English areas of influence around the Pale appear to have contracted, and the economy of the colony slowed to the benefit of Irish lords. In contrast, others have pointed to continuity in the form of the building of friaries in the decades after the Black Death, and the ongoing nature of Gaelic-English economic co-operation.[45] In the economy a shift from mainly arable to pastoral practices mirrored a European trend from exporting general produce to concentrating on those goods specifically suited to each region. The arrival of huge herring shoals off the south-west and west coasts has been described as the greatest single economic event of the period 1300-1500. The trade benefited both Irish and English lords, allowing for the building of tower-houses and halls in western Ireland and the maintenance of armies in a period characterised by political unrest.[46] In terms of shipping, the fortunes of individual Irish ports appear to have varied during this period. Many on the east coast responded well to the changes in the rural economy, with an emphasis on the export of herds, hides and wool.[47] The ports of Dublin and Drogheda remained relatively stable, and even though their hinterland had contracted they were able to maintain links from Iceland and Scotland to Brittany and Spain.[48] Waterford and New Ross also adapted quickly while Wexford went into decline.

Major developments were also taking place on the continent from the late fifteenth century. Portuguese and Spanish voyages of exploration were to have far-reaching effects on the politics and fortunes of European states. The opening up of vast areas of the Americas and Asia to trade and imperial ambition was dependent on technological advances, both in shipping and navigation. The trade to the east was dominated by the ships of Spain and Portugal and these countries also controlled many of the overland routes to China, India and Indonesia. England had long tried to gain a foothold into this market but it was inhibited by the dominance of the other countries and its position on the extremity of north-west Europe.

Profound changes in the method of ship construction began to occur early in the fifteenth century in Europe.[49] The carvel technique became the more common building method employed on larger craft, while the clinker technique continued to be used on smaller, more localised boats. The introduction of the carvel technique, probably from the Mediterranean region, meant that shipwrights could build larger vessels, which were more economical and structurally sound. The clinker technique had become complex and wasteful of timber as demands for larger vessels grew. The carvel technique, on the other hand, used less timber and required fewer skilled labourers. The main benefit was that it allowed larger superstructures to be accommodated upon ships' hulls. This was particularly useful for military vessels, as larger fighting platforms could then be built. For the first time, gunports could be pierced through the hulls, an important development as naval tactics increasingly depended on artillery. The development of the broadside armament of cannon reduced the sheer of ships' hulls and required consideration of stability and the use of space. Two or three masts were added to ships to increase speed, and bowsprits became increasingly necessary in order to give proper lead to the bow-lines. The fore- and after-castles were merged into the hull of the vessel and the after-castle, in particular, became much larger and played a more central role in the internal layout of the ship. By the middle of the sixteenth century, hulls had become much more round-bottomed to increase stability and carrying space. Square sterns were added in order to support the superstructure and accommodate larger end-rudders. These developments also led to a more formalised internal social arrangement within the vessel. The captain and officers' quarters were located in the stern section, while ordinary seamen and supplies were accommodated amidships and forward. Large ships were essentially developing into floating settlements equipped with everything that was needed for survival. Equipment on-board ranged from military ordnance through to food supplies, and all classes of soldiers and tradesmen were carried to service the community. It is the loss and subsequent recovery of such vessels which has provided us with an invaluable insight into later medieval life.

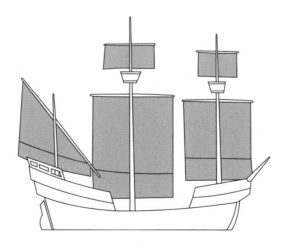

41 Carrack. *After Orpana Strand, 1997*

With the emergence of new ship-building technology, ship design witnessed some radical changes. New, larger vessels emerged and the face of shipping underwent a rapid reformation within a century. The carrack, more than any other ship type, epitomised this change. Although originally developed in the early fourteenth century in the Mediterranean, it quickly evolved and was adopted throughout north-west Europe. Carracks were big, heavy ships with large fore- and after-castle structures *(41)*. Initially they were rigged on the fore and main masts with single square sails but later they essentially became three-masted ships.

Evolutionary trends continued with the emergence of the galleon in the early part of the sixteenth century. Galleons differed from carracks in that they had high, narrow sterns with a lower fore-castle and a low beakhead. This distinctive feature protruding from the hull below the bowsprit was used for ramming and it later provided a platform for handling head sails. Galleons also had a strongly braced hull adopted for almost continuous use in Atlantic conditions. There were many variants of this ship type throughout Europe with different regions displaying characteristics, which were adopted to suit local needs. Although primarily associated with naval functions, galleons were also frequently used for mercantile and fishing purposes.

The majority of the evidence for these medieval ship types in Irish waters comes from that famous naval episode in medieval European maritime history, the Spanish Armada of 1588. The more common vessels around our coastline continue to be noted in documentary sources. The balinger originated in the Bay of Biscay as a whaler and became common in the fifteenth century when it superseded the galleys in use by the English. This oared fishing vessel had evolved into a two-masted sailing boat of 20-50 tons. Balingers appear to have functioned as ordinary trading vessels, transports and warships. One such vessel was the *Katerine* of Waterford, requisitioned in 1414 for the King's service in Bristol.[50] The trade in fish with English ports such as Chester reveals the names of some of the smaller vessels, e.g. pickards. In 1467-'68 the Irish vessel, *Jenicot Pykard*, under *Blak Patrick* was trading regularly with Chester.[51] Pickards appear to have been smaller versions of the balinger and were mainly involved in fishing.[52]

Galleys under the command of both Irish and English captains continued to be employed. Betelius's map of Ireland, dated around 1560, and now in the possession of the British Library, indicates the form of galleys in the latter half of the sixteenth century *(42)*. The map depicts two galley ships off the east coast of Ireland. One lies off Dublin and is the larger of the two vessels shown. It has a large central mast and has 34 oars on either side, in keeping with descriptions of this type of vessel in the written sources, e.g. the 32-oar galley at Rindoon.[53] The vessel shown further south appears to have somewhere between 16-20 oars and carries its sail lowered and furled on a yard. Both of the decks on the vessels are covered with some form of protective canopy and both have pendants on their sterns indicating that they were probably in royal

42 Beteliuss' map of Ireland, *c.*1560. *Courtesy of the British Library*

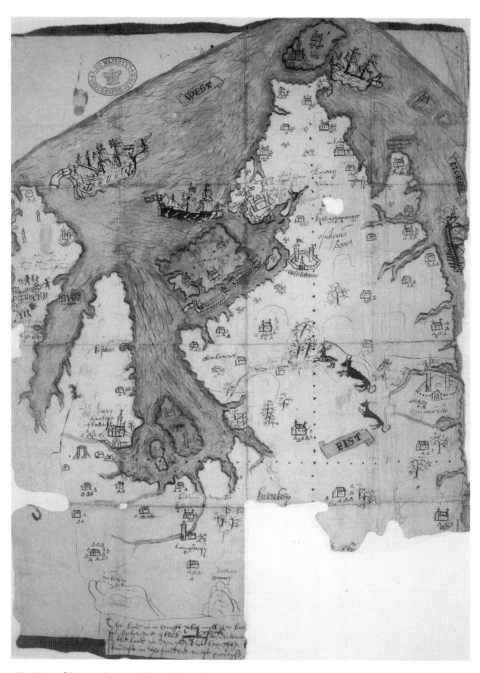

43 Map of Bantry Bay, *c.*1558 *(MPF/1/94, PRO London)*

service. A later sixteenth–century map of Beare and Bantry, Co. Cork, depicts two oared galleys being rowed up the Bere Island Sound towards Dunboy Castle *(43)*.[54] Unfortunately the structural elements of the ships are less clear. Neither vessel has a sail but one flies a flag displaying a simple cross. The leading galley has a trumpeter in the bow, while the second has a man blowing a horn in its stern. These illustrations indicate the type of large, naval galleys that operated off the east and south coasts; however, like the various forms of iconography these representations of vessels are not always accurate. One map dating to about 1602 shows a number of ships off the north coast of Ireland with square sterns, awning and long pointed bows, very much in the style of Mediterranean galleys. The cartographer's annotation states that these vessels are

> fleetes of shippes and Gallies, or rather Skulles of open boates, and woodden Barges… to shewe the frequent and usualle navigations of those wilde beggers the Redshankes alonge the Irish coastes to robbe and spoile *(colour plate 7)*.[55]

A similar depiction of a galley at sea between Antrim and Kintyre appears on a map by Francis Jobson dating to about 1590 and has also been interpreted as a highland vessel.[56] In reality, the form of sixteenth–century highland galleys was more in keeping with the old Scandinavian tradition. A more accurate representation of the vessels is to be found in funerary monuments and graffiti

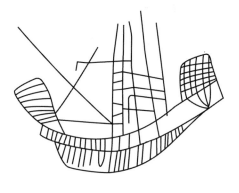

44 Two examples of ship graffiti from Moyne Priory, Co. Mayo. *After Macalister, 1943*

45 Ship carving on
tomb of A. MacLeod,
Scotland. *After Steer
and Bannerman, 1977*

located across the Atlantic seaboard from Mayo to the western isles of Scotland
(44). These stone carvings were created by the communities that used such
vessels and valued them as symbols of wealth and naval power.[57]

Traditional highland galleys were a common feature of north-coast traffic
into the sixteenth and even seventeenth centuries. The island lords of western
Scotland had a major influence on the society and economy of regions like
north Antrim and there was regular traffic between the two areas. The vessels
taking part in this interchange would have varied greatly from warships to large
cargo carriers and humble fishing boats. The galleys depicted on Scottish
funerary monuments were probably the elite vessels among these coastal fleets;
they were reliable sea-going vessels and were well-suited to the Gaelic mode
of combat and raiding. They were capable of high speed over short distances
(6-7 knots) and their shallow draught allowed them to penetrate estuaries and
approach beaches with no formal landing facilities. One of the finest examples
of such a galley is carved on the tomb of Alexander MacLeod *(45)*. It dates to
1528 and is found in St Clement's Church at Rodel on the island of Harris in
the Outer Hebrides. In a Crown charter dated 1498, the MacLeods were
granted estates in Skye and Harris and they were required to keep a number
of ships in the service of the King, one of 26 oars and two of 16 oars apiece.
The ship shown on the tomb is clearly of the highland galley type and it is
paralleled on other tombs in western Scotland in the late medieval period. The
carving is of a double-ended, clinker-built vessel with a high prow and stern.
It has a central mast with one cross yard lashed fore and aft, and its large rectangular sail is unfurled. Seventeen oar ports are visible on its starboard side. In

contrast to its Scandinavian ancestors, a large, stern-mounted rudder with two large pintles is featured.[58]

The galley depicted in graffiti at Dunluce castle illustrates a similar vessel.[59] The castle is sited in a commanding position on a promontory overlooking much of the north coast and across to Scotland. This seaboard enjoyed close links with the Scottish lords of the Isles through the powerful McDonnell family, who occupied a number of coastal fortifications, including Dunluce. The vessel is incised on a stone within a gatehouse, which was erected after 1584 following the demolition of the earlier one. It depicts a double-ended ship with a zoomorphic figure on the stem and stern *(46)*. A single, central mast with one yard is shown, its sail is furled, and rigging takes the form of fore and aft stays. Along the hull 22-23 oar ports are visible. The graffiti probably represents a galley either lying alongside a quay or at anchor. On the other hand the apparent bend in the two braces at either end of the yard may instead represent the sail of the vessel underway – the rather crude nature of the piece allows either interpretation. Either case may explain the rough nature of the representation. The artist might have been attempting to draw one of the many galleys that must have passed the castle on their way to favourable landing areas. Alternatively, the vessel may have been sketched while it was lying some distance off the promontory at anchor, in which case smaller tenders or local craft would have brought the crew or cargo ashore. The similarity between the depiction of this craft and those from contemporary Scottish tombs is an interesting example of funerary carvings and graffiti reinforcing

46 Galley carving at Dunluce Castle, Co. Antrim

47 O'Malley family crest from a stone plaque on Clare Island, Co. Mayo. *Courtesy of DEHLG, the Heritage Service*

historical accounts of the strong links between these two regions. It is impossible to say whether the vessel was of Scottish origin or was locally based, but in many ways this is irrelevant. Whatever its origin the vessel was sufficiently impressive for the artist to record. No observer would have failed to have been impressed by the sleek lines of the relatively large craft, which would undoubtedly have belonged to a well-known lord.

Another example of the Gaelic galley tradition is found on a memorial plaque in the abbey of Clare Island, off the west coast of Co. Mayo *(47)*. The plaque, which is thought to date to the early seventeenth century, is traditionally believed to commemorate '*Granuaile*', or Grace O'Malley, the notorious pirate queen.[60] The O'Malley's were one of the most famous nautical Gaelic families along the west coast, their motto being 'Powerful by Land and Sea'. The vessel depicted is a clinker-built, double-ended boat again with a single, central mast. The vessel is shown with six oars on one side, indicating that it was a relatively small vessel. These boats may have been the most common medium-sized vessels in Irish waters in the later medieval period, larger galleys are known to have been in the possession of Granuaile – three galleys capable of carrying 300 men each were noted in 1599.[61]

There is also evidence in stone carvings of the continued use of early medieval vessels, for example hulcs. Two depictions of hulc-like vessels survive on the sides of tomb chests in churches in Thurles and Cashel, Co. Tipperary.[62] The example from Thurles, which dates to around 1520, shows a bearded ecclesiastic, presumably St Simon, holding a ship in both hands at waist level.[63] The vessel has a rounded hull profile with a pronounced after-castle, which appears to be incorporated into the hull. There are indications that a similar structure was present at the bow. There is a single, central mast with two stays running fore and aft respectively. A large, castellated crow's nest sits on top of the mast, which is out of proportion to the rest of the vessel. A similar representation survives in Cashel, on the north side of the tomb chest, which dates to the first half of the sixteenth century.[64] Again Simon is shown holding a ship in front of him in both hands *(48)*. The vessel is clearly of clinker construction with a large, central mast held by four stays, two each running fore and aft. A disproportional crow's nest is shown on top of the mast and it is barrel-like in shape and build. Two castle-like structures are clearly shown at both ends where they are integral parts of the hull. Although allowances have to be made for artistic licence and the stone mason's ability to represent ships accurately, both ships bear a clear resemblance to a ship shown on Betelius' 1560 map of Ireland. The vessel, shown sailing with the wind off Ardglass, Co. Down, has a rounded, clinker-built hull with integral fore- and after- castles. No crow's nest is shown but the sail appears to be tied off on a bowsprit, which is helping the sail take full advantage of the wind. The vessels depicted on the tombs represent the retention of Scandinavian techniques with local modifications. While the trend in shipbuilding was turning toward carvel-built craft for

48 Ship carving
from Cashel,
Co. Tipperary. *Photo:*
A. O'Sullivan

ocean-going voyages, the clinker-built vessels – so well adapted for northern coastal areas – persisted indeed into recent centuries, where they survived as smaller fishing boats.

In addition to the vessels depicted on early charts, carvings and graffito, town seals and charters continue to be of use in providing information about ships at this time. They too demonstrate that clinker-built ships continued to be employed not only in Gaelic areas, but also in busy Irish ports under English control, for example, Youghal and Waterford. A number of seals from the town of Youghal depict a clinker-built vessel, double-ended with a high prow and stern and a single central mast *(49)*. The sail on these vessels is shown furled on a yard hanging from the mast. The earliest of the seals is from a later medieval document dated 12 June 1527, but they continued in use into the seventeenth century.[65]

The Waterford seals are particularly valuable in showing the evolution and development of English naval galleys guarding the city over a period of 200 years. In 1461 the O'Driscolls of Baltimore, Co. Cork, landed at Tramore in Waterford on a raiding mission. There had traditionally been a great deal of enmity between the two regions and frequent raiding appears to have taken place. On this occasion the men of Waterford defeated the raiders and captured three galleys from the West Cork men. The three galleys on the seals of Waterford are believed to celebrate this victory.[66] The earliest charter portraying the three vessels is that of Henry VIII, which dates to 1510. The charter of Philip and Mary, dated to 1556, also depicts the three vessels on the top right corner. These wooden, clinker-built vessels are shown with high curved bows and what appear to be square sterns with tents erected. The vessels have a single, central mast with furled sails tied on yards. Eleven oar ports are visible on the sheer strakes of the vessels. Three galleys are again shown on Elizabeth's charter of 1574. A later seal of Waterford Corporation, from a deed dated 1663, now on display at the museum of Mount Sion Monastery, depicts three slender galleys which have evolved considerably from the small, wooden vessels shown on the charter of 1510.[67] These vessels have long, curved, slender lines with a pointed bow and a slightly raised stern castle section *(50 a and b)*. Between 11 and 13 oars are shown protruding from rectangular oar ports on the sheer strakes of the vessels and the uppermost vessel is shown with two or three masts. Waterford's harbour was one of the busiest in the country throughout the medieval period and it came under constant attack from pirates and rebel forces from outside the town. In 1497 a fleet of 11 ships and 2,400 men under Perkin Warbeck, pretender to the English throne, and the Earl of Desmond besieged Waterford, which was held by forces loyal to the king. One of the ships was bulged and sunk by the ordnance from Dundory. Warbeck escaped to Cork and from there sailed to Cornwall pursued by four ships. A breech-loading cannon (see appendix 2) typical of the period was dredged from the River Suir, opposite Reginald's Tower, by the town's harbour commissioner during dredging operations in January 1901.[68] Ship timbers were recovered at the same time but these were destroyed. The cannon is currently on display at the Civic Museum. It measures just under 2m long and is mounted on a movable support. It appears to be intact and its breech-block is in situ. By 1537 Waterford had what was described as its own 'great galley', which carried artillery and was well stocked for the defence of the town.[69]

49 Youghal Seal. *After McCaughan and Appleby, 1989*

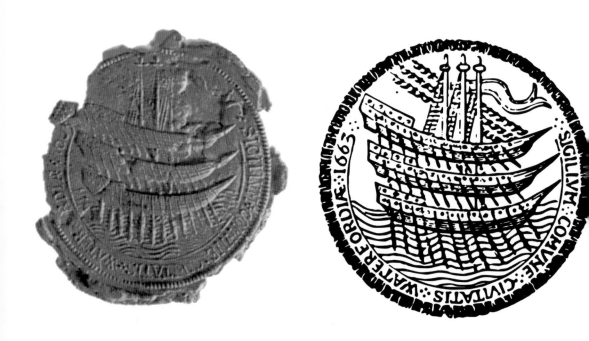

50 (a) Seal of Waterford, from a deed dating to 1662. *Courtesy of Mount Sion Monastery Museum, Waterford;* (b) Drawing of Seal of Waterford

Evidence for Mediterranean ships in Irish waters is generally limited. Vessels such as Portuguese-style carvels are known to have visited ports such as Passage East in Co. Waterford in the fifteenth century, and Gaelic chiefs conducted a lucrative trade with Spanish and French fishing fleets in the sixteenth century.[70] No vessels associated with these trading networks have been located. Mediterranean ships fitted for war are, however, well represented due to the Spanish attempt to invade England in 1588 and the subsequent dispersal of their fleets along the Irish coastline.

THE SPANISH ARMADA (1588)

On 17 July 1579 three Spanish ships under the command of James Fitzmaurice, son of the Earl of Desmond and a known opponent of English rule in Ireland, landed on the North Kerry coast and occupied Dun an Óir, the old promontory fort overlooking Smerwick Harbour *(colour plate 8)*.[71] This small force made several incursions inland, but met with a great deal of resistance from the English forces, and as a result they were forced to over-winter at Smerwick. The following summer, reinforcements consisting of 800 soldiers commanded by Don Juan Martinez de Recalde, arrived at Smerwick and set up an artillery fortification at Dun an Óir. An English naval squadron under William Wynter arrived at the harbour in order to counter this new threat. It set about destroying the fortification with incessant ordnance bombardment from its larger ships. The three largest ships in the squadron, the *Revenge, Swiftsure* and *Aid*, carried out the primary bombardment from their decks while three smaller vessels, the *Merlin, Achates* and the *Tiger*, sailed close to shore and subjected the encampment to a lesser assault. The attack finally ended when the English landed a force of soldiers near the camp and the garrison quickly surrendered. One of the original ships of the Spanish garrison is depicted being broken on the rocks below the encampment in a contemporary map of the engagement.[72] This small episode in the continuing conflict between Elizabeth I's England and Philip II's Spain was to set the stage for a much greater assault on England by a Spanish naval force in 1588.

One of Spain's greatest naval leaders, the Marquis of Santa Cruz, drew up an elaborate invasion plan of England in 1586 and submitted it to Philip II for consideration. The plan was overly ambitious in its original form and a scaled-down version was adopted and put in motion in 1587. The refined plan involved a large fleet of ships, which would sail from Spain to Flanders where it would meet with the successful Spanish army waiting there under the Duke of Parma. The naval fleet would then escort the army across the Channel to England and, once landed, the invasion of England would begin. During protracted preparations Santa Cruz died and subsequently the Duke of Medina Sidonia took command of the enterprise. Finally, in May 1588 a large armada of ships left Lisbon. The fleet consisted of 130 ships divided into 10 squadrons, each based on the type and function of the vessels involved, or the vessels' region of origin, e.g. the Biscay squadron. Altogether it consisted of 65 warships, 25 transports, four galleys and and galleasses as well as 32 smaller vessels.[73] The vessels were essentially small floating towns carrying enough equipment and cargo on-board to keep some 29,453 sailors and soldiers going for weeks at sea.[74]

The Armada arrived in the English Channel in late July 1588 after experiencing a number of problems, including the loss of a vessel as a result of poor organisation during departure. It was met almost immediately by the English fleet off the coast of Devon. Six days of conflict ensued, at the end of which the Spaniards were in effect defeated. On the night of 6 August the English set eight fireships adrift into the main Armada formation. The fireships were small vessels loaded with pitch and faggots, which were set alight and floated toward the enemy to disperse their defensive formation. This succeeded in breaking up the grouping and scattering it around the Channel. The winds began to pick up, and, by the following day, much of the Armada had moved into the North Sea. The venture was effectively finished and the fleet was ordered home. Rather than risk going back into the Channel the fleet instead chose to round Scotland and return home via the west coast of Ireland. On this passage the homeward-bound Armada had to contend with very stormy weather combined with freezing fog and unfamiliar coastlines. Many of the ships had suffered during the week-long conflict and were storm damaged. Over 30 ships were lost on the return voyage with as many as 26 lost around the Irish coast. Less than 75% of the Armada made it home to Spain; the 'Enterprise of England' had truly failed. As Drake later remarked, 'God breathed and England was saved'.[75]

While much has been made of the size of the Spanish fleet and its apparent strength it has become clear that the Armada was probably doomed before it set out. The ships themselves were hastily brought together as a fleet and were supplied very rapidly. The subsequent delay in their departure led to the decay of many of the supplies and this had serious consequences when the fleet was fleeing down the west coast of Ireland. The effects of rationing and the constant struggle to control the ships through foul weather would have weakened many of those on-board the ships. The vessels requisitioned for service in the Armada were not, in many cases, suited to the waters of north-west Europe. They were built for the sheltered, calmer waters of the Mediterranean and were stretched, in many cases beyond their limits, in the subsequent storms during the late summer of 1588. The weather, which included particularly violent gales, played a significant role in leading many vessels to their end on the coasts of Ireland and Scotland.[76]

The readiness of the English fleet in meeting the threat of the Armada was also a major factor in the campaign's failure. The English fleet was actually much larger than that of the Spanish and it was armed with larger and heavier

1 Broighter Boat. *Courtesy of National Museum of Ireland, Dublin*

2 Captain Phillip's 1670 drawing 'Portable Vessel of Wicker'. *Courtesy of Pepys Library, Magdalene College, Cambridge*

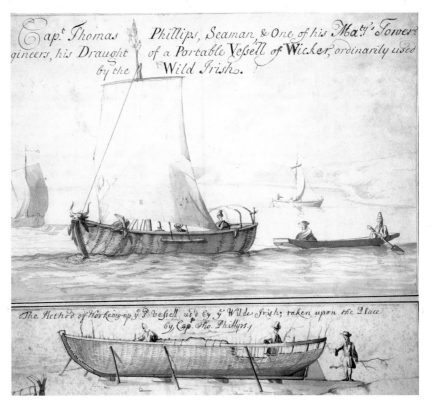

Cap.ᵗ Thomas Phillips, Seaman, & One of his Ma.ᵗˢ Tower engineers, his Draught of a Portable Vessell of Wicker, ordinarily used by the Wild Irish.

The Method of Working up y.ᵉ Vessell used by y.ᵉ Wilde Irish; taken upon the Place by Cap. Tho. Phillips.

3 *Above left:* Archaeologists lifting the Lough Lene boat

4 *Above right:* Kilnaruane Pillar Stone, Bantry, Co. Cork. *Photo: W. Forsythe*

5 *Left:* Illustration from 1370 Waterford City Charter Roll. *Courtesy of Waterford Museum of Treasures*

6 Sir R. Bingham's Map of Streedagh Strand, 1589. *MPF 1/91, PRO London*

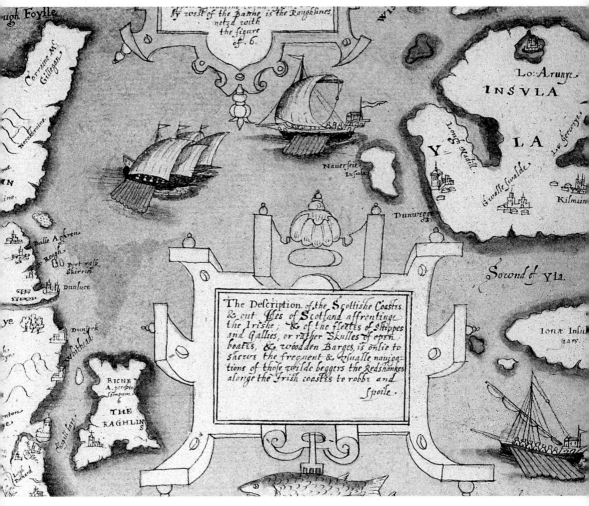

7 *Above:* Map of East Ulster, *c.*1602, showing a number of ships. *Dartmouth map 25, courtesy of National Maritime Museum, Greenwich*

8 *Right:* Early seventeenth-century map of Smerwick Harbour, Co. Kerry. *MPF 75, PRO London*

9 Illustration of raft at Charlesmont Fort, by Bartlett. *After Hayes-McCoy, 1964*

10 Painting of *La Surveillante* by Robert Dodd, 1748–1815. *Courtesy of National Maritime Museum, BHC0426*

11 Artefacts from the *Taymouth Castle. G. Pollock, EHS Belfast*

12 Wrecks of two Seine fishing boats in Co. Cork. *Photo: W. Forsythe*

13 Abandoned seine fishing boat on Dursey Island, Co. Cork

14 Boat shelter in Mill Bay, Rathlin Island

ordnance well suited to the tactics adopted by the English navy. Rather than engage the Spanish vessels at close range, which would have suited the Mediterranean craft and Spanish tactics, the English ships stood off and bombarded the Spaniards from a distance. It is highly unlikely that the large siege guns carried on-board the Spanish ships for use during the conflict on land would have been manageable at sea and so would not have featured in the naval conflict. Research on the ordnance recovered from the Spanish wrecks indicates that many of the pieces were of substandard construction and a lot of the actual ammunition was ineffective and dangerous to use.[77] The English ships were also much closer to home and did not need to be provisioned or equipped to the same degree as their Spanish counterparts. This would in turn have freed up much more space on-board and would not have tied the ships to the sea for any considerable time. It would have been relatively easy for them to slip into port to re-arm and equip almost at will.

The experience of the seamen in both navies also played a major part in the outcome of the venture. Medina Sidonia readily acknowledged that the seamen in the Spanish fleet were too inexperienced. This repeatedly showed itself during the short campaign. Their lack of knowledge of the waters of northern Scotland and western Ireland also may have played its part in the wrecking of so many ships around these coasts. Certainly the contemporary charts of these areas were highly inaccurate and would not have aided the Armada's safe return home. Medina Sidonia had urged the retreating vessels to steer well clear of the west coast of Ireland, but this advice was either unheeded or the ships were unable to follow it because of the heavy weather.

An account of the wrecking of three Armada vessels at Streedagh Strand in Co. Sligo is recorded in the testimony of Don Francisco de Cuellár, who escaped from the wreckage, and local scavengers, who robbed anybody that reached the shore and killed those who resisted. The three ships had rounded Scotland in very bad weather, suffering heavy damage by the time they reached the west coast of Ireland. They were unable to round Erris Head on the Mayo coast and were forced to anchor more than half-a-league from the shore off Streedagh. After five days lying at anchor, the ships were driven from their moorings and blown onto:

> a strand covered with very fine sand, shut in on one side and the other by great rocks... and within the space of an hour, all three ships were broken in pieces.[78]

Over 1,000 men were either drowned or killed on the beach by the locals, who proceeded to salvage the riches on-board one of the vessels. De Cuellár only just managed to escape by lying on a timber which was carried ashore and then by hiding until night fell. The three vessels wrecked, the Sicilian *Juliana* (860 tons), the Venetian *Lavia* (728 tons) and the smaller *Santa Maria de Vision* (666 tons),

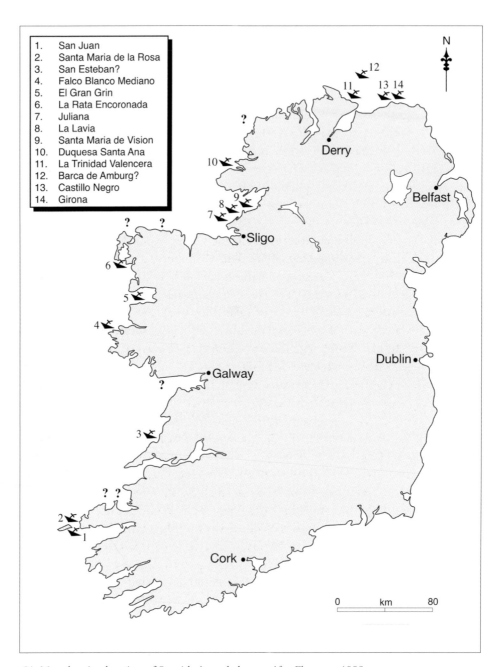

1. San Juan
2. Santa Maria de la Rosa
3. San Esteban?
4. Falco Blanco Mediano
5. El Gran Grin
6. La Rata Encoronada
7. Juliana
8. La Lavia
9. Santa Maria de Vision
10. Duquesa Santa Ana
11. La Trinidad Valencera
12. Barca de Amburg?
13. Castillo Negro
14. Girona

51 Map showing location of Spanish Armada losses. *After Flanagan, 1988*

were all from the Levantine squadron. This squadron was made up of large Mediterranean merchant vessels that had originally been built to carry vast quantities of grain and elements of the siege train for the use of troops once ashore.[79] A map drawn by Sir Richard Bingham and dated 20 April 1589 shows the three vessels breaking up in the surf at Streedagh *(colour plate 6)*. Allingham records that in the late nineteenth century, some cannon and cannon balls were brought to the surface in the area and that bones from Spaniards buried in the sands had been exposed.[80] The site of the wrecking was found in 1985 by a group of English divers who subsequently recovered three guns. The cannons consisted of two pedreros – short-barrelled guns with reduced powder chambers used for firing stone shot, and one saker with a foundry date of 1570, which was probably Sicilian. The saker was bored off-centre originally and a hole was blown out of the gun close to the muzzle during firing. A large rudder with its pintles still intact was also uncovered and photographed on the site but this was later re-buried by sediment movement. The wreck site continues to periodically reveal remains on the seabed – gun carriages, iron and stone shot, anchors, lead sheeting and structural timbers have also been noted.[81]

The north and west coasts were witness to many other Spanish wrecks in the late summer of 1588 *(51)*. Both the *Castillo Negro* and the *Barca de Amburg* were wrecked off the north coast, east of Inishowen.[82] *El Gran Grin*, a ship of 1,160 tons, was driven ashore on Clare Island off Mayo, while a smaller vessel was lost off Mutton Island, Co. Galway. The *San Esteban* of the Guipúzcoan squadron was probably wrecked at Doonbeg in Co. Clare, while the 703 ton *Anunciada* was scuttled near Scattery Roads near Kilrush. A pinnace, a small two-masted vessel of about 20 tons, was abandoned and fired near Tralee, while the merchantman, *San Juan* was lost in Blasket Sound in Co. Kerry, north of where another vessel was lost near Valentia. The *Duqesa Santa Ana* was lost in Loughros Mor Bay in Co. Donegal while the carrack *Rata Santa Maria Encoronada* ran aground at Tullaghan in Blacksod Bay, Co. Mayo.[83] In July 1631, Jacob Johnson sailed from London in a small bark, *Charity*, to salvage the contents of a number of ships including Armada wrecks in Broadhaven, Co. Mayo.[84] Johnsen went ashore with William Brotheridge, a mariner from Kent, to a castle under the command of Michael Cormacke to ascertain the directions to these wrecks. After a couple of weeks arguing with the lord's wife, Johnsen finally managed to dive on one of the sites and recovered a bronze cannon which is likely to have come from an Armada vessel in this area. Cormacke's men immediately seized the piece from him and the venture was aborted after further confrontations.[85] The majority of the Spanish wrecks remain unlocated, but numerous place-names and folklore relating to the recovery of objects from the wrecks attest to the burial sites of these famous wrecks. Indeed the Armada is so well known in coastal folklore that virtually every underwater find around the coast is attributed to the ill-fated, sixteenth-century expedition.

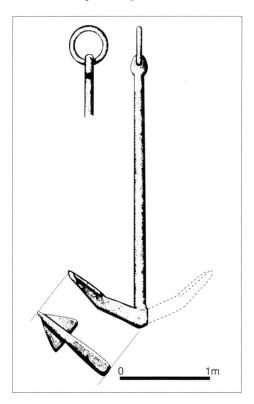

52 Anchor from the *Santa Maria de la Rosa*.
After Wignall, 1982

A number of the Armada wrecks have been excavated in Irish and Scottish waters and they have proved to be of enormous importance, as they provide a unique insight into technology and society of late-sixteenth century Europe. The idea of locating Spanish wrecks in Irish waters was first mooted by Sidney Wignall, an English diver with a tremendous interest in archaeology under-water. From 1963 he led a diving team searching for the wreck of the *San Juan* in the Blasket Sound, Co. Kerry.[86] After a six-year search, a wreck was finally located in 1968. It lay in the Sound 180m south-east of Stromboli Reef. Initially the divers thought they had found the *San Juan* but this identification was quickly discounted in favour of the *Santa Maria de la Rosa*. The *Santa Maria* was the vice-flagship of the Guipúzcoan squadron under the command of Miguel de Oquendo. It weighed 945 tons, carried 297 men, and was armed with 26 pieces of ordnance.[87] The vessel had suffered from a number of problems during the Armada venture. Soon after the original departure of the fleet, it had to put into Corunna, in north-west Spain, having lost its mainmast. It sustained a number of direct hits on its hull during the engagement in the English Channel and as a result began taking in water. By the time it reached the coast of Kerry it was in a poor state and barely able to fight the weather. Eventually, having lost a number of anchors off the Blasket Islands, it was driven onto the reef where it perished *(52)*. All that remained of the wreck on the seabed in 1968 was a large, tightly-packed ballast mound of limestone blocks, 33m in length and 40m wide running on a north-south axis. The mound lay in 40m of water on a flat, shingle bottom and survived to a height of just under 1m.[88] The site produced structural elements from the lowermost part of the hull *(53)*. A section of the scarf-jointed keelson was uncovered as well as portions of a number of stanchions, which would have supported the orlop beams. A complex mast step with a surrounding wooden box survived on the keelson, which was excavated during the course of the project. The structure showed signs of being hurriedly put together and may represent the step repaired at Corunna prior to departure. A series of ground timbers and an assortment of artefacts also survived beneath the mound. Lead ingots, shot, guns including arquebuses and muskets, as well as the fragmentary skeletal remains of a mariner were recovered during the course of the excavation. Two of the pewter plates recovered confirmed the identity of the ship. Both were engraved with the name 'Matute' and belonged to Francisco Ruiz Matute, an infantry captain who was among those on-board. Martin interpreted this section of the remains as being from the bow end of the ship on the basis of the position of ballast in ships of that period and on the position of the mast step.[89]

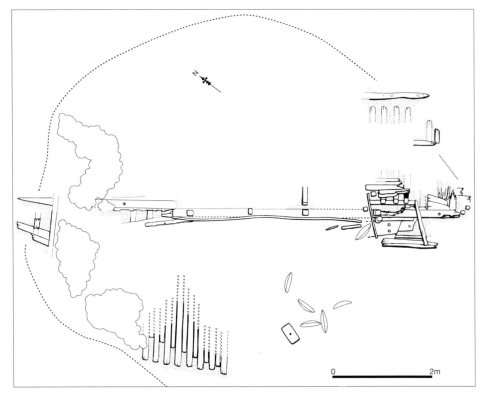

53 Site plan, showing the timbers of the *Santa Maria de la Rosa. After Wignall, 1982*

The site formation processes on the wreck are of note. It appears that the super-structure of the vessel could not withstand the dynamics of Blasket Sound and must have been destroyed quite quickly. It was only the protective cover of the ballast mound which led to the preservation of the remains underneath. This process can be seen on other sites in these waters, where the formation of such a 'cover' can lead to the preservation of organic material in even the most dynamic of environments.

In 1967, Robert Sténuit, a Belgian salvage expert, came to Ireland in search of Spanish wrecks.[90] He had originally planned to concentrate his efforts on Blasket Sound but, finding the English group at work there, he switched his attention to the north coast. According to a number of historians, the wreck of *La Girona*, a galleass of the Naples squadron, had occurred along the Co. Antrim coast in the vicinity of Dunluce Castle or the Giants Causeway. Sténuit was attracted to a bay east of the Giant's Causeway, which the ordnance survey maps labelled *Port-na-Spaniagh*, or Port of the Spaniards, an obvious indicator of a Spanish connection. On his first dive around Lacada Point, Sténuit recovered a number of Spanish coins and noted the presence of a range of other artefactual remains including the distinctively-shaped lead ingots, items commonly carried onboard the Armada vessels. These ingots would have been melted down later to make lead shot once the invasion force had landed. Sténuit returned the following year (1968) with a dive team and a range of equipment that would enable him to carry out a large-scale salvage job. Work continued on the site for another season and ended in 1969, by which time an incredible assortment of objects had been recovered *(54)*. Unlike the *Santa Maria*, no hull structure was found. The topography of the seabed at this location and the shallowness of the site mitigated against the survival of such a large structure. Once the vessel had been driven onto the rocks, the forces of the sea would have quickly broken up the hull. There is no sediment of any depth on the seabed around the Point, which would have allowed for the burial of the structure so instead objects such as ordnance or personal items were either covered by stones or buried into pockets of sand and shingle below large boulders. The continual movement of these stones over the centuries allowed many artefacts to become even more deeply buried. Work in this environment was extremely difficult but very rewarding. The largest items recovered from the site were three guns, including one bronze half-saker and one bronze esmeril. The muzzle of a third gun was also recovered. The ship had an original complement of up to 50 guns but many of these were salvaged at the time by local chieftains and by an English salvage operation mounted soon after the wrecking. An impressive assortment of personal items was found including religious crosses, jewellery and kitchen utensils. Recent work by a licensed diver, under the conditions of the Protection of Wrecks Act (1973), has recovered further personal items and located two more iron cannons and part of an anchor.

Both the *Santa Maria* and *La Girona* were found as a result of systematic

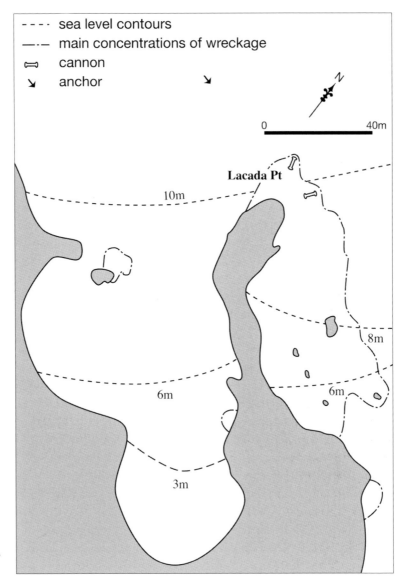

sea level contours
main concentrations of wreckage
cannon
anchor

Lacada Pt

0 ———————— 40m

10m

8m

6m

6m

3m

54 Site plan showing main areas of wreckage of the *Girona*. *After Flanagan, 1974*

searches. The site of *La Trinidad Valencera* however was found by chance by the City of Derry Sub-Aqua Club in 1971. During the course of a training dive, club members found a number of guns, one of which was cast in 1556 and is inscribed with the royal arms of Philip II of Spain. The club decided immediately that the site should be investigated scientifically and it invited Colin Martin to come and direct the operations *(55)*. The Spanish authorities in Sicily had originally requisitioned the ship in 1587 for use in supplying the proposed Armada but she was later incorporated into the Armada itself and sailed as part of the Levant squadron. The ship, because of its bulk-carrying abilities, was fitted with three large siege guns that were to be used on land once the army had been successfully landed in England. Two of the siege guns were later recovered during the course of the excavation. They had come from a Flemish foundry and fired 40-pound cannon balls. The ship also carried 29 other pieces of ordnance, 79 mariners and 281 soldiers.[91]

No intact portion of the hull structure survived in the areas under excavation. However oak planking was found on the site. This appears to have been exclusively fastened by iron bolts, as there was no apparent evidence for the use of treenails. The rusting and corrosion of these fastenings would have quickly broken down the structural integrity of the hull, causing its gradual collapse. This process would have been accelerated by the influence of the natural dynamics of the area. The hull would have rested in only a few metres of water and was thus fully prone to the destructive effects of wave action. As the wreck broke up, sections of it scoured into pockets of soft sand on the seabed and were quickly covered over. The subsequent excavation of these shallow pits revealed a good deal of organic material as well as a variety of ship and personal items. The organic specimens included wood, leather, textile and bone pieces, all of which underwent conservation at the Ulster Museum in Belfast.[92] The survival of these items in such quantities enabled the excavator to paint a much more detailed picture of the functionality of a ship from this period than was possible from the other sites.

By the late sixteenth century, even though the English had been in Ireland for four centuries, they had not succeeded in conquering the whole country. With an increasing involvement in European power struggles and religious warfare, the English became fearful that the resentful Irish would provide a platform for their enemies' attacks on England. The Spanish Armada was among the incursions that provided the English with a clear need to complete their conquest and this led to a change of policy in Ireland from one of maintenance to one of aggression. The result of this policy was to lead to the Nine Years War in the 1590s, a conflict which again brought Spanish vessels to Irish shores, but this time, as the English feared, to aid the Irish lords fighting against English rule. The Crown had attempted to isolate Irish strongholds and blockade the seas in order to stop supplies reaching them, particularly from Scotland. This blockade was continually broken by numerous Scottish vessels, which arrived on the northern coast week after week with supplies. Early in 1594, at the beginning of the war, Byran McArt led an expedition into Dufferin, Co. Down and burned twelve towns, attacking Killyleagh and Ringhaddy. He subsequently took the castle at Ringhaddy as his personal residence and went about garrisoning it. McArt had extensive trading contacts with Scotland, and a letter in the *Calendar of State papers* refers to Scottish barques (sailing vessels) 'sometimes twenty in a week', loaded with provisions 'lying at road [at anchor] under the castle wall'.[93] The war continued for the next seven years undergoing periods of conflict and truce before culminating in the decisive Battle of Kinsale in 1601. In September, prior to the battle,

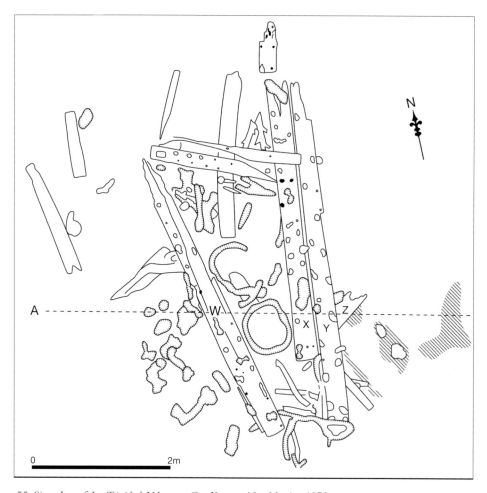

55 Site plan of *La Trinidad Valencera*, Co. Kerry. *After Martin, 1979*

Spanish forces landed at Kinsale, Co. Cork, captured the town and then waited for the Irish from the north to join them. However, before help arrived they were besieged by English forces.

KINSALE 1601

In December 1601 a fleet of six Spanish vessels under the command of Don Pedro de Zubiaur (Vice-Admiral de Zubiaur, commonly known as Seriago) attempted to reach Kinsale to support the besieged Spanish garrison. De Zubiaur's ships had tried to reach Ireland with the main invasion force in September, but they were separated from the fleet and eventually returned to Spain. The missing ships had been carrying important supplies, ordnance and ammunition that were desperately needed. The second attempt by De Zubiaur to reach Kinsale failed and the fleet was instead guided into Castlehaven by the O'Driscoll's, who were sympathetic to the Spanish. The O'Driscoll's were the main Irish family in this southern area of Munster and they had a number of coastal castles at Baltimore, Sherkin Island and Castlehaven, from which they controlled this section of the coast. They handed over a small tower house on the western side of the haven entrance to the Spanish fleet on 28 November. Eighteen days later, on 16 December, an English squadron under the command of Sir Richard Leveson arrived from Kinsale at Castlehaven, having heard that the Spanish had landed. It appears that just prior to the English engagement all the Spanish ships were either lying aground on Castle Strand or at anchor below the castle. The English proceeded to fire on the Spanish ships. There are conflicting reports on the extent of damage inflicted on the Spanish vessels, but it appears that one ship was sunk and two more were driven onto rocks. The testimony of a captured Spanish solider records that one vessel sunk was laden with '300 quintales of biscuit and 400 barrels of wheat'. He goes on to report that one vessel escaped and, of the four that remained, two belonged to the King and two were merchant ships.[94] The vessel lost is named as the *Maria Francesa* in de Zubiaur's accounts.[95] A second vessel, the *Cisne Camillo*, was so badly damaged that the Vice-Admiral intended making landing stages and magazines from its hull.

The vessel that went down was sunk by the *Warspite*, the flagship of Admiral Leveson, and one of the ships driven ashore was de Zubiaur's flagship. An English report refers to the flagship ashore as being bulged and half-sunk.[96] De Zubiaur himself records that the flagship was high and dry on 20 December, but he was hopeful that she could be refloated. This was achieved by Christmas Eve but the vessel lost its rudder the following day.

The story of the remainder of this ill-fated expedition is complicated. The Spanish recovered ordnance from the wrecked vessels and placed eight cannon in a battery just south of Castle Strand. They fired on the English fleet from there and they appear to have inflicted considerable damage to Leveson's vessel. The bombardment eventually resulted in the withdrawal of the English fleet back to Castlehaven. Much of the Spanish contingent now left for Kinsale and the surrounding region in order to support the ultimately unsuccessful efforts of the Irish and Spanish forces there. A small garrison was left at Castlehaven to protect the castle at this strategic location.[97] Some 30-40 Spaniards who had been killed in the conflict were buried at Reen or Spanish Point directly across the haven from the castle. It is interesting to note that the tip of this Point is also called Galleon Point. A number of weeks later, in the aftermath of Kinsale, the Spanish withdrew and returned home. De Zubiaur was later brought to account over his role in the whole affair and died a broken man in 1608.[98]

Throughout this period, the tradition of building skin-covered craft was still very much evident in Ireland. In 1602, the Irish chief, O'Sullivan Beare made a final stand for Gaelic power in the south-west after the defeat of Kinsale. He too was finally defeated at Dunboy Castle, Co. Cork, and was forced to retreat northwards under pressure from English forces under the Earl of Thomond. Having reached the River Shannon north of Lough Derg, his band found that they were unable to cross the river as the local people had been ordered to hide their boats in case they were commandeered by the retreating force.[99] To overcome this obstacle they built a small fortification near the river and killed some of the horses in the company to provide much-needed food and also hides, to be used as hull coverings for the boats they set about building. In a contemporary account of the retreat published in Lisbon in 1621, O'Sullivan Beare records the manner in which the boats were constructed:

> In two days they built two boats of osiers and timber; twelve horses were killed and their hides used to cover the boats... The boat which Dermot designed was built in the following way: Osiers fixed in the earth by their thicker ends and bent back to the centre towards one another, were bound in place with cords and these formed the hull of the vessel. To this stout wooden gunwales and thwarts inside were added. The exterior was covered with the hides of eleven horses; oars and thole pins were also added. The bottom, because of the nature of the material and for the purpose of avoiding rocks and jagged points, was flat. The length was 7.9m, the width 1.8m and the height 1.5m except at the prow which was raised a little higher to throw off the waves. The construction of the second boat was in the hands of O'Malley's horsemen. It was made of osiers without cross-pieces; the bottom was shaped like a circular shield and the sides much deeper than the bottom required. A single horse hide was sufficient to cover the bottom.[100]

The *Annals of the Four Masters* record the same instance in 1602:

> Not finding cots or boats in readiness, they killed their horses, in order to eat and carry with them their flesh, and to place their hides on pliant and elastic osiers, to make currachs for conveying themselves across the green-streamed Shannon.

The larger of the boats described by O'Sullivan Beare is very clearly a currach similar to the modern examples still in use on the south-west coast, while the second boat seems to be a large coracle. On completion, both vessels were carried on the backs of the soldiers to the riverside. The *Annals of the Four Masters* state that the soldiers then crossed the river at AthCoille-ruaidhe (the ford of Red-Wood, opposite Kiltaroe Castle, in the parish of Lorha, Co. Tipperary) without incident, while O'Sullivan Beare records that they crossed at Portland in the same parish. O'Sullivan Beare's account also states that the coracle tried to carry ten men across the river but quickly overturned while the larger currach carried 30 men across at a time with horses tied to the stern of the boat swimming behind them.[101]

Another form of craft in evidence in the early seventeenth century is the raft, an example acting as a ferry is depicted in Bartlett's map of Charlemont fort, on the River Blackwater near Armagh *(colour plate 9)*[102] The map dates to around 1602 and shows a large raft being punted across the river by a single man with a large pole. The raft is built of seven rows of wooden barrels, each row consisting of three barrels. A platform of 12 roughly-cut planks sits on top of them. The raft must have been used for ferrying large goods across the river as a narrow timber bridge traverses the water downstream of the vessel.

FOUR

THE EARLY MODERN PERIOD
c.1600 - 1920

The seventeenth century in Ireland was a time of great change, as the Gaelic lords were dispossessed and the English carved up great portions of the land for themselves. Ireland's economic development was now completely dominated and at times restricted by England. Under the new system cattle, butter and wool became more important exports than traditional commodities such as fish, furs and hides. Ireland found a new market in the emerging trade with the Americas and the East Indies and in doing so found a continuing role in European trade ventures, albeit ancillary. As trade grew in the second half of the century, small ports serving their own narrow hinterland were overtaken by those in more favourable locations. Cork expanded at the expense of Youghal and Kinsale, Belfast overtook Carrickfergus and Dublin developed rapidly through the traffic of English coal.[1]

The great innovations of the period in ship design were stimulated by large-scale mercantile businesses carrying goods from around the world to Europe. Several incorporated companies were founded in Europe at the beginning of the seventeenth century for the exploitation of trade with the countries on the fringe of the Indian Ocean. These were known as the East India Companies and the most successful were those of the Netherlands and England. For much of the seventeenth century there was a great deal of competition and hostility between the Iberian nations who had originally discovered the new maritime trading routes, and the up-and-coming northern maritime companies. The companies exploited the overseas trade routes to meet European demand for eastern commodities, particularly spices and silks. The spices of the Far East were of great value to the economies of the countries of western Europe, as they could be used to preserve food, and also greatly added to its flavour. Trade with the west coast of Africa was also commonplace throughout the seventeenth and eighteenth centuries. Much of this traffic was associated with the slave trade and the ports on England's western seaboard, especially Bristol and Liverpool. The trade was based on a triangular route between the African Gold Coast, Europe and the Caribbean. Manufactured goods were traded with Africa for slaves, who were packed on-board ships, which returned to Europe with sugar and money.

The English East India Company (EIC) was established in 1600 by a group of London merchantmen. A trading network was quickly established throughout the East with factories and trading centres being established at Bantam, India, Sumatra and Persia. The company exported metals, cloth and bullion from England in return for spices, and in particular pepper. The EIC was later expelled from many areas of eastern Asia by their much more powerful Dutch opponent, and as a result it concentrated its efforts in Western Asia, establishing trade relations in Iran and around the Gulf. The company was dissolved in 1858 following the removal of its monopolies on all trade with India and with China's tea trade.[2]

In 1602 the Dutch East India Company (*Verenigde Oostindische Compagnie* or VOC) was formed. The company was essentially an amalgamation of a number of Dutch overseas trading companies and interests which sought to create a monopoly on their extensive trade network throughout Asia. In the middle of the seventeenth century, at the height of its success, the company had over 250 trading offices with 40 warships, 150 armed merchantmen and over 10,000 soldiers. With its eastern headquarters at Batavia, its outlying trading posts became established as fortified centres. The company had the powers to enlist its own militia, had extensive legal powers and autonomy over its own land. It had in effect become a state within a state. However, Dutch naval influence began to wane in the eighteenth century and eventually changes in ship technology and shifts in economic bases resulted in the demise of the company by the 1800s.[3]

With the ever-increasing dominance of the VOC over the eastern trade routes in the seventeenth century, the Netherlands looked westwards for further financial gains. The *West Indische Compagnie* (WIC) was founded in 1621 to develop Dutch trading interests in the Americas and Africa, but more importantly it was established to harass the Spanish fleets on the Atlantic and Caribbean oceans. The company was particularly interested in the returning treasure fleets of the Spanish from the gold mines of South America. It enjoyed formidable success in its first two decades of operation. During this period it sent out over 800 ships to the Americas and by 1636 had taken 600 Spanish ships as prizes.[4] By the 1640s they were the masters of the transatlantic traffic; however, when hostilities with Spain ceased in 1648 the WIC's sole asset was the African slave trade. They had some success in North America where they founded New Amsterdam, a settlement that was seized by the English in 1664 and renamed New York. Thereafter they primarily concentrated again on the African slave trade, even though their clergy had decided it was immoral.[5] The WIC was ultimately less successful than the VOC and was dissolved in 1791.

The emergence the East Indiamen ships in the seventeenth century was a direct response to the need for greater cargo-carrying capacity and the demands of the ever-longer trading voyages.[6] These vessels were characterised by high sterns, three masts, a combination of square and lateen sails and complex rigging. The vessels became larger in size and design, to over 600 tons by the mid-eighteenth century and over 1,000 tons by the end of the century, at which point they even exceeded warships.[7] By this time their lines had become bluffer, their hulls more squat and they carried more artillery. There were also improvements to the masts and rigging, the anchor arrangements and there was a reduction in the flamboyant, decorative carvings around the beakhead and stern which were so popular in the seventeenth century.[8] An important internal distinction between the large merchantmen and naval vessels was the lack of division in the hold for naval stores and platforms.[9]

East Indiamen were produced by traditional methods with no drafted design and a flexible approach to each buyer's requirements, however, by the eighteenth-century shipwrights were committing their designs and innovations to paper. The demand for ships led to some standardisation of construction techniques and the streamlining of the shipbuilding process in order to increase productivity. This was most notable in the shipbuilding industry's relationship with timber yards, which began to produce pre-cut components for ships.

Unsurprisingly the EIC was the company with which Ireland was most directly associated. By the seventeenth century most of the woodlands of England had been cleared and a major attraction of Ireland was the proximity of forest to the coast. This timber, required for shipbuilding and general purposes, could be approached through navigable rivers. The company developed a number of commercial interests, establishing a base at Dundaniel, Co. Cork, and a yard at Limerick at the beginning of the seventeenth century.[10] A shipyard and ironworks were set up at Dundaniel.[11] Three settlements Hope, Bandon and Bantham were established to house 300 workers and 22 armed guards.[12] By 1613, Dundaniel had a dock where two vessels of 400 and 500 tons apiece were built. Houses, storehouses, offices, smiths' forges and an iron works were also built at the site to facilitate the works and accommodate the 300 English inhabitants. The plantation was strongly opposed by

Walter Coppinger, the local lord, as well as by others with local interests. As a result the settlement was under constant threat of attack. It failed to reach its full potential and was abandoned in 1641.[13] Other towns on the south coast took part in the West Indies trade. Cork and Castletownsend became centres for trade and provisioning, notably exporting salted meat, pickled butter and candles and importing sugar and coffee.[14] Some of the meat was carried directly from Ireland but a significant portion was moved to other European ports before crossing the Atlantic.[15] Cork merchants maintained their association with the West Indies trade up to 1864, sending brigs, barques and schooners across the Atlantic.[16]

A number of ships belonging to the various companies were wrecked around the Irish coast and accounts of some of these events are documented in the records of the Admiralty courts as well as newspapers of the day. For example, the Admiralty court in London records the wrecking and subsequent salvage of an East Indiaman ship, the *Pearl*, which belonged to the EIC.[17] In 1610 this vessel sailed for the East Indies under the command of Captain Castleton. After trading in the east (and possibly becoming involved in some piracy) she returned home in 1613 with two other company ships. During the return passage the ships encountered heavy weather and lost a number of men. The small fleet eventually reached the Irish coast in September 1613 and the authorities, fearing that it would be attacked by pirates, took measures to secure it. The vessels at this stage were in poor condition, having suffered badly during the storms. The *Pearl* seems to have been the most badly affected and ran aground near Dursey Island, off the coast of Co. Cork. One of the accompanying vessels, the *Thomas*, was similarly in a poor state but managed to return to London after discharging a portion of its cargo to the care of Sir Richard Bingely. The third ship, *Peppercorn*, was able to get as far as Waterford. Walter Rockwell, a crew member aboard the *Pearl*, later recounted the circumstances of the wrecking and the subsequent salvage of the cargo from the vessel. He indicated that Bingley, captain of the naval ship the *Dreadnought*, came to assist the *Pearl* and recover its cargo. Bingley went to Berehaven and hired three fishing barks, the *Blessing* of Fowey, the *Speedwell* of Oreston and the *Desire* of Millbrook to carry the cargo from the stricken ship onto his own vessel. The three boats were still employed in December of that year when Rockwell mentions that they were carrying goods to Dingle, Co. Kerry. The *Pearl* is described as having her 'bulk broken or made altogether unprofitable' in the *Chichester Letter Book* dated 6 November 1613.[18] The deposition of a second crew-member aboard the *Pearl* recounts that the three barks worked until the following April on the stricken vessel.[19]

In 1952 wreckage began to appear on the foreshore after a heavy storm at Tra na Pferla (the beach of the *Pearl*), on the Cork coast north-east of Dursey. It consisted of a ship's oak ribs with treenails. Further timbers and cannon balls have been washed ashore periodically since then. One of the timbers has been dated on typological grounds to the early seventeenth century, or more specifically by the spacing of the dowel holes, the nature of the carving and the presence of iron-sheathing nails on the outer face of the planking. The recovery of these early seventeenth-century artefacts coupled with the beach's place-name strongly supports the theory that the wreck lies close by. Initial diver surveys in the area have failed to uncover any structural evidence of it on the seabed but future underwater work may yet locate the wreck.[20]

The *London Gazette* records the wrecking of another EIC ship on the coast of Co. Kerry. On 12 July 1685 the 400-ton, 20-gun ship *Henry*, of London, was on passage from India to England under Captain Hudson with a cargo valued at £75,000. The ship took shelter in Ventry Harbour. There it was attacked and boarded by 100 men from a 20-gun French privateer. However, the English captain ordered that the round deck house be blown up, thus setting fire to the vessel and causing the ship to be run ashore. The French ship then fled the scene leaving the party of boarders at the mercy of the English who killed most of them. The vessel was burnt to the middle deck but the goods in the hold were undamaged and were brought to Kinsale the following February.

Artefactual material, including anchors and cables found at Poulatomish, Co. Mayo, may be from a VOC vessel, the *Zeepard*, which was lost in December 1665. A salvage attempt on a possible Dutch ship was carried out in August 1666 near this location and a naval ship was sent to recover the anchors and cables.[21] To date just one wreck associated with the WIC has been recorded. A WIC fleet, under Admiral Piet Heyn, captured a Spanish galleon, the *Santa Anna Maria*, off Cuba in 1628. While on the passage back to Amsterdam the galleon was separated from the Dutch fleet during the course of a storm. A British vessel the *Dragon*, under Captain James, subsequently took it as a prize.[22] The galleon was taken into Castlehaven, Co. Cork, but was wrecked in shallow water two-three fathoms deep. In 1630 some ordnance was recovered by Jacob Johnston, the famous salvor, including eighteen bronze cannon and a number of iron cannon. Bronze and iron cannon were rediscovered at the site in 1970. The crest and date of one demi-culverine indicates that it belonged to Don Pacheco, Sargent of the Spanish silver fleet which was captured in 1628 by the Dutch company.[23]

A number of vessels engaged on the African trade routes were also wrecked on the Irish coastline. In 1796 a certain Mr Hamilton was demolishing a number of old buildings at Tyrella, Co. Down, when he unexpectedly discovered that the beams, lintels and other structural supports were made of cedar wood.[24] Local people informed him that there was a tradition that a large ship, from the coast of Guinea, laden with slaves, ivory, and gold dust, had been wrecked many years previously, in Dundrum Bay. It was believed that a considerable portion of her hull had been swallowed up in the sands near Tyrella. The site of the wreck was marked by the locals and became known as the 'Cedar Ship'. Although the shoreline had undergone considerable changes in the intervening years, the wreck site was still well remembered locally. Hamilton carried out an excavation on the site around 1815 and discovered the 'upper works of the ship'. He recovered six elephant's tusks, a silver goblet, wood and chains, which were thought to have been used to imprison slaves. Hamilton's son re-visited the site in November 1829 and recovered six more tusks, wood, four cannon and the remains of a number of swords, muskets and chains. A number of exotic shells were also recovered.

In November 1775 the *Fame*, a Liverpool ship of 300 tons burthen, was homeward-bound from Africa and Jamaica with a cargo of rum, sugar and ivory when it was lost at Groomsport in Belfast Lough.[25] The ship had struck the Briggs rocks before losing her rudder and being driven ashore by gale-force winds. Diver inspections around the 'Fame Rock' in Groomsport harbour have so far failed to locate any remains of the vessel, although scattered glassware of possible eighteenth-century date was noted. Twenty-one years later in 1796, a Guinea trader, the Sisters, also working out of Liverpool was destroyed by the French Armada in Bantry Bay near the site where *La Surveillante* was scuttled.[26]

Finally, a number of recent discoveries, which seem to date to the seventeenth century, are throwing new light on a range of vessels from the period. Underwater surveys at Baltimore, Co. Cork, have sought to inspect the remains of HMS *Looe*, a British fifth-rate man-of-war, which sank after hitting a rock in 1697. The wreck site revealed that some 14 cannon had come to rest in a series of gullies, with an anchor, cannonballs and red brick also in the area.[27] Another naval vessel fitted with cannon has been uncovered at Duncannon, Co. Waterford. It has tentatively been identified by Connie Kelleher (UAU) as the *Great Lewis* (which sank during action against Royalist forces holding Duncannon fort in 1645) or the *Hastings* (a 32-gun frigate which sank in 1697). Lastly a carvel-built vessel was uncovered at Sutton, Dublin Bay, during dredging operations. It had become completely buried in the sandy intertidal area and initial inspection indicated it may have been stripped on abandonment in this shallow area before slowly succumbing to the sands. Attempts to date the timbers by dendrochronology failed to find a matching tree-ring sequence from any local records, implying that the vessel had been built abroad and possibly was a visiting trader.[28]

A variety of locally built boats continued to be used around the coast and on inland waterways. In 1993 fishermen trawled up an almost complete section of a wooden boat from the southern end of Lough Neagh and this was subsequently recorded by archaeologists from the Environment and Heritage Service *(56)*.[29] The remains consisted of the lowermost part of a carvel-built, relatively flat-bottomed boat with strakes surviving to the turn of the bilge. A large, oak keel measuring 3.37m long ran from stem to stern. Three oak strakes survived on either side of the keel with a section of a fourth visible on the port side. Ten floor timbers crossed the hull joining the keel to the lowermost

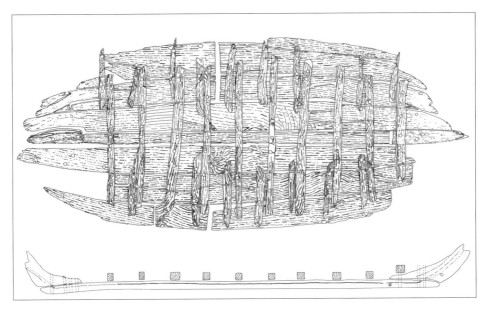

56 Lough Neagh boat. *After Wilkinson and Williams, 1996*

strakes. The timbers were of ash and were joined to the keel with oak treenails. A series of irregularly-shaped ash futtocks survived above the floor timbers and these were similarly fastened. Iron nails were also used to fit the bottom boards below the surface level of the planking. No evidence for a mast step or fitting was found and the evidence suggests that rowing was probably the only form of propulsion. Dendrochronological dating of some wood samples recovered from the boat indicated that the felling date of the tree used for the boat was AD 1718±9 years. The carvel construction of this vessel is of particular importance as documentary sources and local information indicate that clinker-built boats were the dominant tradition on the lough.[30] The vernacular boats used into this century were exclusively clinker, so the location of a carvel vessel is a significant addition to the local record.

The use of skin-covered craft continued throughout the seventeenth century; in one of the earliest discussions (1665) of ancient Irish boats, Roderic O'Flaherty states:

> The ancient Irish had, besides, boats and canoes, which we even use yet in crossing ferries, these small wicker boats…They are called in Irish Corach or Noemhog.[31]

A contemporary drawing of such a vessel was produced by Captain Thomas Phillips in 1670 for Samuel Pepys, the famous diarist. In his drawing of a 'portable vessel of wicker, ordinarily used by the wild Irish', a large currach-like vessel is shown.[32] The vessel depicted however, appears to be much larger than many of the modern-day currachs. While no scale accompanies the drawing, dimensions can be attributed to the craft if it is taken that the figure standing at the stern of the vessel is just under 2m in height. Using this as a base line measurement the vessel would have been in the region of 12m long and around 1.2m deep. The vessel has a wooden frame with an obvious keel and a rounded stem post. Evenly-spaced ribs about 0.3m apart lead to a square transom with an end-mounted rudder. There is a small cross on the transom and this has been compared to the cross on the stern of the Bantry boat (see chapter 1). Two curved timbers cover the helmsman at the bow and these must have been covered with a cloth or hide to provide protection during bad weather. The hull is covered with a number of hides, which appear to be stitched together. A single large mast stands slightly forward with a large, rectangular sail unfurled on a cross yard. An unusual grapple-like anchor hangs over the port side. This larger vessel is either towing or being followed by a very realistically depicted northern-type cot, similar to those visible on early maps of Lough Erne and Enniskillen, Co. Fermanagh – for example the map of Maguire's castle by John Thomas (1593-94). The cot is clearly made of wood, has square ends and is flat-bottomed. The actual size of the larger vessel has raised some doubts as to its authenticity, although in comparison with nineteenth-century descriptions of the Umiak boats of the Canadian Indians, it is not an unrealistic size for a skin-covered boat. These Canadian boats had internal wooden frames, were 12-14m long and could carry a cargo of two tons. It is important to realise that boats are continually changing and studies of modern survivors should not rely too heavily on individual past examples. Even the logboat, in use well into the eighteenth century, probably witnessed subtle changes at different times, although a clear chronological development from crude to well-fashioned vessels is not evident.[33] The currachs remain one of the most enduring vernacular boat types in this country. Gabriel Beranger in his *Tour of Connaught* in 1779 describes a currach from Inishmurray, Co. Sligo, as being made from basketwork and covered with the hide of a horse or cow. An account book from Rathlin Island, off Co. Antrim, dating to the second half of the eighteenth century, records the payment of 1s 6d for one mare's hide for a boat.[34] References to this boat-type continue into the nineteenth century and indeed until the vessels emerge in their contemporary form.

Logboats are another long-term survival. Interestingly, of the 67 dated logboats in the country, 30 are less than 1,000 years old and 18 are less than 500 years old.[35] This figure shows that 27% of all dated logboats are post-medieval in date. Examples include *Derrygalley 2*, dredged from the River Blackwater in Co. Tyrone in 1988, which was dated to AD 1665±20 and the Moy boat, Co. Tyrone, dated to AD 1705±15. The durability of this vessel type can be accounted for by the abundant amount of timber that was available for its construction. It could be argued that the use of logboats only died out when timber was in short supply in the late eighteenth century and with the

Cotts for the vse of the Campe

57 Image of cots taken from map of the siege of Maguire's Castle, Enniskillen, 1593/94. *After McCaughan, 1969/70*

onset of the Industrial Revolution and its associated social and technological changes.[36] During this period the building of bridges at crossing points along rivers superseded the ferrying role of many of the boats. In the mid–seventeenth century the natural historian Gerard Boate remarked that logboats were very common throughout Ireland and were used on rivers and lakes.[37] Sir James Ware also noted that the 'ancient Irish made use of another kind of boat in their rivers and lakes formed out of an oak wrought hollow, which is yet in use in some places, and called in Irish coitti, in English a cott' *(57)*.[38] Fry has found evidence of their use in Ulster as late as 1796.[39]

MODERN SHIPPING, *c.*1750–1920

During the seventeenth and eighteenth centuries there were few significant developments in the evolution of sailing warships. They increased in overall size, were built to a more uniform design and could carry more guns – up to about 130. A system of rating was introduced for fighting ships in the middle of the eighteenth century by the British Admiralty.[40] The system was based on the number of guns that were carried on-board. The ships that were third–rate and larger were considered powerful enough to take their place in the line of battle, and so were known as ships-of-the-line. The line of battle was the common naval formation, which became formalised in the seventeenth century.[41] The tactic sought to maximise the effect of ships carrying broadside armaments that could not be effectively trained fore and aft. The fleet would form a single line and attempt to break the enemy line by sailing parallel to it, or head-on. The tactic required the support of smaller warships, such as frigates, for communication by a system of flags and reconnaissance duties. A first rate ship carried 100 guns or more, while a second rate carried 90 to 98 guns. These vessels were known as three deckers as they mostly carried their armament on three gun decks. They were the largest military vessels of their time and usually functioned as Admiral's flagships. A third-rate ship normally carried 74 guns but could carry between 64 and 84. The armaments were carried on two decks so became known as two deckers. Uncommon fourth-rate ships carried 50 to 60 guns while a fifth-rate carried 32 to 44 guns and the sixth-rates carried 20 to 28 guns.[42] The latter two rates accommodated their cannon on a single gun deck. Ships carrying 28 or more guns were called frigates, which were smaller, faster and more manoeuvrable than the ships-of-the-line. While their primary function was to act as reconnaissance vessels, they also provided protection for convoys and fleets.[43] A 20-gun ship was called a sloop of war and was the smallest, three-masted vessel in the navies of north-west Europe. All of the ratings carried the standard three masts: the foremast, mainmast and mizzen. Each mast was sectioned into the lower mast, topmast and gallant mast. The masts carried square-rigged sails while the bowsprit was also rigged with a jib boom. The sail plan in the eighteenth century had become much more complicated as the number of sails greatly increased. New terms for both large and small vessels appeared which depended as much on the rigging arrangements as the hull design (see Appendix 1). The general result of these changes was improved performance when sailing into the wind, while retaining the efficient square-rig when the winds were fair.[44]

Many of the smaller naval vessels were engaged in patrolling duties, protecting local mercantile vessels against the actions of privateers who plagued the coast. Privateers were privately owned vessels, which were commissioned by their states to prey mainly on the commercial fleets of the enemy. Throughout the latter part of the eighteenth century, French, Spanish, Dutch, American and English privateers were common in Irish waters. These State-sanctioned ships were usually allowed to keep the greater portion of their spoils while the state received one-tenth of their worth. More important was the degree of damage the privateer inflicted on the commerce of its enemy. The British response to the threat took the form of naval action but they also employed their own privateers to meet the enemy. In 1780 the privateer schooner Black Snake, captained by Alexander Fulls, was fitted out at Warrenpoint for a three-month cruise 'against the Dutch and other enemies of Great Britain and Ireland'. A notice advertised for 'spirited seamen', who wished to make their fortune to man her.[45] The *Amazon* was a British privateer fitted out in the Bangor area of Co. Down and it was also engaged in repelling the enemies of the king off the coast of Down and Antrim.[46] The vessel was carrying 14 six-pounder guns (see Appendix 2) and was captained by George

Colvill. She first saw action in September 1779 off Bangor against a 22-gun Spanish brig. During this fight several of her crew were killed. The vessel was wrecked in a storm the following February at Ballyholme, Co. Down, and all her crew were lost. In 1900 timbers from the wreck could still be seen at low tide and one of the six-pounder guns could also be seen at Rathgael, to the west of the wreck site.[47] George Colvill's tombstone is in the grounds of the old abbey church at Bangor and reads:

> Captain George Colvill, of the private ship of war *Amazon*, and only son of Robert Colvill, of Bangor, was wrecked near this ground, 25th Feb., 1780, in ye 29th year of his Age.

American privateer activity increased greatly after that country's Declaration of Independence in 1776. The Americans were unable to match English naval power in their battle for independence so their young government resorted to encouraging privateers to disrupt English commerce. In 1777 the collector of customs in Glasgow wrote to his counterpart at Belfast, asking him to inform the merchants and traders that three American privateers – the *Reprisal* with 18 six-pounder guns, the brig *Lexington* with 16 four-pounders and the cutter *Dolphin* with 10 four-pounders, were cruising between Belfast Lough and the Mull of Galloway.[48] The sloop of war *Wolf* was among the naval vessels sent to counter this threat, however, it was later lost on rocks at Ballywalter, Co. Down. Later in September of that year another sloop of war, HMS *Drake* also arrived, with 20 guns. The vessel was later captured after engaging the famous pirate John Paul Jones, aboard his equally armed sloop, *Ranger*, off Donaghadee, Co. Down.[49]

On 13 August 1781 the surveyor of customs at Waterford wrote that the port was completely blocked by privateers, one of which, the *Princess de Norrice*, carried 26 guns (9- and 12-pounders). One month later the *Apollo*, a privateer from Bristol, arrived at Castletownsend having engaged three American privateers off the Cork coast. The ship had been overpowered by the Americans and the crew had thrown all her 18-pounder guns and ammunition overboard before retreating. Amongst the American privateers were the Essex and the *Pilgrim*, which had been cruising off Cape Clear on the west Cork coast before being captured by the English ship the *Queen Charlotte*.[50] While the threat from the Americans was troublesome and costly it was short lived. The French on the other hand posed a more permanent threat and their interest in Ireland was intensified after the French revolution.

FRENCH ARMADAS 1796–98

While the stories of the Spanish Armada are firmly etched in Irish coastal lore, it was not the only such venture. The objective of the Spanish Armada had been to invade England. However, other expeditions have sought to invade and hold Ireland, often as a means of harassing England. One of the better known of the later campaigns was the French Armada of 1796. France, having undergone a revolution in 1789, was at war with England by 1793. Within Ireland in the 1790s a home-grown revolutionary movement was building up. The United Irishmen was an organisation that modelled itself on the ideals of the French Revolution. One of its leaders, Theobald Wolfe Tone, arrived in France in February 1796 in order to seek French support for a proposed invasion of Ireland which would lead to the country's emancipation from British rule. While Wolfe Tone's pleas were initially met with scepticism he eventually managed to convince the French authorities of the viability of such a strategy and the advantages for the French campaign against England. The invasion fleet began to assemble in the summer of 1796. Despite a number of serious setbacks, a fleet of 48 vessels finally left Brest harbour on 15 December for Bantry Bay, Co. Cork. Tone had proposed landing in Ulster or Leinster, but the French were nervous of a superior British naval presence there and favoured Galway Bay. However, this choice had been leaked to the British government and so Bantry Bay was finally chosen. It offered a superb natural harbour which would serve as a base from which an attack on the important naval town of Cork could be launched.[51] The fleet consisted of 19 ships-of-the-line, 13 frigates, six corvettes and nine transports under the command of Vice-Admiral Morand de Galles. It also carried over 13,000 troops and cavalry under one of France's most noted generals, Lazare Hoche. On departure, the Armada immediately met with problems, one ship was wrecked while leaving the harbour and the fleet became dispersed soon afterwards due to heavy weather and poor communications. As a result only a small number of vessels made it into Bantry Bay in late December. The frigate *La Surveillante* arrived severely storm damaged and leaking *(colour plate 10)*. Her compliment of 600 cavalry under General Mermet was transferred to other ships and a number of guns were thrown overboard before her crew scuttled her on 2 January 1797. In a letter dated 3 January 1797, Major John Brown of the Royal Engineers wrote to the Earl of Camden, Lord Lieutenant at Dublin Castle:

> The weather has been so hazy and so very stormy that although I have been looking out all day from Whiddy Island, I could only see two frigates, one off the west end of Whiddy Island and the other under the north shore. I could plainly see the top mast of the frigate which they scuttled and sank last night...[52]

La Surveillante was built at Lorient in 1778 and had enjoyed a successful if not glorious naval career, having defeated the English frigate *Quebec* in a single ship to ship encounter off Ushent. The vessel was designed along the lines of *La Belle Poule*, built by the shipwright Guignace in 1765 and used as a model for future French frigates.[53] *La Surveillante* was originally three-masted with two main decks, the lower being the gun deck. Measuring over 43m the vessel initially carried 32 guns and a crew of over 200 men. By 1780 the frigate was one of only 12 French ships to have their hull copper-sheathed, having being coppered during a refit in 1779. This modification prevented fouling and protected her lower hull against impregnation by marine organisms such as *teredo navalis* or shipworm.[54]

Over the years local fishermen came to know the area in the vicinity of the wreck, to the north of Whiddy Island, as foul ground. Items such as copper sheeting were continually being brought to the surface by trawlers, even though the exact position of the wreck was unknown. A 16cwt anchor was also brought to the surface and this was mounted on a plinth outside Bantry. Following the Whiddy Island oil disaster in 1979 the wreck was located during a seabed-clearance operation on a side-scan sonar trace. Divers under the direction of Tony Balfe visited the wreck, carried out a photographic survey of the site and confirmed it as belonging to the 1796 Armada. During subsequent surveys two of the original compliment of 40 cannons were raised *(58)*. The wreck was surveyed in 1990 by a team of archaeological divers from the *Mary Rose* Trust on behalf of the Bantry Armada Trust, which had been set up to develop the wreck as a tourist amenity and co-ordinate further research on the site. The survey team mapped the basic outline of the ship and the positions of a variety of artefacts were noted on the site plan.[55] Orientated approximately NE-SW, with her bow to the south-west, the wreck is around 40m long and 10m wide amidships. Copper sheathing is visible to a height of 4.3m above the seabed and is highest at what appears to be the stem. No timbers are recorded above this line although they may have collapsed into silt.

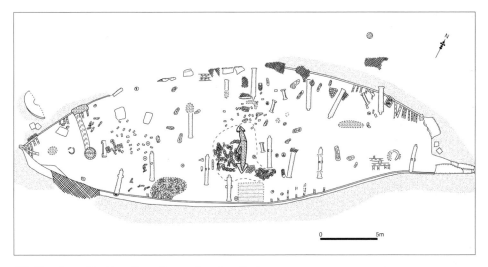

58 Site plan of *La Surveillante*, Bantry Bay, Co. Cork

Alex Hildred, the survey leader, has suggested that the orlop (lowermost) deck and the hold may therefore be preserved. Geophysical survey was undertaken at the site in May 1998. During the course of the survey, a chirp sub-bottom profiler was deployed over the wreck *(59)*. Analysis of the data derived from this survey would suggest that the wreck lies in 2m of silt and rests on hard strata, which is probably a gravel layer.[56] This may indicate that the orlop has collapsed and now rests within the hull. Most of the wreck remains are contained within the sheathing, including 14 guns, one anchor, numerous rigging elements, a collapsed galley structure and smaller artefacts. A bell was lifted from the vessel by local divers and archaeologists from the MSMR in May 1997. This bronze bell is 0.3m high and may be a signal bell from the ship. It is un-inscribed and is plainly decorated apart from a fleur-de-lis mount from which the bell would have been hung. The presence of this type of decoration, which is royalist in origin, strongly suggests that the bell was made prior to the French revolution. A longboat from the French fleet, which was captured when it came ashore in Berehaven, is currently on view at the Maritime Museum in Dún Laoghaire.[57] The slender boat, which was probably an admiral's barge, would have chiefly acted as a transport for officers between the shore and their frigate.

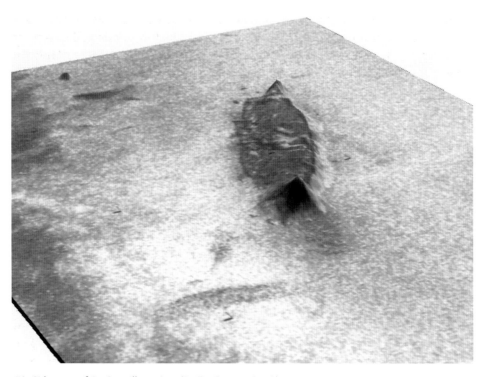

59 Side scan of *La Surveillante* site. *(Dr R. Quinn, CMA)*

Four days before *La Surveillante* was scuttled, a second French frigate, *L'Impatiente*, commanded by Captain de Vaisseau Deniau was wrecked below Mizzen head. She was attempting to make her return voyage to France. This *frigate-bombardiere* armed with 20 or 21 cannon and a mortar, was built in Lorient in 1794-'95. There were only seven survivors from an original crew of 560-70. The victims are reputedly buried in the sands at Barley Cove. The survivors, including the Irish pilot, were taken on-board the British 74-gun *Monarch*.[58] The wreck site of this frigate differs greatly from that of *La Surveillante*. Her remains lie at the base of the steep cliffs of Mizzen Head near rocks known as Coosanisky. Eleven cannon have been seen on the site by divers, lying in a gully 15-20m deep. A wide assortment of shot, including mortar shot, lies scattered about the site along with three anchors, ballast and other wreckage. No hull components have survived though smaller personal pieces may survive buried in pockets of sediment around the wreckage.

The wrecks of the south-west are not the only French vessels to have foundered while attempting to aid the United Irishmen's attempts at revolution. Two years later, in the late spring of 1798, a third frigate, *L'Amite* of Brest, was lost near Sheepland harbour on the coast of Co. Down.[59] The vessel was sailing to Derry, carrying guns to aid the United Irishmen's imminent uprising, when it foundered on the coast. There is a suggestion that the vessel hit an offshore reef before being driven onto the rocky shoreline where it broke up. All on-board were lost except for one sailor who was sheltered in the nearby village of Sheepland. The vessel quickly disintegrated and now consists of a series of iron cannon and cannon balls lying in a shallow, rocky gully north of Ardglass. Local people knew the site of the wreck as the Cannon Hole, as lobster fishermen had seen a number of cannon from the surface. In the 1960s divers from the Belfast SAC dived on the site and found seven cannon, which were cast-iron with trunnions (see Appendix 2). They measured on average 2.7m in length, 0.34m in diameter at the breech, 0.15m at the muzzle and had a 0.10m bore. Six of the cannon were partially buried in the sediment while one was lying loose; it was recovered and found to be a demi-culverin, capable of firing a nine-pound shot. A number of other cannon were later lifted and temporarily deposited on the harbour bed in Ardglass. One of these was erected in the village of Ballyhornan as a jostle stone and is still visible there today. Of the remaining two cannon on the seabed, one was removed illegally from the site in 1995; it was later recovered and is currently undergoing conservation.[60]

Following the failed French invasions of 1796 and 1798, the British initiated a construction programme of new fortifications to monitor shipping around the coast. Among the measures taken was the erection of numerous martello and signal towers as well as increasing the naval presence along the coast. The towers were erected between 1809 and 1814 and extended southwards from Dublin Bay around the south and west coasts, as far north as Lough Foyle in

Derry. Particular emphasis was placed on large bays affording the enemy shelter to disembark troops, notably Lough Swilly, the Shannon estuary and Bantry Bay.[61] One of the naval vessels charged with patrolling the coast was the *Saldanha*, which was wrecked at a great loss to the navy in December 1811. This frigate, built in 1809, was a fifth-rate ship-of-the-line carrying 36 guns. She weighed 951 tons, 44m long with a beam of 12.9m. On 19 November the ship, under Captain W. Pakenham, left Cork to relieve the naval vessel *Endymion*, which was on patrol duties off Lough Swilly. A contemporary letter recounts that at Lough Swilly she met with both the *Endymion* and another vessel, the sloop of war *Talbot*, and sailed westwards on 30 November. Three days later the three vessels met with very heavy weather and the following night the *Saldanha* was wrecked as it was unable to weather the storm at Ballymastoker Bay, on the west side of Lough Swilly. The vessel may have hit rocks at the entrance to the harbour and was then driven ashore where it was totally wrecked and all on-board were lost. Timbers from the wreck were salvaged and used in the construction of the local church.[62] An anchor was found in the 1980s and lies on the coast near the wreck spot. The *Saldanha* was only one of a number of naval vessels to be lost on the Irish coast during this period. Two troop transports, *Rochdale* and the *Prince of Wales*, were wrecked

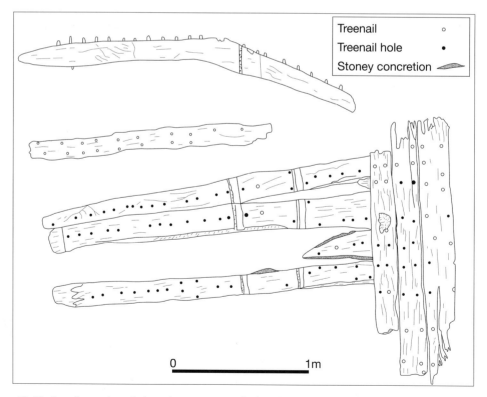

60 Timbers from a late eigtheenth-century wreck, found in Ballycastle Harbour

near Seapoint in Dublin Bay in November 1807 during a north-easterly gale. Over 700 lives were lost and as a result of the ensuing public outcry the east pier was constructed at Dún Laoghaire in 1815 to improve harbour safety.[63]

The English vessels stationed around the coast also attempted to restrict smuggling, which was rife in the decades around the turn of the nineteenth century *(60)*. There had been an increase in duties during the long Napoleonic wars, and with the cessation of the conflict smuggling activities soared. A number of commodities such as tobacco, spirits, tea and silks were highly sought after. Cullen highlights the importance of the Irish Sea area in this business, as it was bounded by rich and bustling seaports and involved the separate customs jurisdictions of Ireland and Scotland, divided by the narrow North Channel.[64] Many small, lightly armed coastal traders were involved in this illicit trade. Most were active on the less well-known stretches of coast and operated at night. This type of activity carried inherent risks and many vessels were wrecked while attempting a landfall. One possible wreck site was surveyed in Derrynane Harbour, Co. Kerry in June 1994.[65] Divers led by Andrew Thoma from the Inbher Sceine SAC found an artefactual spread of six cannon and two anchors lying on the seabed, which was subsequently mapped by IUART *(61)*. Of the guns, the three largest were probably six-pounders. A

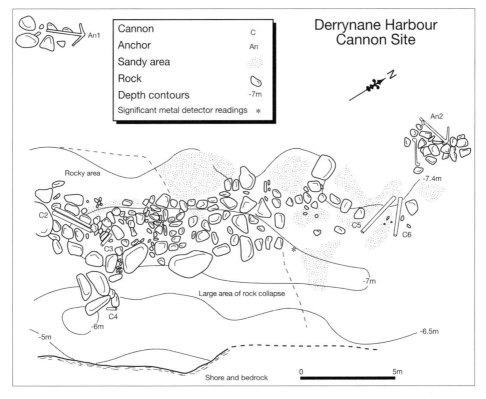

61 Site plan of Derrynane Harbour Cannon Site, Co. Kerry. After Breen, 2000b

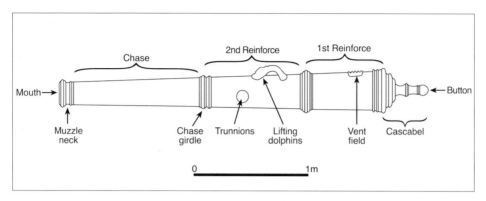

62 Main features of a cannon. *After Breen, 2000b*

fourth is possibly a four-pounder (see Appendix 2). Smaller still are the fifth and sixth guns which are most likely to be carronades, as other small guns, like the fowlers and falcons, had become obsolete in the mid-1600s. As such, the armament and anchors from this site would suggest a date of around 1790 for this wreck site.

This late eighteenth-century date ties in with what is known about smuggling in this locality. At this time the O'Connell's were living in Derrynane and local tradition has it that they were heavily involved in such activities. It is unlikely that anyone other than local mariners would have known about the harbour, least of all try to enter it. It is tempting to suggest that the wreckage on the seabed represents an ill-fated smuggling trip which ended in disaster. The vessel may have been caught in heavy weather and made a run for the harbour. For whatever reason, the wrong entrance was chosen and the vessel was dashed on the rocks.

An artefactual spread of a similar date was surveyed in July 1997 again by IUART divers in tandem with the diving unit from *Dúchas*.[66] The wreck material lay in 34m of water in a deep, rocky gully below the western face of the Little Skellig Island. Six cannon were noted during the course of the survey, five of which were almost certainly carronades that fired three to six-pound cannon balls. The guns were heavily abraded due to the movement of rocks and few distinctive features survived, aside from cascabels and indications of trunnions on one example *(62)*. An anchor was visible south of the main concentration of guns displaying a distinctive arrow-shaped crown, which would date it to pre-1820. This site is believed to be the remains of the *Lady Nelson*, wrecked in October 1809, while sailing from Oporto to Liverpool with wine. Contemporary newspaper reports suggest the vessel was lost off the Lemon Rock, to the south-east of Little Skellig, so the identification of the wreck remains hypothetical.[67]

The battle of Waterloo in 1815 signalled the end of French military interest in Ireland and a period of relative peace from external forces ensued until the two World Wars of the twentieth century. During the course of demobilisation following the war, three vessels were wrecked off the southern Irish coast, in January 1816. The vessels, the *Seahorse*, the *Boadicea* and *Lord Melville* were travelling in convoy from Ramsgate to Cork, transporting soldiers and their families as well as equipment for garrison duty. They got into difficulties when they encountered an easterly gale while crossing the Irish Sea. The *Seahorse*, a 350-ton transport, was carrying five companies of the 2nd battalion of the 59th regiment, and including wives and children the total complement was 394. The mate, who was the only one familiar with the Irish coastline, fell from the rigging and broke his legs and so was unable to guide the vessel effectively. The ship failed to round Brownstown Head near Tramore Bay, Co. Waterford, and foundered about a mile from shore after losing her masts and rudder. Of all the people on-board, only 29 were saved, including the captain. British Admiralty records note that in the 1970s some cannon, which were believed to date to the same period as the *Seahorse*, were found in 10m of water to the south of Glass Island. Seabed movement has since covered the finds, so that no traces are now visible.[68]

The *Boadicea* and the *Lord Melville* were both lost in Courtmacsherry Bay, Co. Cork. The *Boadicea* was a brig also carrying troops from the 2nd battalion of the 59th regiment. It was driven ashore in the bay to the west of the Old Head of Kinsale, with the loss of over 220 lives. The bodies were initially buried in a mound on the beach, but were later re-interred in the churchyard at Old Court on the Old Head. The *Lord Melville*, an 818-ton former East India ship, was carrying men from two regiments – 380 men from the 59th and 90 from the 82nd – as well as a number of horses. It was driven onto rocks after her anchor had parted. A small boat launched from the stricken ship was lost but the majority of those on-board managed to make it safely ashore aided by locals.[69]

INDUSTRIAL SHIPPING

The relative peace of the eighteenth century had seen an impressive growth in Ireland's economy and by 1800 the country's prospects continued to seem promising. Most of the major developments in ship technology were driven by changing economic climates and increased prosperity. Exports had increased dramatically and faster vessels were required, which were able to deliver cargoes quickly in an increasingly competitive commercial environment. One development that facilitated these changes was the Industrial Revolution in the late eighteenth century. Ireland embraced the new technology which had extensive repercussions on transport and economic organisation.[70] The advent of the steam engine, iron hulls and the screw propeller transformed shipping, especially after 1820 when the technology came into widespread use. This period of increased prosperity is reflected in the large volume of coastal trade and shipping witnessed at ports around the island. Much of this trade was involved with importing coal and raw materials, such as iron ore, to drive industry. It also involved the distribution of the by-products of these industries. The booming herring and fishing industries around the coast also contributed to an increase in shipping and led to the emergence and development of many lesser ports and harbours. The early years of this coastal trade was dominated by the well-established wooden sailing vessels such as schooners, brigs, brigantines and snows (see Appendix 1). Literally hundreds of wrecks from this period survive around the coast and bear testimony to the extent of trade in the nineteenth century. An example of one such vessel that has been investigated is the schooner *Nimble*. This Penzance-registered vessel was sailing from Glasgow to Dublin with a general cargo in February 1850. The 77-ton ship, under Captain Savage, was lost when it caught fire in Ballyhenry Bay, Co. Down. Divers and archaeologists from IUART surveyed her wreck in June 1995 *(63)*. The vessel lay in 14m of water at the base of a steep slope, near the entrance to Strangford Narrows. Only the lower part of the hull has survived, with much of the starboard side lying buried in sediment. A large, timber keelson ran from an upstanding stern post for a length of 27m before it became buried in the seabed. Framing and floor timbers ran out from this keelson on the port side and were covered on their underside by copper sheathing. A mast step survived about 12m from the stern post[71]

Wooden sailing vessels continued to be used into the early twentieth century but were doomed once the technology of steam and iron began to develop. Experiments with steam-driven vessels had begun in the late eighteenth century in America, France and Britain, but the first really successful and commercially viable steam vessels were developed in the first decade of the nineteenth century. The steam tugboat *Charlotte Dundas* was built in Scotland in 1801 and has been described as 'the first practical steamboat'.[72] The first merchant steamship, Comet, was built in 1812 again in Scotland. At first steamships were confined to rivers and estuaries, but as the technology improved their use became more widespread and they became increasingly popular. The first steam vessels were paddle steamers, propelled by various forms of paddle wheels placed amidships on a common shaft. By the middle

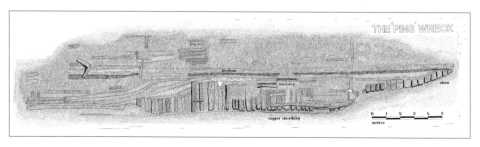

63 Site plan of the wreck of the *Nimble*, Co. Down. *After Breen, 1996b*

of the century the disadvantages of paddle propulsion for ocean-going vessels were limiting progress; these included the vulnerability of the paddle shaft and wheels and the damage incurred to engines in heavy seas. These factors led to the adoption of the fully immersed screw propeller, which proved its superiority in tests around the middle of the century. Although the paddle steamers survived as ocean-going vessels into the 1860s, increasingly they once again became confined to inland waterways.[73]

In 1815, Andrew and Michael Hennessy constructed the hull of the first Irish-built, paddle steamer at their yard in Passage, Co. Cork, although the engine was a British import. A year later they built the hull of a second steamer but this time the engine was made at the Hive Iron Works in Cork city, the first marine engine to be made in Ireland.[74] By 1820 the first steamer had been built in Belfast, its engine being constructed at the Lagan foundry.[75] One early Irish-owned steamship, the *Sirius*, secured her place in maritime history. Built in 1837 in Scotland, she became the first vessel powered by steam to cross the Atlantic from Europe to America. The ship set out from Cork on 14 April 1838, under Lieutenant Richard Roberts, and reached New York 18 days later on 22 April. However, later in 1847 the vessel was lost on the rocks at Ballycotton on the east coast of Cork.[76]

The first iron-built steamer was constructed in Cork in 1845, and in 1847 the Neptune Iron Works for shipbuilding was opened at Waterford.[77] Six years later an iron shipyard was established on Queen's Island in Belfast by Robert Hickson & Co., who appointed Edward Harland as shipyard manager. Harland hired the German draughtsman Gustav Wolff in 1857 and a year later Harland bought the business and formally took over the yard. Wolff proved so capable that Harland took him into partnership in 1867 and so began Belfast's famous shipping firm, Harland and Wolff. It was not the only successful shipping firm to become established in Belfast. Another shipyard, opened by Frank Workman in 1877, steadily expanded when a partnership was formed with George Clark in 1880.[78] By the early years of the twentieth century both Workman Clark and Harland & Wolff were among the UK's leading shipbuilding companies. The two Belfast companies accounted for almost 8 per cent of the world's shipping output by 1914. This period of high growth and productivity was the result of an abundant supply of low-cost, unskilled labour as well as the formal and informal links the companies had with the world's largest merchant shipping fleets, which helped to secure markets.

During the First World War there was a great increase in demand for naval tonnage and for the first time in its history Harland & Wolff received substantial orders from the Admiralty. Despite this, the years between the two World Wars were not good for shipbuilders. After a brief post-war boom, in which the merchant shipping lost during the war was replaced, there was a reduction in the demand for ships across the world. During this period both Harland & Wolff and Workman Clark faced difficulties. Harland & Wolff ran up a number of substantial liabilities and debts, which it was unable to repay. As a result, control of its finances and management were handed over to its creditors, and a modest recovery had been made by 1934. During the same period Workman Clark was not so fortunate. Excess capacity and deficient demand had been compounded by the successful prosecution of a legal case against them, which forced the firm, in 1927, into temporary liquidation. The following year it saw a temporary revival but it finally closed in 1935 when it was taken over by the National Shipbuilders Security Ltd.[79]

COMPOSITE SHIPS

Commercial iron shipbuilding began in the first half of the nineteenth century. In order to produce such vessels there was a need for fundamental changes to ship design. The Industrial Revolution had provided an economic means of producing iron, enabling the development of the steam engine and new technology to begin to address the growing difficulties associated with wooden vessels. These difficulties included a lack of cheap timber for shipbuilding reflecting the depletion of woodlands throughout Europe. The technical limitations of using wood were also becoming evident, single, large components such as stem and stern posts could only be as large as the timber available, this in turn restricted the size of the hull.[80] Iron provided for a much stronger hull and required less internal support so leaving more room for cargo. It had become a common ship-building material in the 1820s but was slow to become widely adopted for a number of reasons including limited availability as well as the fact that iron interfered with ships' compasses. By 1839 the problem with compasses had been solved by a method of placing magnets and pieces of un-magnetized iron around the compass.[81] The use of iron for shipbuilding was also developed in response to the competition between America and Britain in the race to produce faster and safer ships.

In the early days shipyards simply translated wooden components into iron, an inefficient and unsuitable practice that was done away with by up-and-coming, innovative engineers, notably Brunel. Many yards were uneasy about constructing ships completely from iron and so individual iron components were combined with wooden structural elements to form composite ships.[82] Many of the great clipper ships of the later 1800s were composite built, the *Cutty Sark* probably being the most famous example surviving from this period. Iron began to be used for the inner 'skeleton' of the ship to give it additional strength while the outer hull was still planked with wood *(64)*. The wooden hulls were also sheathed in copper to prevent fouling, as iron fouling was still a problem.

As to when composite shipbuilding first developed, there is some controversy. The first patent for the construction of a composite ship was to a Mr William Watson of Dublin in 1839, who proposed the substitution of iron for

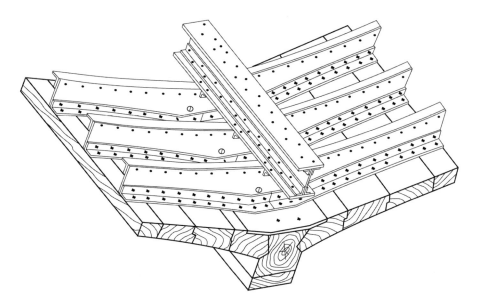

64 Line drawing of composite ship. *After McGregor, 1983*

wood in the framing of a ship. The idea involved using iron T-bars as frames, to which the outer wooden planking was secured using bolts. In the same year the *Assam*, which was described as a composite steamer, was built in India by Captain Andrew Henderson, but no plan exists to qualify this.[83] Throughout the 1840s and '50s a number of patents were applied for to build composite ships. The schooner *Excelsior*, built by Jordan & Getty of Liverpool in July 1850, had iron frames and wooden planking – a method of construction which was patented by Jordan.[84] Two similarly constructed vessels, the barque *Marion Macintyre* and the ship *Tubal Cain*, were built by the same company the following year, in 1851 The *Marion Macintyre* was probably the first composite ship to trade with China, carrying tea in 1853. In January of that year Alexander Hall launched the *Cairngorm* whose main deck beams and half of her hold beams were made of patent iron. The *Red Riding Hood* was the first composite ship launched by Bilbe and Perry of Rotherhithe, London in 1857. They have often been credited with building the first composite ship. Bilbe devised the system of compound frames, which became a common feature of composite ships. Here the spaces between two frames were filled with wood. Bolts attached outer planking to the framing through this filling without ever having to touch metal, reducing the corrosion between copper and iron considerably.[85]

Advances in the use of iron in shipbuilding continued, especially in vessels where speed was not a necessary pre-requisite. Yet despite the advances, there were other factors dictating the use of iron or wooden ships. Vessels involved in the tea trade remained wooden hulled, as it was believed that the condensation or 'sweating', which occurred within iron vessels as they travelled through the tropics, ruined the cargo of tea. It is likely that both the ship owners and builders who were involved in the tea trade kept a close eye on the developments made in the use of iron. There was a great surge in the number of composite vessels constructed in 1862 and 1863 as their advantages over both fully wooden and fully iron ships were realised. Compared with wooden ships they could carry a larger cargo, were stronger, and so lasted longer and delivered their cargo in excellent condition. When compared to iron ships they were lighter and so could travel faster, especially in light winds, and did not spoil their cargo as a result of 'sweating'.

One experimentally-built composite ship that was wrecked off Ireland was the *Taymouth Castle*. It was contstructed in July 1865 in Glasgow by the Connell Company and was subsequently registered with Lloyds in August as an 'A1' ship, indicating that it was in good condition. She was one of the castle line of ships, a series of composite ships all bearing the 'castle' suffix. The *Taymouth* was owned by T. Skinner & Co., of the Glasgow and Asiatic Shipping Company. She was a fully rigged ship, with three masts and square sails measuring 52m in length, 9m in breadth and 5.5m in depth.[86]

The *Taymouth* left Scotland on Thursday 3 January 1867 bound for Singapore. She was under the command of Captain Millen and had a crew of 19 men as well as a number of passengers on-board. It was the vessel's second voyage, her maiden trip had also been to Singapore, and she was carrying a valuable general cargo consisting of spirits, beer, cotton, pottery and saddlery valued at £50,000. Two days later it appears that the ship was caught in severe gales, which swept across the North Channel. She was wrecked that night between Tor Point and Tornamoney Point, near Cushendun on the Antrim coast, and was discovered at daylight the next day by the *Laura*, an Austrian brig. At this stage the ship was almost totally submerged and a dead seaman was seen lashed to the mizzen mast, which protruded above the water. Over the following days, 11 were recovered. Amongst the personal items recovered was a piece of linen inscribed 'Wm. Fullerton, No. 9, Ardrossan', which belonged to one of the sailors aboard the ship.[87]

Little is known about what happened to the wreck subsequently. Local tradition suggests that hard-hat divers carried out salvage on the site in the early part of this century. The wreck was relocated in the 1970s by local sports divers and was heavily plundered over the following twenty years. Divers from the Ballymena SAC, who were researching the wreck, approached the DOE (NI) to highlight the state of the site. Archaeologists subsequently visited and assessed the wreck. In September 1995 a survey and short excavation was carried out by MAU in order to obtain a representative sample of the cargo.[88] The wreck site lies in 15m of water, 70m offshore at the base of steep boulder cliffs. The remains of the ship on the site would suggest that it was heavily damaged and torn apart during the initial wrecking incident *(65)*. Subsequent natural conditions also seem to have played a part in its destruction. A large section of the iron framing was seen to the south of the boulder slope. It was made up of thin iron beams welded together forming a single, complex frame on top of which lay a fragment of iron plating, some 3.5m in length. The iron framing appeared to be the forward body of the vessel. It measured over 7m in width and would have originally been slightly wider at this point conforming to the beam of the *Taymouth Castle*, her maximum breadth being just over 9m at its mid-section. A large windlass was attached to this section at its western end, consisting of a large, cylindrical, iron drum with wooden components lying on a horizontal shaft. A protrusion from its northern end seemed to constitute the remains of the ship's rotary gear. Here bars could have been fitted to enable the windlass to be manually turned in order to lower the anchor. A windlass is normally carried in the fore part of the ship, which would give another indication that this iron framing was part of the bow of the Taymouth. A series of iron links from an anchor chain were visible, concreted on the windlass. These led from the windlass off the iron framing into the sand on the starboard side of the structure. The presence of these links may suggest that during the wrecking, the *Taymouth* tried to drop her anchor in order to keep off the rocks. The anchor either did not hold, or was not strong enough and the ship was subsequently dashed onto the shore.

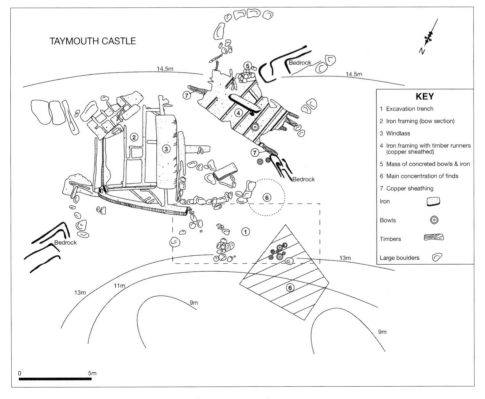

65 Site plan of the *Taymouth Castle. After Breen, 1996b*

A large composite section of iron plating, over 7m in length, lay exposed on the surface directly to the west of the iron framing. Four timber beams lay attached to the underside of this piece. These were copper-sheathed, suggesting that they formed part of the outer ship's hull structure, probably the outer planking. A number of bowls lay in clusters around this section of the wreck. These bowls were part of the original cargo. Each cluster consisted of a number of iron bowls packed inside each other with straw dunnage between the individual bowls. It has been suggested that they were used for cooking rice. The bowls had been concreted together and formed a protective cover over organic material underneath. Excavation of the mound revealed extensive pottery associated with wooden packing cases as well as a number of bottles still corked and retaining their contents *(colour plate 11)*. Preservation of this kind demonstrates the fact that material of a fragile and organic nature can survive on underwater sites, even on the most exposed sections of the Irish coast. This type of survival may be the result of sediment burial, deposition in a deep gully or an unusual type of site formation process like that evident on the *Taymouth* site, where part of the cargo itself protected the delicate material underneath.[89]

The navy also adopted composite-built vessels. The British composite gunboat HMS *Wasp* was built in 1880 by Vickers in England, weighed 465 tons and was 44m long. Although powered by steam she also had schooner-rigged sails. The vessel was armed with two 64-pound guns, two 20-pounders and two machine guns. While on passage from Westport, Co. Mayo, to Moville, Co. Donegal, in September 1884 she hit a rock, *an Feadan*, near the Tory lighthouse. The ship's boats were launched but they were battered by the waves. The ship sank into deeper water leaving only her masts visible. The captain T.J.D. Nicholls and 50 of the crew were drowned. Some of these are buried near the lighthouse. Eight survivors were rescued by HMS *Valliant* and taken to Lough Swilly. In November 1910 the wreck was sold by the Cornish Salvage Company and years later was investigated by divers who recovered a number of artefacts from the wreck site including the ship's bell.[90]

IRON–BUILT VESSELS

Shipyards willing to embrace iron hulls could increase the length of their ships safely, although new methods had to be devised for the internal arrangements. Isambard Kingdom Brunel devised a number of features in the middle of the century, including iron stringers running the full length of the vessel to give longitudinal strength, transverse bulkheads capable of sealing water-tight compartments and an inner and outer bottom, which gave an iron vessel strength throughout its hull.

A number of early iron-built ships were wrecked in Irish waters. The *John Tayleur* was built by the Bankquay foundry near Liverpool in 1853 at cost of

66 The *John Tayleur. After Branigan, undated*

£34,000 *(66)*. She was the largest iron-built, barque-rigged sailing clipper of her time.[91] She had a length of 76m, a beam of 12m, a draught of 6m and had four decks over her lower hold. The vessel was built for the Australian passenger trade by the White Star Line of Australian Packets and was capable of carrying 4,000 tons of cargo. No proper trials were made before she left Liverpool en route for the Australian gold fields on 19 January 1854, carrying 660 passengers and a severely depleted crew of 26 (there was normally 80). Cargo weighing almost 2,000 tons was carried on-board including farm machinery, 40,000 roof slates, 10,000 bricks, slate fireplaces, headstones, crockery, general kitchen items, lamps, linen tinplate and the hull of a river steamer. She quickly encountered severe weather and was driven onto rocks at the south-eastern point of Lambay Island, Co. Dublin, before sinking in deeper water. Almost 400 lives were lost. One passenger managed to reach the shore with a line, by which the rest of the survivors were saved.[92]

A report on the wreck site in 1977 found that the remains were lying on a NNW–SSE axis in 15m of water.[93] The wreckage lay in one section and consisted of iron plates collapsed in on the vessel's ribs. A mast, over 10m long, was still visible lying collapsed on the seabed. A number of girders, plating and other general material were lying around the site.[94] A small boiler with a diameter of around 1.5m lay on top of the wreckage to a height of 1m above the seabed. Much of the cargo was still in situ with roofing slates, around 60 headstones, crockery, wine and beer bottles visible. The seabed adjacent to the wreck was littered with sherds of willow-pattern pottery. The site has been subjected to extensive plundering by divers over the years and much of the material raised from the seabed has been dispersed around the country. A kedge anchor from the wreck was placed in the main street in Rush, Co. Dublin, while a bell from the wreck and a half-model of the ship are kept in the Dublin Civic Museum.

Ironclads were ships with an iron hull or a wooden hull protected with iron plates. The audacious-class ironclad battleship *Vanguard* was lost 12 miles east of Bray Head, Co. Wicklow on 1 September 1875. The vessel was built between 1867 and 1870 in Birkenhead, England, and launched in September 1870. She had three masts and measured over 93m in length with a beam of 18m and a draught of 8m. Weighing 6,034 gross tons, she was powered by twin, steam-powered screw propellers and by sails and was capable of reaching speeds of up to 13 knots. The twin screws were disconnected while sailing, which also allowed the vessel to enter shallow harbours. The *Vanguard* had a double hull, the iron hull was 0.2m thick and this was reinforced in some parts with 0.25m of teak to protect against ramming. The double hull also allowed water to be pumped in or out of the various compartments which greatly added to the safety of the vessel. However, the vessel had no wing passages, leaving the main compartment open to flooding should she be breached above the double bottom. Her armament consisted of an iron ram attached to her bow and an assortment of guns and muzzle-loading rifles.[95]

On the day the *Vanguard* was wrecked she was part of a fleet of five vessels leaving Dún Laoghaire for Cobh. She was captained by R. Dawkin and carried 360 crew and passengers on-board. A heavy fog descended on the vessels after the Kish lightship and the *Vanguard* collided with another ship of the fleet, the *Iron Duke*. The engine room quickly flooded and the crew abandoned the ship, which sank in 70 minutes. Some salvage work was carried out by the Admiralty at the time and it was hoped that she could be raised with cranes. Bad weather hampered the operation and any further attempt to recover the vessel was abandoned. The wreck currently lies in 32-46m of water and stands 15m proud of the seabed. The ship is almost fully intact except for some of the wooden hull components. Her hold, gun ports, davits and the iron base of the mast step have been recorded on site by divers and the double propellers can be seen on the starboard shaft.[96]

In the late nineteenth century, ocean-going steamships took the same form as sailing ships and were rigged to accommodate sails. As steel began to replace iron from the 1870s onwards, the old sailing ships went into decline. The great sailing vessels such as the clipper ships had remained competitive on the long voyages through dangerous seas. The clippers were fast ships, credited with 22 knots, and they also had a greater cargo capacity than steamers in the absence of engines and fuel. However, the additional strength of steel reduced the amount of plating and other metal components required for the hull by 25 per cent.

This lightened the ship and as a result it was more efficient. Steel also enabled more powerful, high-pressure engines to be developed. Compound engines, with one high- and one low-pressure cylinder were introduced in 1854. These improved power and efficiency from 20lb per square inch boiler pressure to 60lb. By 1874 the first triple expansion engine was fitted to a ship, which used steam in three cylinders at 120lb per square inch. The first turbine-propelled vessel was the *Turbinia*, unveiled in 1897. Reaching speeds in excess of 30 knots it was heralded with great acclaim and interest, especially by the navy.[97] The turbine engine's improved power to weight ratio was quickly adopted by shipyards and the navy. The resulting vessels were cheap, reliable and could offer, for the first time, a competitive cargo capacity over the sailing ship. The new technology gave rise to the great period of liners and warships, exemplified in most peoples' minds by the RMS *Titanic*, built in Belfast between 1909 and 1912, and lost in the Atlantic after hitting an iceberg *(67)*. The most famous wreck in Irish waters and one of enormous historical importance is the RMS *Lusitania*. She was lost on 7 May 1915, 11.8 miles south of the Old Head of Kinsale, in 100m of water.[98] The ship was built by John Brown & Co., Clydebank, for the Cunard Line and was launched on 6 June 1906 before making her maiden voyage on 7 September 1907 from Liverpool to New York. She weighed 32,500 tons gross and could reach a speed of 25 knots with

67 Photograph of the *Titanic* at Queen's Island alongside a wooden schooner moored in Victoria Channel, Belfast, 1911. *Courtesy of Ulster Folk and Transport Museum*

68 The *Aud. Branigan, undated*

a 30,000-ton, turbine-driven, quadruple-screw engine. She was 239m long
with a 27m beam and had a draught of 10m. The British government had
given a £2.6 million low-interest loan to the Cunard Line to build two fast
Atlantic liners. In return the Admiralty required that the liners be capable of
24 knots and have all vital gear below the waterline, in addition to having
armour steel protection at the waterline. They also agreed to make an annual
payment to Cunard on the condition that the two ships were capable of being
armed and that the government would have a claim on their services in times
of national emergency. In May 1913, at the Admiralty's request, the reserve
coal bunker forward of boiler No. 1, and a mailroom at the stern were
converted to magazines and shell racking was installed. Twelve revolving
wheels bearing gun rings for six-inch guns were also installed into the deck.
The ship was en route from New York to Liverpool in May 1915 with a crew
of 702 and 1,257 passengers as well as a large general cargo, including
armaments. She was struck on the starboard side by a torpedo fired from a
German submarine U–20, under Captain Schweiger, and this was followed by
another explosion soon afterwards. The ship became unmanageable and sank in
20 minutes with the loss of nearly 1,200 lives. The outrage generated by the
sinking of the *Lusitania* has been considered as one of the factors which led
America into the First World War, given that 124 American citizens perished.[99]

A number of diving expeditions and salvage operations have taken place on
the wreck, carried out by the Admiralty and various international teams.[100]
These have resulted in the propellers being raised as well as an assortment of

shells, spoons and other small objects, some of which are on display at Kinsale Museum. The wreck currently lies 8m proud of the muddy seabed at a depth of 87m. The wreck is leaning to starboard and orientated SW–NE.[101] It has collapsed onto itself as a result of the weight of the longitudinal bulkheads bearing down on weak transverse supports, while the rivets have corroded badly due to galvanic action. This has resulted in the outer hull plates separating and moving. The decks, originally 3m high, are now only 0.6m apart. Modern fishing nets, having snagged on the wreck, drape the upper deck rails. An Underwater Heritage Order was placed on the site in January 1995.[102]

A second wreck, the *Aud*, played a significant if unsuccessful role in recent Irish history and is currently the subject of a second heritage order *(68)*. The frustration at the delay of home rule for Ireland at the beginning of the twentieth century led to the arming of new groups to fight for, or against, Irish independence. In the run up to the Easter Rising the Irish Republican Brotherhood was arming itself with imported weapons; guns had already been landed at Howth and Kilcoole. Roger Casement went to America and on to Germany where he published the Irish cause in the German national newspapers. The Germans, as the French had done before them in 1796, saw an opportunity in the planned insurrection to disrupt the British war effort. They were more cautious than the French enterprise and eventually agreed to send a consignment of arms to be met off the Maharee Islands, Co. Kerry. Originally named *Castro*, the *Aud* had been owned by the Wilson Line of Hull, England. It was captured by the Germans in 1914 and renamed *Libau*.[103] The ship was chosen to carry arms to Ireland and was disguised and renamed the *Aud*, after a vessel which she resembled in tonnage and profile. In April 1916 the vessel set sail from Lubeck for Kerry under Captain Karl Spindler, with 20,000 rifles, three machine guns and one million rounds of ammunition. The *Aud* arrived off Tralee on 20 April, but the pilot boat had been briefed to expect the ship on 23 April off Inis Tuaiscirt. The vessel was sighted by Tralee volunteers but, suspecting it was a British decoy, they waited. After a close encounter with a British ship, Spindler decided to abandon his attempt and return to Germany.[104] However, the ship was intercepted by the British destroyer HMS *Bluebell* off the southern Irish coast. Rather than let her be captured, the crew scuttled the vessel off the Daunt light vessel, Co. Cork, on 21 April. The wreck was later depth charged by the British during the Second World War, as they believed it was a submarine. The vessel currently lies in around 42m of water. Inspections have shown that the vessel is broken up, although her lower hull is intact. A large boiler is lying nearby. The seabed in the vicinity of the wreck is littered with ammunition and other assorted artefacts, many of which have been removed in the past.[105]

The nineteenth century had begun with an expanding economy and thriving coastal trade. Nevertheless, the underlying social and economic situation was precarious. The full extent of this weakness was tragically borne out by the Great Famine and mass emigration. Coastal shipping found new competition in the second half of the century from the expanding railway network and many of the smaller ports suffered stagnation. Recovery only really took hold in the 1890s and it was evident that the large industrial centres such as Dublin and Belfast were the real survivors. These cities had experienced growth and were massive exporters of foodstuffs, textiles and shipping. By the twentieth century, Ireland was playing a full role in international shipping, particularly through her shipyards which were producing the state of the art vessels of the day. In 1907 Harland & Wolff was the world's leading shipbuilding firm, constructing the world's biggest ships in the world's biggest shipyard.[106] Yet, ever since this heyday, the shipping industry in Ireland has been in almost constant decline, so that today the industry is a rather fragile shadow of its former self.

FIVE

VERNACULAR BOATS

Until recently the study of the traditional boats used around the coast and on the inland waterways of Ireland had received little attention. However, a major research project investigating them has been established, the preliminary results of which indicate that about 70 traditional boat types have been in use here over the last 150 years.[1] Many of these working boats have been on the verge of 'extinction' but the concerted effort of a number of individuals and societies has raised interest in them and they are once more becoming popular. The study of these vessels is important as in some cases their ancestry can be traced back to prehistoric times. Certainly the currachs of the west coast and the coracles of the Rivers Boyne and Shannon have their origins in the skin-covered craft of prehistory. The arrival of various peoples to this country has also left its mark in surviving boat traditions. The Vikings in particular have left a legacy of clinker building and a wide range of nautical terminology (see chapter 2). The shallow cots of the south-eastern rivers and the north-western lakes also have had a long ancestry and were adopted to suit their local conditions. Other vessels, such as yawls, zulus and nobbys are more recent arrivals, although they have been developed to cater for a specific need or changing economic conditions. The study of these boats is complex, as the vessels have been and, indeed, are in a continuous state of evolution. Traditional boats were constructed by local builders, or were imported and modified to suit local

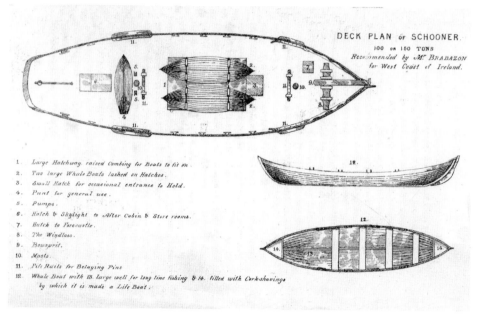

69 Deck plan of a schooner recommended for the West Coast of Ireland. *After Brabazon, 1848*

conditions *(69)*. Unlike industrial shipping where vessels were built to detailed plans and specifications, there was rarely a formal plan for their construction, as the techniques and designs were handed down from one generation of boat-building families to the next. The predominant materials for their construction were wood and skin – either from cattle or horse hides. Many of the boat types lasted for generations while others, which were found to be unsuitable, died out quickly. They were designed to carry out a variety of tasks ranging from inshore and offshore fishing to the transportation of cattle, seaweed, turf and stone. The brief survey of the main wooden and skin-covered vessels which follows demonstrates the diversity and richness of this aspect of our maritime heritage.

SKIN-COVERED BOATS

Currachs/Naomhóg

Few people can fail to be impressed at the sight of a currach moving gracefully over the waves of the Atlantic Ocean. This vessel, which is still widely used along the western seaboard, can trace its ancestry back to the earliest skin-covered boats from prehistoric times and it continues to serve its owners well in this technological age. They are lightly built boats consisting of hides stretched over a wooden, ribbed frame. Currachs were generally used for fishing, kelp gathering or for the ferrying of goods and passengers along the Atlantic coast of Ireland. At first sight the boat appears to be an unsuitable vessel for the rough seas of the west coast, yet its survival through the centuries attests to a very different story. The wooden frame of the boat is flexible yet very strong and its smooth hull allows the boat to glide over the water. Much of its success is due to the skill of the boatmen who row the craft and occasionally sail it with the use of a small sail erected forward in the bow. The methodical study of skin-boats in Ireland was pioneered by James Hornell.[2] In the 1930s, he toured the west coast describing variants of the currach and much of his work has never been superseded.

To what extent the currach has changed and evolved over time is not clear and, likewise, exactly when this boat-building technique first developed in Ireland is also unknown. The earliest evidence indicating the possible use of such vessels is the Broighter boat model, which dates to the first century BC (p. 40). While modern-day currachs bear little resemblance to this representation, their similarity in shape and form is striking when compared to the depiction of a boat on the Kilnaruane pillar stone near Bantry, Co. Cork, which dates to the eighth century AD (p. 52). Documentary sources such as the Law-tracts (p. 45), the *Lives of the Saints* and the voyage tales (p. 47) all refer to such vessels and even give some indications as to how they were built. Details noted by Giraldus Cambrenis (p. 81), O'Sullivan Beare and Gabriel Beranger indicate their continued use in the thirteenth, seventeenth and eighteenth centuries, while Wakefield notes that they were used extensively in the early nineteenth century. In 1811 Wakefield claimed that 9,911 fishermen working in Ireland were operating from:

> the only boats used at present [which] consist merely of a wooden frame,
> covered with a horse's or a bullock's hide.[3]

The Kerry currach, or *naomhóg* as it is more commonly known in the region, is a large example of the craft and arguably the most elegant of the various currachs which are used along the western seaboard *(70)*. Regional variations developed probably as a response to local working needs and the waters of their area. In the 1930s, the Kerry currach had an average length of 7.6m and width of 1.4m. The sheer of the gunwale curved elegantly both fore and aft and the boats carried an average crew of three men. Many of the vessels were fitted with a short mast, less than 4m high, set forward through a thwart. A small mast shoe was nailed onto the ribs to take the mast, which was rigged with a small lug-sail. The sail was tied on a yard and controlled by a sheet and a tack.[4]

The Clare currach – also termed a *naomhóg* – was very similar in form and size to the Aran currachs *(71)*. They differed only in a few minor features such as their near-vertical stem strut, an additional batten along the gunwale to save nets from snagging and an extra thwart at the stern that was employed when hauling lobster pots aboard. Nineteenth-century descriptions of the Aran currach indicate that they varied in length from 2.4m to 7.6m. The smaller

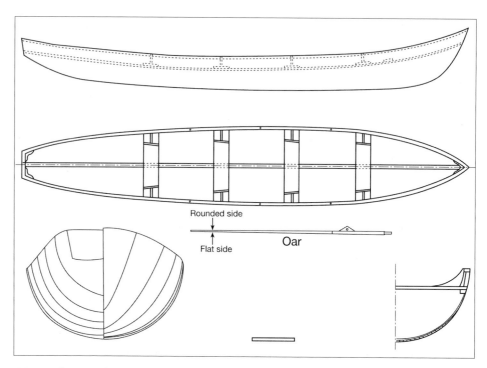

Rounded side

Flat side

Oar

70 Line drawing of a naomhóg. *After Mac Cullagh, 1992*

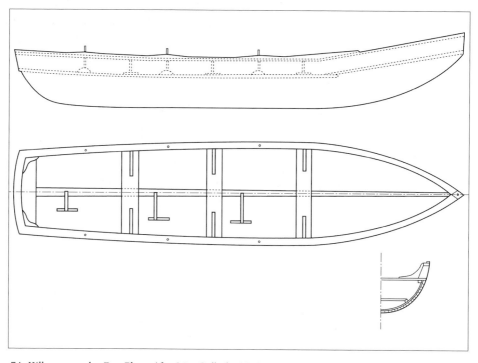

71 Kilkee currach, Co. Clare *After Mac Cullagh, 1992*

vessels had a square transom and pointed bow, and were capable of carrying a crew of three people. The larger carried a four-man crew. Cow hides were used to cover the boats. Hornell describes the boats as having a 'long narrow hull, sharply sheered bows and a low transom stern'.[5] Like the Kerry fishermen, many of the Connemara crews had experimented with wooden boats in the nineteenth century but had also reverted back to the use of currachs on safety grounds. The Connemara boats were smaller than their southern counterparts, averaging between 5-6m long. They carried a double gunwale, had three thwarts and their bottoms were fully planked. Both the Achill Island and Connemara types were closely related.[6]

In North Mayo, from Ballycastle to Broadhaven, the currachs were 2-2.5m long with a double gunwale and their oars were carried between paired thole pins *(72)*. The boats in the Blacksod Bay and Iniskea areas had single gunwales and like the Achill boats used broad-bladed, feathering oars pivoting on a single pin.[7] Along the coast of Donegal the currachs were particularly distinctive *(73)*. They were smaller and more rounded than the currachs to the south, and are often designed to carry a single man. The Tory currachs, for example, were originally designed to be paddled and not rowed. This is unique in the modern skin-boat tradition along the west coast. In the nineteenth century another development occurred in the building of currachs; canvas hulls sealed with tar were adopted to replace the age-old hides. Canvas was far cheaper and easier to obtain and it is still used today. All the currach types described by Hornell still survive and continue to be built by a small number of specialists around the coast. Many of the boats enjoy an active working life, with a small outboard engine being the only concession to modern technology.

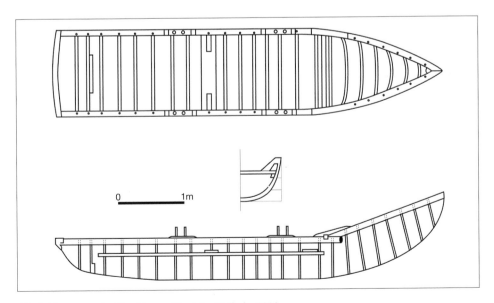

72 Iniskea currach, Co. Mayo. *After Mac Cullagh, 1992*

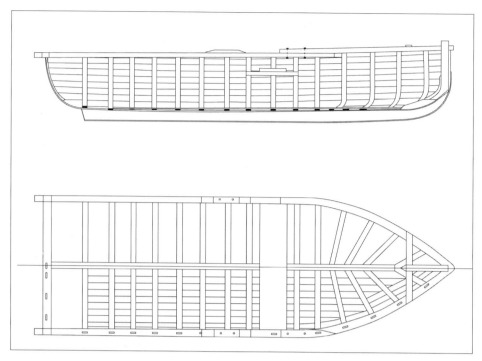

73 Donegal Keel/Stem currach. *Courtesy of H. Madill*

Coracles

Coracles, like currachs, have a long ancestry in Ireland. While currachs were traditionally sea-going craft working in near-shore areas, coracles were used on the inland waterways for fishing and ferrying *(74)*. In 1848 Wakeman described the hulls of coracles on the River Boyne as basket-work, bound with willow rope, and covered with untanned cow or horse hides. The small craft carried a single thwart and was on average 2.4m long. Four years later in 1852 he noted that coracles formed of wattles and covered with cow hides were in use above Lough Ree.[8] The hide was the most valuable part of the boat, while the wooden wickerwork frame was the least durable portion of the boat. The frame suffered from repeated wetting and wear and may have been changed a number of times during the craft's lifetime.

The earliest information regarding coracles is recorded in the Irish law-texts, which differentiate between a small, wickerwork coracle – a clíab and a large boat – a náu (p. 45). Some of these texts indicate that the coracles were covered with single hides – *curach óenseichi* (p. 47). Records from Mellifont Abbey, Co. Louth indicate their continued use for fishing, haulage and carriage during the thirteenth and fourteenth centuries (p. 81), while O'Sullivan Beare describes the construction of one at the beginning of the seventeenth century (p. 107). In the nineteenth century Wakeman noted that the vessels being used by fishermen on the River Boyne included punts, cots and coracles. Wakeman believed that the Boyne coracle was an example of the 'true currach' and he recorded it in detail because he believed that these vessels would be the last to be constructed for use on the river.[9] They were used in the salmon fishery within the estuary and for work on a number of fish traps on the river. They provided a quick and easy means of access to the traps for the collection of fish and the repair of the netting. The boats were built locally but were covered with imported ox hides. During the 1940s the coracles were again regarded as being on the verge of extinction but the tradition of their building has survived and a number of organisations are making them today.

Reed-buoyed craft

While hides and wood are the main materials associated with traditional boat-building, Wakeman refers to the use of bulrushes in the construction of vessels which he describes as primitive and a 'rude substitute for a boat'.[10] These vessels, which were used on Lough Erne, Co. Fermanagh until around 1840, were constructed by using 'wreaths of bull-rushes tied upon a frame, or raft, made of rough branches of trees, or saplings'. Wakeman noted another rush-buoyed craft on Lough Coolermer, near Letterbreen, Co. Fermanagh in the late 1860s.[11] Other examples of reed craft have been reported from counties Leitrim, Longford, Clare and Mayo.[12] As recently as the late 1950s a reed raft was recorded in use on the River Suck, Co. Roscommon.[13] In this case bundles of reeds were fastened together with withies to form a buoyant raft and

74 Coracle. *Photograph: R. McConkey*

support for a light timber superstructure. The craft had a pointed bow and square stern, one centrally placed thwart and two thole pins holding oars. It was designed to carry one man and must have been used primarily for ferrying and for laying nets. The above examples are composite wood and reed craft with the bulrushes providing buoyancy and acting as a water sealant for the craft. Unfortunately no original examples of reed boats survive, but the folklife department of the NMI commissioned a reproduction, which is on display in the new museum of Irish Folklife at Turlough, Co. Mayo *(75).*[14]

Wooden Boats

In his many studies of Irish vernacular craft, Michael McCaughan has identified the 1836 *Report into the State of Irish Fisheries* as a base line for the study of wooden boats.[15] This report was very important as it was the first comprehensive inquiry into coastal communities in Ireland and it recorded in detail their living conditions, maritime activities and types of boats. Results from the study indicate that the average boat size of the Irish fleet was small and that it was mainly engaged in local inshore fishing. The majority of the boats – 73 per cent – were open rowing boats, while 17 per cent were open sailing boats.[16]

75 Turlough reed boat. *National Museum of Ireland*

Few boats were involved in what could be termed offshore fishing as decked sailing vessels represented only 2 per cent of the total fleet. A noticeable difference in boat-building techniques is one of the most striking aspects of the report. The clinker technique of construction dominated along the north-east coast, and was also present along the Cork and Sligo coasts, while the carvel technique was more popular and was recorded everywhere except along the north-east coast.

One of the most interesting areas mentioned in the 1836 report is the Claddagh, the fishing suburb of Galway city. At this time the district had a population of over 2,000 who made their living from the waters of Galway Bay. The community was fiercely traditional and jealously guarded its fishing grounds, and it would go to any extreme to protect them. The fishermen used carvel-built hookers ranging from 6-13 tons burthen. The larger 13 ton vessels were made from oak and had no cabins. They averaged 10.1m long and 9.2m wide. Twenty new hookers were built in the Claddagh in 1835, bringing the Galway fleet to over 100 vessels. The boats were predominantly used for fishing and the transportation of turf and seaweed but they also carried other general cargoes. They fished along the western seaboard and are recorded as fishing off Kerry along with Kinsale hookers in 1804.[17] Hookers have a very distinctive shape, being sturdily built with a raking transom stern and a deep-heeled keel. They were traditionally open or half-decked and their hulls were blackened with tar. The vessels were smack rigged, the larger boats having a foresail and jib and also carrying a strong weather helm.

Galway Hookers

Scott lists four broad local classifications for the most well-known type of hookers, the Galway vessels *(76)*.[18] These are the *Bád Mór* or large boat, the *Leath Bhád* or half boat and the *Gleoiteog* and *Púcán*. The *Bád Mór* averaged 11-13m in length while the *Leath Bhád* was normally about 10m long. The other two vessels had similar lines to the larger hookers but were smaller in size and were generally open and undecked. The *gleoiteog* was normally 7-8.5m long, while the *púcán* was similar in size but rigged differently.[19] Some writers have attributed a Dutch origin to the hookers claiming that the boat developed as a result of contact with Dutch herring fleets, which were common off the coast in the post-medieval period. However, it is more likely that the boat-type developed indigenously around 1790 from smaller local craft.[20] The origins of these smaller prototypes, prior to 1790, are unknown.

The hookers were the most common working boat in the Galway region throughout the nineteenth century. However, with the advent of steam and the development of the road network, the boat slowly began to die out and by the 1960s it was on the verge of extinction. In recent times though, thanks to the efforts of a number of enthusiasts, the hooker is enjoying a revival as evidenced by the numerous hooker regattas on the west coast and the restoration of a number of the boats around the country.

76 Galway Hooker, section and sail plan. *After Scott, 1996*

Kinsale Hookers

While the Galway vessels are the most well-known type of hooker, another regional variation emerged in Kinsale, Co. Cork *(77)*. Like the Galway vessels these may also have Dutch origins. An early reference to hookers in Kinsale dates to 1671.[21] These hookers differed from the Galway type in that they were almost twice as big, ranging from 15-25 tons. They were also deeper and had narrower hulls. Plans published in the *Washington Report* of 1849 into British and Irish fishing vessels show a vessel 12m long, 3m wide with a hold depth of 2m. The vessel carried six men, was smack rigged and cost £120 to build. The Kinsale boats were primarily engaged in offshore line fishing but with the development of the mackerel fisheries after 1860, new boats were introduced from Britain and the hooker slowly became redundant. No Kinsale hookers survive afloat but in the summer of 1996 a team from IUART surveyed the remains of two of these boats in a muddy creek in Cork Harbour. Only the lowermost portion of the hulls of the boats survived allowing tentative reconstructions of their original form.

Yawls/Drontheims

A variety of other wooden boat types were in use in different parts of the country. The terms 'Yawl' and 'Drontheim' both refer to the same type of small boat and both names betray their Scandinavian ancestry *(78)*. Yawl is derived from Yol, and Dronthiem is a local corruption of Trondheim, the Norwegian town which exported the boats following the depletion of Ireland's timber resources in the eighteenth century.[22] The yawl was the common boat in the north-east of the country, working from Newcastle, Co. Down, to

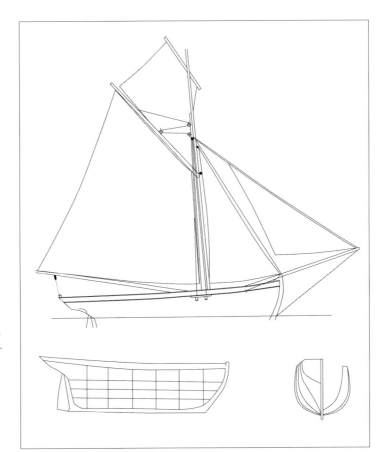

77 Kinsale Hooker,
section and sail plan.
After Thuillier, 2001

78 Plan and side
aspect of a
drontheim. *After
MacPolin, 1999*

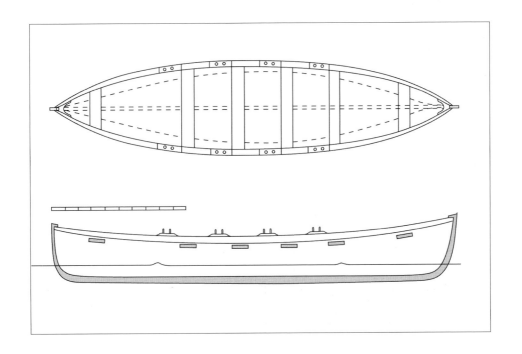

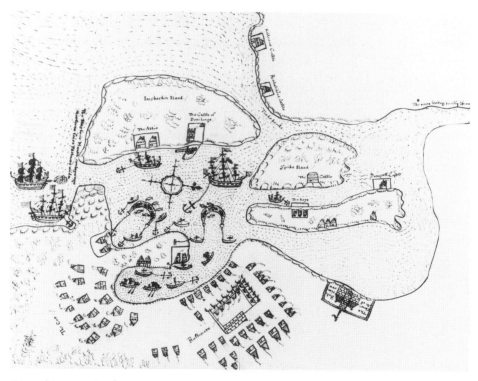

79 Early seventeenth-century folio of Baltimore, Co. Cork, showing seine fishing boats. *Courtesy of Sheffield Archives wwm str p20/100: 8/388/6*

Donegal. They were open, double-ended, clinker-built boats ranging from 5.5-6m long, with a beam of 1.5-1.8m. They were propelled by means of four oars and also carried a set lug or spritsail. Although originally imported from Norway they began to decrease in numbers as local versions were developed, especially during the Napoleonic wars when timber imports ceased. The Norwegians used wide planking but scarce Irish supplies meant narrower planks were cut locally. Irish shipwrights also improved the sailing ability of the boats by straightening the stem and reducing the sheer. The majority of Greencastle yawls spread into Donegal in the 1890s while the 'Druntin Boat' was a popular work boat in recent times in the Portrush area of Co. Antrim.[23] Although they were primarily regarded as the common rowing boat of Ulster, yawls were also popular down the east coast, extending as far as Dublin Bay.[24]

Seine Boats
Seine net fishing is one of the oldest forms of fishing recorded in Ireland. William Petty, writing in 1672, states that 160 gentlemen in Ireland were engaged in seine fishing.[25] Fishing of this type was usually carried out with two boats, the larger leader or seine boat carrying up to 12 oars and the smaller follower or 'faller' carrying four to six oars *(79)*. Both vessels were double-

ended, beamy, open rowing boats and differed only in size. The seine boat was wider and stronger than the faller and had an overall length of about 9m and a beam of about 2m. Seine boat-builders worked on the principle that the boat's length was four-and-a-half times its width. The frames of the boats were made of oak, the keel and stern post of elm, while the rest of its body was made of lighter wood, probably larch *(colour plate 12)*.[26] Copper and later galvanised nails held the planking to the frame. The leader boat was directed out to sea by an experienced fisherman, either standing on the shore or sitting in the stern of the boat. When a shoal of fish was met with, the men were instructed to drop their nets. The leader boat then quickly tried to encircle the shoal with the net while the follower took up the free end of the net and brought it around so that both ends would meet. This method of fishing was particularly common in the south-west of Ireland, but was occasionally seen in the rest of the country.

Nobbys and Zulus
In 1891 the Congested District Board (CDB) was set up to try and develop the infrastructure and economy of Irish coastal communities and, in particular, to develop and upgrade the fishing industry as well as the fishing fleet. The CDB regarded the Irish fleet as being outdated and as a result it introduced a number of new boat types to Ireland, the main ones being Manx nobbys and Scottish zulus. Both were introduced to provide decked, efficient craft for both inshore and offshore fishing. The CDB also brought over instructors to educate

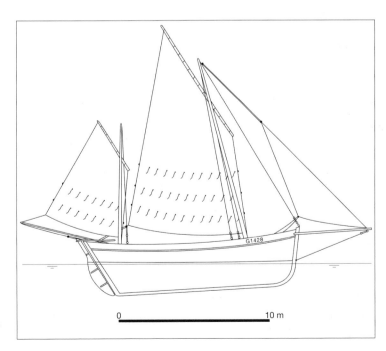

80 Line drawing of a Connemara Nobby. *After Scott, 1996*

local shipbuilders in the construction techniques of the vessels and by 1909 the CDB craft totalled 100 zulus and 87 nobbys.[27]

Of these boat types, nobbys were popular in Connemara, Donegal and along the east coast *(80)*. Soon shipwrights in all these areas began to produce their own versions of the vessels. The nobbys differed greatly from the traditional hooker fishing vessels in both hull form and rigging. They were double-ended with a raked stern and had two masts. Typically they measured some 15m in length and 4.5m in width. They had standing lug sails on their fore and mizzen masts with a jib on a long bowsprit. Their appeal lay in the fact that they could be manned by a reduced crew, and that they were cheaper to build .[28]

The zulu evolved in north-east Scotland and was a broad-beamed, carvel-built boat with a straight stem and raked stern. It was rigged with a dipping lug foresail and standing lug mizzen.[29] In general, Irish zulus were smaller than their Scottish counterparts and measured between 13 and 15m in length. Zulus were favoured in Donegal and Galway. The first Irish zulu was 14m in length and was built at Carna, Co. Galway in 1898. Scott notes a fine example from Inishbofin, Co. Galway whose hull resembled that of a nobby but was narrower and had a more acutely raked stern.[30]

SIX

CONCLUSION

It was stated from the outset of this book that this was not meant to be a definitive study of the history or archaeology of boats and shipwrecks in Ireland. Rather it was written as an introductory study to the subject and will hopefully stimulate further research in this area. The study of this material has a great deal to offer to the study of past maritime traditions on the island of Ireland. Boat and shipwreck remains are tangible links to past coastal activities, which have been largely forgotten, in contemporary Ireland. The dominance of post-medieval English naval activity and later the inward looking nature of the government of newly independent Ireland caused the population of the island to turn away from the sea. The advent of modernity and the general decline in Irish shipping also contributed to this process. There was also a general sense that many of the shipwrecks in Irish waters were of continental origin and were therefore of limited interest to Ireland's cultural past. This view failed to recognise the international nature of maritime traditions and the global context of past trade and communications. Ireland has always played an important role in the Atlantic world in terms of its geographical position in both strategic and economic terms. Its fishery resources greatly contributed to this importance and have attracted visiting fishing fleets for millennia. Many countries in Europe have recognised its strategic importance in terms of creating a bridgehead into Britain and the island has consequently been witness to numerous invasion attempts. Later Ireland played an important role in the development of transatlantic shipping and the movement of large sections of the population across the Atlantic to North America.

While shipwrecks are an important indicator of external contact, boats provide evidence of past activity in a local world context. It is important to appreciate the many scales and levels of activity that were in evidence along the coast. While the large ports of Dublin and Belfast were engaging with the broader North Atlantic world there were many hundreds of other lesser ports and landing places operating within their own areas. In these areas much smaller and often locally built vessels plied their trade up and down the coast. Locally built vessels fished the nearshore waters and their construction reflected the local environment and coastal conditions. However, all of these vessels, from the smallest coracle to the largest warship, were but part of a much broader maritime landscape. A landscape that has many different characters and personalities but which is dynamic, successful and infinitely interesting. Research must continue into these nautical artefacts but all the time recognise that they are but one constituent part of a far broader cultural mosaic. The study of the craft themselves is not an end in itself but rather one piece of a greater story.

The study of boats and shipwrecks in Ireland is in its formative phase. For the first time government is investing in the quantification of the resource and universities and interest groups are advancing studies into particular aspects of the resource. Much however, needs to be done. In terms of the shipwreck resource dedicated programmes of site location and landscape mapping need to continue and expand. In situ site recording utilising the most advanced high resolution marine survey equipment combined with diver survey are important and other researchers from disparate backgrounds need to be integrated into this work. The generation of survey data for management and conservation purposes is important but it is also imperative that research questions and methodologies are formulated. This is ultimately an archaeological and historical resource and one that should be placed not only in a conservation framework but also a research one.

Developing conservation and preservation strategies for the resource is critical. It is not enough to simply map and record these sites; the process needs to be taken a step further. Active programmes of investigation into suitable conservation strategies need to commence recognising the non–renewable nature of this resource and its unique submerged environmental context. Greater integration and recognition of local community and marine user groups needs is also required. The less visible nature of underwater sites has been used in the past to divert attention away from these remains but modern technology and developing knowledge bases negate against this former approach and encourage new and innovative ways of investigating, appreciating and understanding this important resource.

APPENDIX I

SAILING SHIPS AND RIGGING

In the post-medieval period a bewildering assortment of names for sailing boats and ships was introduced. Names like brigs and schooners did not necessarily refer to different hull types and constructional methods, but rather to the different types of rigging that a vessel carried *(81)*. The original arrangement was the square-rig, where the main sails were attached to yards set square to the mast. As vessels increased in size, in the fifteenth and sixteenth centuries, two to three masts were added, all featuring square sails and topsails. A spritsail was fixed below the bowsprit and a spritsail or lateen on the mizzen-mast. In the seventeenth century staysails were added and the jib replaced the bowsprit. The expansion of trade and the further increase in vessel size in the nineteenth century saw elements of the fore-and-aft rig adopted (in use by the Dutch since the fifteenth century) and set on gaffs or stays running longitudinally. The largest most elaborate arrangements of sail and rigging came in the dying years of the great sailing ships. These ships had up to five masts with six-square sails, four jibs, eight staysails and a spanker. The following lists the main types of sailing vessels used during the heyday of sail and tall ships over the last three centuries *(82)*:

Barque	A three or four-masted vessel, square-rigged on the fore-mast and main-mast and fore-and-aft rigged on the mizzen-mast.
Barquentine	A three or four-masted vessel, square-rigged on the foremast only and fore-and-aft rigged on all other masts.

81 Line drawing of a schooner recommended for the west coast fisheries. *After Brabazon, 1848*

Brig	A two-masted vessel, square-rigged on both masts with a gaff sail on the main-mast.
Brigantine	A two-masted vessel, square-rigged on the foremast and fore-and-aft rigged on the main-mast.
Clipper	A fast ship which developed in the middle of the nineteenth century. It had a schooner hull, a raked stem and counter stern, and three square-rigged masts.
Cutter	A small, single-masted vessel with two or more sails carried forward of the mast. In the eighteenth century it carried a gaff mainsail and a square-rigged topsail.
Fully-Rigged	A large, three or four-masted vessel, square-rigged on all masts.
Ketch	A two-masted vessel first developed in England and North America in the mid-seventeenth century. The foremast was taller than the mizzen-mast, which was stepped forward of the rudder-post. Ketches were square-rigged until the nineteenth century, when they were fore-and-aft rigged.
Schooner	A vessel type with many variants, first developed around 1700. By the middle of the eighteenth

century schooners carried two masts with square topsails and up to four foresails on a long, jib boom. Later the vessel adopted a V-shaped amidships section, which was subsequently adopted by yachts, and resulted in long slender vessels. Two to six-masted schooners were common in the nineteenth century, while two-masted, staysail schooners with higher aft masts and three-masted topsail schooners are still sailed today.

Sloop	A single-masted fore-and-aft rigged boat.
Smack	A 15-50 ton ketch-rigged near shore sailing vessel.
Snow	A two-masted vessel rigged as a brig, but with a small try-sail mast abaft the main-mast.
Yawl	A small, clinker-built, two-masted vessel. The foremast is taller and the aft mast stepped behind the steering position.

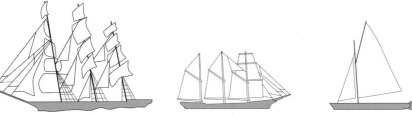

82 Various types of ships: (a) barque. *After Orpana Strand, 1997*; (b) barquentine. After *Orpana Strand, 1997*; (c) brig. *After Orpana Strand, 1997*; (d) clipper. *After Roberts, 1996*; (e) 3-masted Schooner. *After Orpana, Strand 1997*; (f) sloop. *After Roberts, 1996.*

APPENDIX II

SHIPS' ARMAMENTS

Prior to the introduction of gunpowder, naval conflicts consisted of close ship-to-ship fighting. Boarding an opponent's vessel was the main objective of the engagement and a variety of weapons such as longbows, crossbows and spears were used in the initial assault. In the Mediterranean, in the first and second millennia BC, rams were fitted to the front of oared vessels (galleys) to pierce and inflict hull damage on the enemy ship. The rise of the sailing ship sent the ram into decline until the advent of the ironclads in the nineteenth century. Sailing vessels initially used high fore- and after-castles to afford their soldiers a superior fighting position. Grappling irons were used to fasten the ships together and once crews boarded the other vessel hand-to-hand combat with swords and clubs ensued. Essentially such engagements were little more than land battles carried out on mobile platforms at sea. The introduction of gunpowder radically changed the nature of naval warfare. There is a range of names for the ordnance carried on-board ships; from the seventeenth century they were generally referred to as cannon or simply guns. The evolution of weaponry and ballistics is a substantial field of study in itself and the following is intended only as a brief summary.

The Chinese developed gunpowder in the eleventh century AD and it was being used in Europe by the middle of the thirteenth century. Around this time small thunder barrels and falconets were introduced and these light-loading guns were mounted on ship's railings. Heavy cannon could not be mounted on the upper decks or castles for fear of the vessel capsizing. Naval conflict still consisted of close-quarter fighting and the first guns were used primarily as anti-personnel weapons.

The early guns were of bronze or wrought-iron construction and initially were made by blacksmiths and later specialist gun makers. At first complete

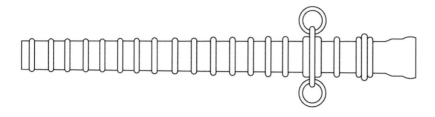

83 Line drawing of a wrought iron gun. *After Martin and Parker, 1988*

barrels could not be cast, the wrought-iron guns featured bars of iron welded together to form a tube and reinforcing rings shrunk to fit over the outside *(83)*. This was in many ways similar to the construction of wooden barrels with staves and rings. Other guns such as the bombardelle were introduced in the late fourteenth century. These guns were placed on a two-wheel carriage and were breech-loading, meaning that a separate chamber holding the powder was placed usually in the rear of the gun while the projectile was placed in the barrel. The kammerbuchsen, introduced in the late fourteenth/early fifteenth centuries, was the first proper ship gun. It was a breech-loading piece, made of reinforced wrought-iron rings, mounted on a block carriage. These early guns had a limited range and were mostly mounted on the fore- or after-castles. They were used in pursuit of enemy ships or for defence purposes during engagements. By the middle of the fifteenth century such guns were common on merchant and military ships throughout Europe. These ordnance pieces fired a variety of shot depending on their size, ranging from stone or iron balls to lead pellets and composite projectiles.

Guns continually developed throughout the fifteenth and sixteenth centuries, giving rise to a plethora of terms that were sometimes interchanged such as drake, basilisk, falcon, serpentine, saker, mortar, perier and base.[1] Technology was advancing, although these weapons were mainly muzzle-loaded – all the materials including the projectile and powder was placed in the muzzle. By the sixteenth century the casting of bronze cannon was proving to be more cost effective and reliable *(84)*. These weapons are often referred to as 'brass guns' as they were made from a copper alloy, primarily copper and tin but also of lead and zinc. The bronze cannon quickly became the predominant larger pieces of ordnance used at sea with the older wrought-iron cannon being discarded on safety grounds. Another major development at this time was the emergence of the hinged, watertight gunport, thought to have been invented around 1500.[2] While gunports did exist prior to this they were difficult to open or close quickly. It was also difficult to make them watertight on clinker-built hulls. The change to carvel construction solved this problem and allowed guns to be mounted on the lower decks reducing their effect on

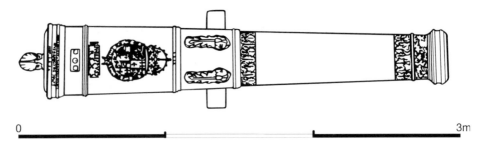

84 Line drawing of a bronze cannon from the *La Trinidad Valencera. After Martin, 1989*

the overall stability of the vessel. The increased size of ships resulted in greater firepower capable of inflicting more damage on enemy vessels without coming into contact. This gave rise to new naval strategies with ships standing off and firing broadsides at each other. This change of naval tactic was grasped early by the English who used it to decisively defeat the Spanish Armada in 1588.

The main classes of ordnance in the fifteenth and sixteenth centuries ranged from the large cannon to the small falcon. The cannon were often ornately inscribed with the maker's name, the owner's name and coat of arms on the barrel. The Royal Cannon was the largest type of gun with a 0.22m bore, firing a 66-pound shot. The cannon was a typically large piece about 3.6m long and with a 0.18m bore. Most experts in this field disagree over the comparative range of guns but a cannon seems to have fired a 60-pound shot. Demi-cannon fired 24-30 pound shot, depending on which authority is accepted while a culverin fired a 17-20 pound shot and a demi-culverin fired a 9-10 pound shot. Culverins measured 2.4-3.6m in length with a 0.13m bore while a demi-culverin measured just over 3m and had a 0.10m bore. A saker was 3m long with a 0.09m bore and fired a 6-pound shot while minions were 2.6m long with a 0.08m bore and 4-pound shot. Falcons were the smallest guns carried on-board and were 2m long with a 0.07m bore and fired a 3-pound shot.[3]

In 1543 the first cast-iron guns were made in England and they were in common use by the late seventeenth century.[4] The iron guns, in common with their bronze counterparts, were muzzle loaded. Cast-iron guns were considerably cheaper to produce than bronze and far greater quantities could be produced. In 1610 the *Prince Royal* became the first English warship to carry guns on three decks.[5] This multi-decked gun arrangement gradually gave rise to another fundamental change in naval battle tactics at sea where ships sailed in a line (giving rise to the term ship-of-the-line) and fired broadsides at the opposing enemy line (see chapter 4). In the middle of the eighteenth century cannon began to be categorised by the size of the balls they fired. The old names such as culverin and saker were discarded and guns were now referred to as 6-pounders, 18-pounders, etc. Other developments included refinements to gunpowder, new arrangements for absorbing recoil and firing, and most significantly the introduction of the carronade. This gun was first made in 1759 in the Carron iron foundry near Falkirk in Scotland. It consisted of a small, light-chambered gun capable of firing a relatively heavy shot.[6] It became popular as it required smaller gun crews and less space. The guns were solid cast and bored and were initially supported by a loop on the underside. The largest carronade developed fired a 68-pound shot and measured just under 1.5m in length while 42, 32, 24, 18, 12 and 6-pounders were also produced.[7] They were adopted widely on both naval and merchant vessels and were only really surpassed by the large iron and steel cannon adopted by European navies in the late nineteenth century. These later guns were developed in response to armoured vessels and resulted in continuous competition between bigger guns and thicker hull plating. Gunnery advances were witnessed in improved propellants, higher muzzle velocity, the rifling of barrels, efficient breech-loading techniques and greater rates of fire. With the new ballistic technology of explosive and armour-piercing shells these developments offered the prospect of accurate and devastating firepower to naval shipping.

NOTES

GLOSSARY

ABBREVIATIONS

BIBLIOGRAPHY

INDEX

NOTES

INTRODUCTION
1 Roddie, 1976.
2 Rule, 1982.
3 Wood-Martin, 1886.
4 Muckleroy 1978; UNESCO 1972.
5 Farrell, 1989.
6 *ibid.*, 226-227.
7 Unpublished, NMS files.
8 C. Martin, pers comm.
9 Breen and Barton, 1998.
10 Williams, 1995.
11 Breen, 1996b.
12 eg., Forsythe *et al.* 2000, Breen 2000a, Brady and Kelleher forthcoming.
13 Breen and Callaghan, 2001; Forsythe 2002.
14 Bourke, 1994, 1998, 2001; Wilson, 1997; Hocking 1969.
15 See Flanagan, 1988b.
16 AU.
17 AFM, 1022.
18 Appleby, 1992; 1985.
19 PRO MPF91.
20 Brady, Shipman and Martin, 1997, 179.

CHAPTER I
Mesolithic
1 Woodman, 1985, 175.
2 *ibid.*, 1986, 34.
3 e.g. Mitchell 1990, 64-65; Woodman, 1994, 94.

4 *ibid.*, 1978, 203, 205; 1994, 96.
5 Hornell, 1938, 148-9.
6 McGrail, 1987, 185.
7 *ibid.*, 86.
8 McGrail, 1998, 56-63.
9 Johnstone, 1980, 17.
10 Clark, 1954, 23, 177-8; McGrail 1987, 34.
11 McCormick, 1999, 359-360.
12 Van Wijngaarden-Bakker. 1985, 131-132; McGrail, 1987, 176; Hornell 1970.
13 AB, 1818, 201.
14 Johnstone, 1980, 27-28.
15 Movius, 1940, 5.
16 Woodman, 1985, 159.
17 Woodman *et al*, 1999, 89.
18 Woodman, 1978, 51; Fry 2000, 116.
19 *ibid.*
20 Based on Lanting and Brindley, 1996, 85, 91; and Fry, 2000, 123-128.

Neolithic
21 Johnstone, 1980, 102-106.
22 *ibid.*, 113.
23 Fry, 2000, 117-118.
24 *ibid.*, 24.
25 Forsythe, 2002.
26 Wilde, 1857, 203.
27 N. Brady, pers comm., anon 2002, 6.
28 Lanting and Brindley, 1996, 91,

Fry 2000, 106.

Bronze Age

29 O'Brien, 2000, 4.

30 Albelda, 1923.

31 Johnstone, 1980, 107-8.

32 Kaul, 1995, 61-3.

33 Sheppard, 1901, 1902, McGrail, 1987, 84.

34 Denford and Farrell, 1980.

35 Watkins, 1980.

36 McGrail, 1987, 132.

37 Wright, 1990, 7.

38 Wright *et al.*, 2001, 732.

39 *ibid.*, 1976, 32.

40 McGrail, 1987, 133.

41 Parfitt, 1993; Marsden, 1997, 27.

42 *ibid.*, 24.

43 Gregory 1998, 32; Robinson *et al.*, 1999.

44 *ibid.*, 906-7.

45 Lanting and Brindley, 1996, 89.

46 Moloney *et al.*, 1993, 127.

Iron Age

47 Lynn 1997, 120-124.

48 McGrail, 1995, 139.

49 Marsden, 1974, 119-122.

50 McGrail, 1995, 140.

51 Nayling *et al.*, 1994.

52 Freeman, 1995, 11.

53 Berthelot, 1934, 34.

54 Hope 1990, 11.

55 see Raftery, 1994; Freeman, 1995; 2001.

56 Natural History, 4, 102-103.

57 Agricola, 24

58 Satire, 2.

59 Agricola, 24.

60 O'Rahilly, 1964, 3-6.

61 Pseudo-Orpheus, 1165-1181; Freeman 1995, 12.

62 Collingwood and Taylor, 1934, 220-1; Ó Ríordáin, 1947, 65; Bateson,

1973, 77.

63 Bateson *ibid.*, 30; Freeman, 2001, 8.

64 Anon., 1925, 137; Kelly, 1983.

65 Farrell and Penny, 1975, 19.

66 *ibid.*, 24.

67 Cochrane, 1902-3, 215.

68 Bowen, 1972, 187.

69 Farrell and Penny, 1975.

70 *ibid.*, 19.

71 Ó hEailidhe, 1992, 185.

72 Farrell 1989, 226-227.

73 Brindley and Lanting, 1991, 70.

74 e.g. Wooding, 2001a, 80.

CHAPTER 2

Early Medieval

1 Bruce-Mitford, 1975, Christensen, 1994.

2 Bruce-Mitford, 1975; Greene 1988.

3 Bruce-Mitford, 1952.

4 Kelly 1997, 7, 13.

5 *ibid.*, 290.

6 *ibid.*, 499.

7 *ibid.*, 55.

8 *ibid.*, 1988, 61.

9 O'Kelly, 1958, 133; White Marshall and Walsh, 1994, 110.

10 O'Kelly, *ibid.*

11 Kelly, 1997, 296-7.

12 *ibid.*, 1988, 150.

13 Sharpe, 1991, 10-12.

14 Anderson and Anderson, 1961; Little 1957.

15 Anderson and Anderson, *ibid.*, 452-455.

16 *ibid.*, 264-5.

17 Binchy, 1978; Wooding 1996, 10.

18 Little, 1957, 76.

19 Wooding. 1996.

20 Anderson and Anderson, 1961, 328-329, 117; Reeves, 1988, 72.

21 Anderson and Anderson *ibid.*, 386-387; O'Meara 1994.

22 *ibid.* 117, 406-407, 282-283.
23 Wooding, 2001a.
24 *ibid.* 444-445; Reeves 1988, 105.
25 Wooding 1996; Pochin Mould, 2001, 18.
26 Sharpe 1995, 125-126; Anderson and Anderson, *ibid.* 246-247.
27 *ibid.* 456-457; Reeves, 1988, 109.
28 Sharpe, *ibid.*, 163.
29 Reeves, 1988, 103.
30 *ibid.*, 50.
31 Reeves, 1988.
32 Stokes, 1995, 335, 258.
33 *ibid.*, 196.
34 Reeves, 1988, 63.
35 Stokes, 1995, 218.
36 *ibid.*, 257, 253.
37 Flangan, 1975, 5; Stokes, 1995.
38 Reeves. 1988, 55.
39 Meyer, 1994, 21.
40 Oskamp 1970, 105, 107
41 Stokes 1893, 51
42 Wooding 2000, xiv; Dumville 2000
43 Reeves 1988
44 O'Meara 1994, 34
45 *ibid.* 36-8
46 *ibid.* 24
47 Kelly 1997, 55
48 O'Meara 1994, 24
49 Severin 1978, 16-17
50 *ibid.* 1977, 774
51 Hourihane and Hourihane 1979, 65; Wooding 2001b
52 Harbison 1992, 254
53 Pochin Mould 2001
54 Hourihane and Hourihane 1979, 69
55 Johnstone 1980, 128, 130
56 Henry 1940,108; Roe 1965; Harbison 1992
57 Johnstone 1980, 128
58 Harbison 1992, 254-255
59 Hourihane and Hourihane 1979, 70
60 Wallace 1941, 155

The Coming of the Vikings
61 O'Corráin 1997, 103
62 *ibid.* 104; Lucas 1966, 71
63 Greene 1978, 121
64 Christensen 1972, Crumlin-Pederesen 1978
65 McGrail 1980, 48
66 Crumlin-Pedersen 1970
67 *ibid.* 1977, 28
68 Brøgger and Shetelig 1951; Sjøvold 1979
69 Olsen and Crumlin-Pedersen 1967
70 Baillie 1978, 261; Bonde 1998
71 Crumlin-Pederson 1978, 36-7
72 Harbison 1992, 16
73 *ibid.* 197-198
74 *ibid.* 48, 94, 148
75 Barrow 1979, 187-190; O'Reilly 1901, 393-394
76 CS; AFM
77 Little 1945, 66, 115-116
78 Gwynn and Hadcock 1988, 43
79 McGrail 1993
80 O'Sullivan 2000
81 Sjøvold 1979, 62; O'Sullivan 2000, 119-120
82 Hurley and Sculley 1997
83 McGrail 1997
84 *ibid.* 636, 638
85 *ibid.* 640
86 Ed Bourke, pers. comm.
87 Christensen 1988, 15
88 *ibid.* 14, 16
89 *ibid.* 17-18
90 *ibid.* 19-23
91 Briggs 1974, 158
92 EHS SMR, 001:080
93 Hencken 1936, 133
94 Lanting and Brindley 1996, 90

CHAPTER 3
High Medieval Period

1 Ellmers 1979; Gardiner 1994

2 Ellmers 1994, 44

3 Marsden 1997, 65

4 Hutchinson 1997, 5; Unger 1994, 8

5 e.g. Crumlin-Pedersen 1972, 190-1

6 Rodgers 1997, 67; Tinniswood 1949

7 O'Neill 1987, 112

8 *ibid.* 116, 108, 111

9 De Courcy Ireland 1986, 70

10 CSPI 1210, 62

11 *ibid.* 64

12 CSPI 1222, 161

13 O'Neill 1987, 112

14 McGrail 1993, 87

15 CSPI 1244, 401

16 O'Neill 1987, 120

17 Bradley 1984

18 Cal. Just. Rolls Irl. Edward I

19 CSPI 1212-13, 74

20 *ibid.* 1225, 188

21 *ibid.* 1210, 67

22 AOC 127

23 O'Neill 1987, 120

24 Riley 1863, 437

25 Armstrong 1913; Strickland 1923, 122, Plate I

26 McGrail 1993, 78

27 P.M.O. 1834; O'Reilly 1901, 393-394; Moore 1996, 162

28 Walton 1992, 6

29 Wallace 1985, 404, 406

30 Spencer 1988, 37

31 *ibid.* 38; Wallace *ibid.*

32 Armstrong 1913, 21

33 McGrail 1993, 96

34 *ibid.* 98; Hutchison 1997, 151

35 McGrail 1997, 638

36 *ibid.* 640

37 Tinniswood 1949, 283-4

38 O'Neill 1987, 109

39 NMS unpublished files

40 MSMR unpublished files

41 O'Meara 1982, 111

42 Stout 1997, 35

43 Lanting and Brindley 1996, 91; Fry 2000

44 Anon 1997, 5

Late Medieval Period

45 Mallory and McNeill 1991, 283

46 O'Neill 1987, 131

47 Barry 1987, 179

48 O'Neill 1987, 131

49 Unger 1994, 8

50 O'Neill 1987, 109

51 De Courcy Ireland 1986, 79

52 O'Neill 1987, 111

53 Cal. Just. Rolls Irl. Edward I

54 O'Keeffe 1958, 28

55 National Maritime Museum, Greenwich, Dartmouth maps 25

56 Hayes-McCoy 1949-53, 158, 164

57 see e.g. MacInnes 1974

58 Steer and Bannerman 1977, 180-2; IJNA 1981, 275

59 Farrell 1978; McErlean et al. 1998, vol. II, 25

60 Chambers 1998, 18

61 CSPI 1599, 335

62 Hunt 1994

63 *ibid.* vol. I, 230, vol. II, 326

64 *ibid.* vol. I, 222, vol. II, 323

65 Armstrong 1913, 36

66 Walton 1992, 25

67 *ibid.* 39

68 Wheeler Cuffe 1901, 37, 56

69 Smith 1969, 140

70 O'Neill 1987, 111; Breen 2001a, 426-427

The Spanish Armada

71 Martin and Parker 1988, 90

72 NMM P/49/31; Glasgow 1966b

73 Fallon 1978, 209

74 Martin and Parker 1988, 63

75 *ibid.* 227

76 Douglas 1978, 4-5

77 Martin 1989, 68
78 Allingham 1894, 179
79 Martin 1989, 65
80 Allingham 1894, 181
81 Birch and McElvogue 1999
82 Flanagan 1988a, 17-18
83 Martin and Parker 1988, 241-2
84 Appleby 1992, 203
85 Roddie 1976, 267-8
86 Branigan undated, 2
87 Martin and Parker 1988, 63
88 Martin 1978, 95
89 *ibid*. 118-122
90 Sténuit 1972
91 Martin 1989, 61, 66-67
92 Flanagan 1988a, 30
93 CSPI 1601-3, 502

Kinsale 1601
94 Boyle-Somerville 1965, 45-50
95 Coombes and Ware 1978, 53
96 Boyle-Somerville *ibid*., 51
97 *ibid*. 52; Byrne 1903, 142-144
98 Coombes and Ware 1978, 50
99 O'Grady 1896, 658
100 Historia Catholicae Iberniae
    Compendium; Hornell 1938, 28-29
101 Hornell *ibid*.
102 NLI Ms. 2656

CHAPTER 4
Post Medieval Period
1 Cullen 1987, 19
2 Scammell 1981
3 Gardiner 1995
4 Scammell 1981, 418
5 *ibid*. 419-420
6 Hope 1990; Marsden 1997;
    Scammell 1981
7 French 1995, 25
8 Hoving 1995, 43-44
9 French 1995, 20
10 McCracken 1970, 67

11 CSPI James I 1613, 360
12 Bourke 1998, 188-9
13 O'Sullivan 1988; Power 1992, 384
14 Anderson 1984, 102
15 Cullen 1987, 12
16 Anderson 1984, 103
17 Appleby 1992, 140, Notes 616-17
18 NMS unpublished files
19 Appleby 1992, 140
20 Breen 1994, 6
21 Bourke 1998, 186
22 Appleby 1992, 179
23 Bourke 1994, 122
24 Hamilton 1847, 248
25 Belfast News Letter,
    14 November 1775
26 Bourke, 1994, 146
27 Brady and Kelleher 1999
28 Brady 2001
29 Wilkinson and Williams 1996, 95
30 *ibid*. 103
31 O'Flaherty 1793, 121
32 Pepys library, Magdalene Colledge,
    Cambridge; MacAlister 1926
33 Fry 2000, 8-9
34 Evans 1989, 238
35 Lanting and Brindley 1996, 91
36 see e.g. Lucas 1963, 66
37 Boate 1726, 37
38 Ware 1745, 47
39 Fry 1995, 13

Modern Shipping
40 Davies 1996, 23-25; Lavery 1989,
    40-41
41 McKee 1972, 234
42 Davies 1996, 23
43 Henderson 1998, 17
44 McKee 1972, 235
45 PRONI 2015/5/5
46 UJA 1901, 30; Belfast Evening
    Telegraph 4 May, 1900; PRO
    D2015/5

47 Belfast Evening Telegraph 4 May, 1900
48 Breen, forthcoming
49 Belfast Evening Telegraph Enniskillen ed. 28 Oct., 1941; PRO 2015/5/5
50 Antiquary's Note Book 1982, 146-147

French Armada
51 Gough 1997, 15-16
52 Kent Archive Office, Pratt Papers, U840/0170/12
53 Boudriot 1993, 409
54 Breen 2001b, 59
55 NMS unpublished files
56 Quinn et al. 2001
57 Breen 1999, 51-53
58 Bourke, 1994, 142-43; Cork City Archive, P. O'Keefe Collection, Box 6, File 32; Box 12, File 8; O'Mahony and Cadogan, 1988, 24
59 Wilson 1997, 37, 143
60 Jeffris and McDonald 1967, 95
61 Kerrigan 1995, 152-5
62 Bourke 1994, 205
63 Bourke 1994, 28, 1998, 53; Gilligan 1980, 43; Irish National Archive, ref. OP/241/15
64 Cullen 1989, 85
65 Breen 2000b
66 C. Kelleher, MSMR unpublished files
67 Liverpool Evening News 1809
68 Admiralty data 1996; Bourke, 1994, 76-77, 92; CSP, 1836, vol. XVII, Appendix No. 7, 280; Cork City Archive, P. O'Keefe Collection, Box 19, File 13
69 Bourke, 1994, 114, 116; CSP 1836; Friday's Mail, London 17.2.1816; O'Sullivan, 1984, 11-12

Industrial Shipping
70 Cullen 1987, 90
71 Breen 1996b, 62
72 Marsden 1997, 105
73 Kemp 1988, 625
74 Bielenberg 1991, 107
75 Moss 1993, 179
76 Bourke, 1994, 95-96, 100; Barry 1920, 22-37; CSP, 1851, vol. LII, 4, 223; Cork Constitution, April 17, 21, May 1, 2, 15, 22 1838; Illustrated London News, 30.1.1847
77 Anderson 1984, 96, 262
78 Moss 1993, 180, 185
79 Geary and Johnston 1989, 43-57

Composite Ships
80 Muckleroy 1980, 91
81 Kemp 1988, 189
82 *ibid.* 790
83 MacGregor 1983, 85
84 Wardle 1948, 131
85 MacGregor 1983, 85-86
86 Breen 1996a, 1996c
87 Belfast Newsletter, 12 Jan. 1867; Glasgow Shipping Register, CE59/11/22
88 Breen, 1996a, 1996c
89 Callaghan and Breen, forthcoming
90 Admiralty Data 1996; The annual register for 1884, 35, 36; Bourke, 1994, 211; Hocking, 1969, 752

Iron Built Vessels
91 MSMR unpublished files
92 CSP 1854-55, vol. XXXIV, 26-27; 1857-1858, vol. LII, 43; Bourke 1994, 15-16; 1998, 40
93 Irish sub-aqua club, NMS files
94 MSMR unpublished files
95 Admiralty data 1996; Bourke 1994, 33, 1998, 162; CSP, 1876, vol. LXVII, 52

96 Featherston 1995, 30–32
97 Kemp 1988, 172; 1978, 190
98 Tapson 1994, 24; Anon. 1995, 19
99 Ballard 1995; Bourke, 1994, 117,
  1998, 161; CSP, 1919, vol. XLII, 6
  (632); Hocking, 1989, 436-7
100 Bourke 1994, 118
101 Ballard 1995
102 MSMR unpublished files
103 Branigan undated
104 Spindler 1965
105 MSMR unpublished files
106 Hope 1990, 339

CHAPTER 5
1 Tully 1999, 33-5

Skin Covered Craft
2 Hornell 1938; 1946
3 De Courcy Ireland 1981, 51
4 Hornell 1938, 29-35
5 *ibid.* 21
6 *ibid.* 14
7 *ibid.* 6-13
8 Wakeman 1872-3, 74
9 *ibid.* 74-6
10 *ibid.* 75-6
11 *ibid.*
12 MacPhilib 2000, 5
13 Delaney 1976
14 MacPhilib, 2000

Wooden Boats
15 McCaughan 1991, 133
16 *ibid.* 1997, 219-31
17 De Courcy Ireland 1981, 51
18 Scott 1996, 19
19 McCaughan 1997, 230; Scott 1996,
  29
20 Scott 1996, 40
21 De Courcy Ireland 1981, 33-35
22 MacPolin 1999, 6
23 *ibid.* 9, 54
24 McCaughan 1988, 35
25 Landsdowne 1937, 30
26 Allihies 1990
27 Scott 1996, 70
28 *ibid.* 121; McGaughan 1997, 231
29 Kemp 1988, 964; White 1950, 45
30 Scott 1996, 70, 73

APPENDIX 2
1 Kemp 1988, 363
2 *ibid.* 362-3; Humble 1983, 42
3 Munday 1998
4 Guilmartin 1994, 149
5 Munday 1998, 9
6 Kemp 1988, 363
7 Lavery 1989, 82-83

GLOSSARY

AMIDSHIPS	The middle of a vessel.
BOW	The forward section of a vessel.
BOWSPRIT	A projecting spar over the bows to hold stays for the foremast and accommodate jibs.
BILGE	Area between sides and bottom of boat.
CAPSTAN	A cylindrical barrel moved manually or engine driven for hauling the anchor.
CARVEL	Construction method where planks are laid edge to edge.
CAULKING	Material inserted between timbers to make the gap watertight.
CLINKER	Construction method where planks are laid partly overlapping each other.
CRANNÓG	A partial or wholly artificial platform constructed in a lake or wetland environment.
DRAFT (DRAUGHT)	The depth a vessel sits in the water.
FLOORS	Transverse timbers in the interior of the boat crossing the keel.
FOREFOOT	The foremost section of a ship's keel
FRAME	A transverse timber set against the side planking, may be a composite timber.
FUTTOCKS	Frames around the bilge.
GUNWALE	A piece of timber attached to the upper strake.
JIB	A triangular sail of the forestays.
KNEE	An angled timber used as a bracket between two timbers.
KEEL	The spine or backbone of a ship or boat.

KEELSON	A longitudinal timber, overlying the keel, running along the centre line of the vessel. It is used to support the weight of vertical mast.
MAST STEP	A fitting for the base of the mast.
PARREL	A wooden device or rope lashing for holding the yard to the mast.
RIB	(As for frame, a single-piece timber).
ROW LOCK	Curved timber or iron piece for holding an oar.
SIDE RUDDER	A large rudder hanging from the side of a ship near the stern.
STAY	Part of the rigging which supports the mast.
STEM	The foremost timber in a vessel.
STERN	The end section of a vessel.
STRAKES	A line of planks on the hull of a vessel.
THOLE	A vertical wooden projection from the sheer line supporting an oar.
THWARTS	Transverse timbers used as seats.
TORC	Torc or neck ring, usually made of twisted gold.
TRANSOM	Timbers which constitute a square stern.
TREENAIL	A wooden peg or fastening.
YARD	A cross-timber on the mast which holds the sail.
ADU	Archaeological Diving Unit

ABBREVATIONS

AFM	*Annals of the Four Masters*
AOC	*Annals of Clonmacnoise*
AU	*Annals of Ulster*
BNL	Belfast Newsletter
CAP	Crannóg Archaeology Project
CCM	*Calendar of the Carew Manuscripts* (London 1870)
CDB	Congested District Board
CFT	*Comhairle Faoi Thoinn* (Irish Underwater Council)
CMA	Centre for Maritime Archaeology
CMAS	*Confédération Mondiale des Activités Subaquatiques*

CRU	Coastal Research Unit
CS	*Chronicum Scotorum*
CSP	Commons Sessional Papers
CSPI	*Calendar of State Papers relating to Ireland* (London 1885)
CZM	Coastal Zone Management
DoE (NI)	Department of the Environment, Northern Ireland
EIC	English East India Company
EHS	Environment and Heritage Service
ES:HMB	Environment Service: Historic Monuments and Buildings
IUART	Irish Underwater Archaeological Research Team
LL	*Lloyd's List*
MAP	Maritime Archaeology Project
MAU	Management for Archaeology Underwater
MSMR	Maritime Sites and Monuments Record
NLI	National Library of Ireland
NMI	National Museum of Ireland
NMM	National Maritime Museum (UK)
NMS	National Monuments Service
OPW	Office of Public Works
RNLI	Royal National Lifeboat Institute
SAC	Sub-Aqua Club
SCUBA	Self-Contained Underwater Breathing Apparatus
SMR	Sites and Monuments Record
VOC	*Verenigde Oostindische Compagnie* (Dutch East India Company)
WIC	*West Indische Compagnie* (Dutch West India Company)

BIBLIOGRAPHY

ABBREVIATIONS:

BAR   *British Archaeological Reports.*

IJNA   *International Journal of Nautical Archaeology.*

JCHAS   *Journal of the Cork Historical and Archaeological Society.*

JRSAI   *Journal of the Royal Society of Antiquaries of Ireland.*

PRIA   *Proceedings of the Royal Irish Academy.*

PRONI   Public Records Office for Northern Ireland

UJA   *Ulster Journal of Archaeology*

A.B., 1818 'An account of the customs, manners and dress of the inhabitants of the Rosses' in Walker, J.C., *Historical Memoirs of the Irish Bards. Dublin.*

Albelda, J., 1923 'Bronzes de Huelva (Espagne)' *Revue Archéologique* 5th ser. **18**, 222-226.

Allihies Folklore Group, 1990 *Seine Boats and Seine Fishing*. Allihies, Co. Cork.

Allingham, H., 1894 'The Spanish Armada: A Spanish captain's experiences in Ulster in 1588', in *UJA* **1**, 178-194.

Anderson, E.B., 1951 (Reprint 1984) *Sailing Ships of Ireland*. Impact Printing, Coleraine.

Anderson, A.O. and Anderson, M.O., (eds.) 1961 *Adomnan's Life of Columba*. Thomas Nelson and Sons Ltd, Edinburgh.

Anon., 1925 'La Tene sword-hilt', in *JRSAI*, 15, 137-138.

    1966 'A Galley on the Shannon' *The Irish Sword*, **7**, (29), 307.

    1982 'Miscellanea, antiquarian reports' *JCHAS*, **87**, 246, 146-47.

    1995 'Diving "The Lusitania" *SubSea*, **80**, (Summer ed.), 19-21.

    1997 'Boyne boat discovered', *Archaeology Ireland*, **11** (3), 5.

    2002 'Gormanston boat discovery' Archaeology Ireland, **16** (3), 6.

Appleby, J.C. (1985) 'The Irish admiralty: its organisation and development, *c.*1570-1640', in *Irish Historical Studies*, **24**, (95), 299-326.

    (ed.) 1992 *A calendar of material relating to Ireland from the high court of admiralty examinations, 1536-1641*. Irish Manuscripts Commission, Dublin.

Armstrong, E.C.R., 1913 *Irish seal-matrices and seals*. Hodges Figgis', Dublin.

Baillie, M.G.L., 1978 'Dating of some ship's timbers from Wood Quay, Dublin', in Fletcher, J. (ed.), *Dendrochronology in Europe*, 259-62. BAR International Series **51**. Oxford.

Ballard, R.D., 1995 *Exploring the Lusitania*. Madison Press, Toronto.

Barrow, G.L., 1979 *The round towers of Ireland a study and gazetteer*. The Academy Press, Dublin.

Barry, T.B., 1987 *The Archaeology of Medieval Ireland*. Methuen, London.

Barry, W. J., 1920 *History of the Port of Cork Steam Navigation*. Guy and Co., Cork.

Bateson, J.D., 1973 'Roman material from Ireland' PRIA, **73**, 21-97.

Berthelot, A., (ed.) 1934 *Festus Avienus, Ora Maritima*. Paris.

Bielenberg, A., 1991 *Cork's industrial revolution 1780-1880: development or decline?* Cork University Press.

Bigger, F.J. and Hughes, H., 1901 'Some notes on the architectural and monumental remains of the old abbey church of Bangor, in the county of Down', *UJA*, **7**, 18-36.

Birch, S. and McElvogue, D.M., 1999 'La Lavia, La Juliana and the Santa Maria de Vison: three Spanish Armada transports lost off Streedagh Strand, Co. Sligo: an interim report' *IJNA*, **28**, 265-276.

Boate, G., 1652 (reprint 1726) *The Natural History of Ireland*. George Grierson, Dublin.

Bonde, N., 1998 'Found in Denmark, but where do they come from?' *Archaeology Ireland*, **12** (3), 24-29.

Boudriot, J., 1993 *The history of the French frigate 1650-1850*. Jean Boudriot Publications, England.

Bourke, E.J., 1994 *Shipwrecks of the Irish coast; 1105-1993*. Dublin.
1998 *Shipwrecks of the Irish coast: 932-1997*, Volume 2. Dublin.
2001 *Shipwrecks of the Irish coast: 1582-2000*, Volume 3. Dublin.

Bowen, E.G., 1972 *Britain and the western seaways*. Thames and Hudson, London.

Boyle Somerville, C.M.G., 1965 'Spanish expedition to Ireland' *The Irish Sword*, **7**, 26, 37-57.

Bradley, J., 1984 *Urban Archaeological Survey – Counties Roscommon and Westmeath* (limited distribution). O.P.W., Dublin.

Brady, K, 2001 'Sutton shipwreck' *Archaeology Ireland*, **15** (3), 5.

Brady, K. and Kelleher, C., 1999 'You're diving me potty!' *Archaeology Ireland*, **13** (4), 22-23.
(forthcoming) *National Inventory of wrecks and wrecking*. Dúchas the Heritage Service, National Monuments and Architectural Protection Division.

Brady, Shipman Martin, 1997 *Coastal zone management: a draft policy for Ireland*. Government of Ireland, Dublin.

Branigan, D., undated *Historic wrecks on Ireland's coasts*. Marine Research, Dublin.

Brabazon, W., 1848 *The deep sea and coast fisheries of Ireland, with suggestions for the working of a fishing company*. James McGlashan, Dublin.

Breen, C., 1994 'The *Pearl*, Trá na Fearla, Allihies', in Bennett, I. (ed.), *Excavations 1993*, **6**. Wordwell, Bray.
1996a 'The excavation of the *Taymouth Castle*' *Archaeology Ireland*, **10**, (1), 30-31.
1996b 'Maritime archaeology in Northern Ireland: an interim statement' *IJNA*, **25**, (1), 55-65.

1996c 'The excavation of a nineteenth-century composite ship' Ulster Local Studies, **18**, (1), 50-58.

(ed.) 1999 'The French frigate *La Surveillante*, lost Bantry bay 1797' unpublished interim report, *Dúchas*.

2000a 'Marine Archaeology', in Buttimer, N. Rynne, C. and Guerin, H., (eds.) *The Heritage of Ireland*. The Collins Press, Cork.

2000b 'An unidentified late eighteenth-century shipwreck in Derrynane Harbour' *Journal of the Kerry Historical and Archaeological Society*, **29**, 135-143.

2001a 'The maritime cultural landscape in Medieval Gaelic Ireland' in Duffy, P.J. Edwards, D. and Fitzpatrick, E., (eds.) *Gaelic Ireland c.1250-c.1650*, 418-435. Four Courts Press, Dublin.

(ed.) 2001b *Integrated marine investigations on the historic shipwreck La Surveillante*. Centre for Maritime Archaeology monograph 1. University of Ulster.

(forthcoming) *The shipwrecks of Northern Ireland*, a historical reference volume. DoE (NI).

Breen, C. and Barton, K., 1998 'Mapping "the Frenchman" in Bantry Bay' *Archaeology Ireland*, **12**, (3), 8-12.

Breen, C. and Callaghan, C., 2001 'The archaeology of post-medieval shipwrecks, harbours and landing places in the Shannon Estuary' in O'Sullivan, A. (ed.) *Foragers, farmers and fishers in a coastal landscape: an intertidal archaeological survey of the Shannon estuary, 1992-7*. Discovery Programme Monograph 5, Dublin.

Briggs, C.S. 1974, 'A boat burial from County Antrim' *Journal of the Society for Medieval Archaeology*, **18**, 158-160.

Brindley, A.L. and Lanting, J.N., 1989/90 'Radiocarbon dates for Neolithic single burials' *Journal of Irish Archaeology*, **5**, 1-7.

1991 'A boat of Mediterranean tradition in Ireland: preliminary note' *IJNA*, **20**, 69-70.

Brøgger, A.W. and Shetelig, H., 1951 *The Viking ships their ancestry and evolution*. Dreyers Forlag, Oslo.

Bruce-Mitford, R.L.S., 1952 'The Snape Boat-grave' *Proceedings of the Suffolk Institute of Archaeology*, **26**, (1), 1-26.

(ed.) 1975 *Sutton Hoo ship burial*, vol. 1. British Museum, London.

Byrne, M.J., 1903 *Ireland under Elizabeth*. Sealy, Bryers and Walker, Dublin.

Callaghan, C. and Breen, C., (forthcoming) 'Investigations on the Taymouth Castle, a 19th Century Composite Ship Lost off the Coast of Northern Ireland'.

Chambers, A., 1998 *Granuaile: the life and times of Grace O' Malley, c.1530-1603*. Wolfhound Press, Dublin.

Christensen, A.E., 1972 'Scandinavian ships from earliest times to the Vikings', in Bass, G.F., (ed.) *A history of seafaring*, 159-80. Thames and Hudson, London.

1988 'Ship graffiti and models', in Wallace, P., (ed.) Miscellanea 1 Medieval Dublin Excavations 1962-81, Series B. **2**. Royal Irish Academy, Dublin. 13-26.

(ed.) 1994 *The earliest ships: the evolution of boats into ships*. Conway Maritime Press.

Clark, J.G.D., 1954 *Excavations at Star Carr*. University Press, Cambridge.

Cochrane, R., 1902-3 'On Broighter, Limavady, Co. Londonderry and the find of gold ornaments there in 1896' *JRSAI*, **23**, 21- 224.

Collingwood, R.G. and Taylor, M.V., 1934 'Roman Britain in 1933' *Journal of Roman Studies*, **24**, 196-221.

Collins, A.E.P. and Seaby, W.A., 1960 'Structures and small finds discovered at Lough Eskragh, Co. Tyrone' *UJA*, 23, 25-37.

Coombes, Rev. J. and Ware, N.J., 1978 'The letter book of General de Zubiaur: a calendar of the 'Irish Letters'' *JCHAS*, **83**, (237), 50-58.

Crumlin-Pedersen, O., 1970 *The Viking Ships of Roskilde*. National Maritime Museum Monographs and Reports 1.
1972 'The Vikings and the Hanseatic merchants: 900-1450' in Bass, G.F. (ed.), *A history of seafaring*, 182-204. Thames and Hudson, London.
1977 *From Viking ship to victory*. National Maritime Museum, Greenwich.
1978 'Ships of the Vikings', in Andersson, T. and Sandred, K.I., (ed.) *The Vikings*, 32-41. University of Uppsala.

Cullen, L.M., 1987 *An economic history of Ireland since 1660*. Batsford, London.
1989 'Smugglers in the Irish Sea in the eighteenth century', in McGaughan, M. and Appleby, J., (eds.) *The Irish Sea aspects of maritime history*, 85-99. The Institute of Irish Studies, QUB and The Ulster Folk and Transport Museum, Belfast.

Davies, D., 1996 *Fighting ships: ships of the line 1793-1815*. Constable, London.

De Courcy Ireland, J., 1981 *Ireland's sea fisheries: a history*. Glendale Press, Dublin.
1983 *Wreck and rescue on the east coast of Ireland*. Glendale Press, Dublin.
1986 *Ireland and the Irish in maritime history*. Glendale Press, Dublin.

Delaney, J., 1976 'Fieldwork in south Roscommon', in Ó Danochair, C., (ed.) *Folk and Farm*, 15-29. Dublin.

Delgado, J.P., 1997 *British Museum: encylopaedia of underwater and maritime archaeology*. British Museum Press, London.

Dempsey, C., 1993 'Recollections of a diver', *The Kinsale Record*, **3**,10-15.

Denford, G.T. and Farrell, A.W., 1980 'The Caergwrle bowl – a possible prehistoric boat model' *IJNA*, **9**, (3), 183-192.

Douglas, K.S., 1978 *A Meteorological Study of July to October 1588: The Spanish Armada Storms*. Climatic Research Unit Research Publication 6.

Dumville, 2000 'Two approaches to the dating of Nauigatio Sancti Brendani', in Wooding, J.M., (ed.) *The otherworld voyage in early Irish literature*. Four Courts Press, Dublin.

Durell, P., 1996 *Discover Dursey*. Ballinacarriga Books, Cork.

ECOPRO, 1996 *Environmentally Friendly Coastal Protection*. Stationary Office, Dublin.

Ellmers, D., 1979 'The cog of Bremen and related boats', in McGrail, S., (ed.) *The archaeology of medieval ships and harbours in Northern Europe*, BAR International Series, **66**, 1-15. Oxford.
1994 'The cog as cargo carrier', in Gardiner, R., (ed.) *Cogs, caravels and galleons:*

The sailing ship 1000-1650. Conway Maritime Press, London.

Evans, E.E., 1989 (6th reprint) *Irish Folkways.* Routledge, London.

Fallon, N., 1978 *The Armada in Ireland.* Stanford Maritime Ltd., London.

Farrell, A.W. and Penny, S., 1975 'The Broighter boat: a reassessment', *Irish Archaeological Research Forum,* **2**, (2), 15-28.

Farrell, A.W., 1978 'The Armagh cross and Dunluce ship representations – some problems of interpretation', *Irish Archaeological Research Forum,* **5**, 47-53.

Farrell, R.T., 1989 'The Crannóg Archaeological Project (CAP), Republic of Ireland II: Lough Lene offshore island survey' *IJNA,* **18**, 221-8.

Fetherston, C., 1995 *Subsea.* (winter), **82**, 30-32.

Flanagan, L., 1974/5 *Girona.* Ulster Museum, Belfast.

1975 'Ships and shipping in pre-Viking Ireland' *Cultura Maritima,* **1**, (2), 3-8.

1988a *Ireland's Armada Legacy.* Gill and MacMillan Ltd. Dublin.

1988b 'Irish annals as a source for maritime history, 1400-1600 A.D.', in MacNiocaill, G. and Wallace, P.F., (eds.) *Keimelia studies in medieval archaeology and history in memory of Tom Delaney,* 500-503.

Forsythe, W., 2002 'Vernacular Boats' in McErlean, T. McConkey, R. and Forsythe, W., (eds.) *Strangford Lough an archaeological survey of the maritime cultural landscape.* Blackstaff Press, Belfast.

2002 'Shipwrecking and maritime casualties in Strangford Lough' in McErlean, T. McConkey, R. and Forsythe, W., (eds.) *Strangford Lough an archaeological survey of the maritime cultural landscape.* Blackstaff Press, Belfast.

Forsythe, W., Breen, C., Callaghan, C., and McConkey, R., 2000 'Historic storms and shipwrecks in Ireland – a preliminary survey of severe synoptic conditions as a causal factor in underwater archaeology' *IJNA,* **29**, (2), 247-259.

Freeman, P.M., 1995 'Greek and Roman views of Ireland: a checklist' *Emania,* **13**, 11-13.

2001 *Ireland and the classical world.* University of Texas Press, Austin.

French, C., 1995 'Merchant shipping of the British Empire', in Gardiner, R., (ed.) *The Heyday of sail: the merchant sailing ship 1650-1830.* Conway Maritime Press, London.

Fry, M., and Martin, A., 1994 'Conservation and copying: logboats, horizontal mills and other larger archaeological timbers from the North of Ireland' *Ulster Local Studies,* **16**, (1), 7-33.

Fry, M., 1995 'Communicating by logboat: Past necessity and present opportunity in the north of Ireland' *Irish Studies Review,* **12**, 11-16.

2000 *Coití: Logboats from Northern Ireland.* Greystone Press, Antrim.

Gardiner, R., (ed.) 1994 *Cogs, caravels and galleons: The sailing ship 1000-1650.* Conway Maritime Press, London.

(ed.) 1995 *The heyday of sail: the merchant sailing ship 1650-1830.* Conway Maritime Press, London.

Geary, F., and Johnston, W., 1989 'Shipbuilding in Belfast, 1861-1986' *Irish Economic and Social History,* **16**, 42-64.

Glasgow, T., 1966a 'The Elizabethan navy in Ireland (1558-1603)' *The Irish Sword*, **7**, (29), 292-307.

1966b 'Elizabethan ships pictured on Smerwick map, 1580' *Mariners Mirror* **52**, 157-165.

Glasson, J., Therivel, R., and Chadwick, A., 1994 (2nd edition) *Introduction to Environmental Impact Assessment*. UCL Press. London.

Gough, H., 1997 'Anatomy of failure', in Murphy, J.A., (ed.) *The French are in the bay: the expedition to Bantry Bay 1796*, 9-24. Mercier, Cork.

Greene, C., 1988 *Sutton Hoo: The Excavations of a Royal Ship-Burial*. Merlin Press, London.

Greene, D., 1978 'The evidence of language and place-names in Ireland', *The Vikings: proceedings of the symposium of the faculty of Arts of Uppsala University*, June 6-9 1977, 119-123. University of Uppsala.

Gregory, N., 1997 'A comparative study of Irish and Scottish logboats'. Unpublished PhD thesis, University of Edinburgh.

1998 'The Lurgan logboat: work in progress – delays expected' *Archaeology Ireland*, **12**, (2), 30-32.

Guilmartin, J.F., 1994 'Guns and gunnery', in Gardiner, R., (ed.) *Cogs, caravels and galleons: The sailing ship 1000-1650*. Conway Maritime Press, London.

Gwynn, A., and Hadcock, R.N., 1970 (Reprint 1988) *Medieval religious houses: Ireland*. Irish Academic Press, Dublin.

Halpin, A., 2000 *The Port of Medieval Dublin*. Four Courts Press, Dublin.

Hamilton, G., 1847 'The cedar ship at Tyrella, Co. Down' *PRIA*, **3**, 248.

Harbison, P., 1992 *The High Crosses of Ireland: an iconographical and photographic survey*. 3 vols. Royal Irish Academy, Dublin.

Hayes-McCoy, G.A., 1949-53 'Medieval and sixteenth century Irish warships' *Irish Sword* **1**, 158.

(ed.) 1964 *Ulster and other Irish maps, c.1600*. Irish Manuscripts Commission, Dublin.

Henry, F., 1940 *Irish Art in the Early Christian Period*. London.

Hencken, H., 1936 'Ballinderry crannóg no. 1' *PRIA*, **43C**, 103-239.

1942 'Ballinderry Crannóg No. 2' *PRIA*, **47C**, 1.

Henderson, J., 1998 *The Frigates*. Wordsworth Editions, England.

Hocking, C., 1969 *Dictionary of disasters at sea during the age of steam, including sailing ships and ships of war lost in action 1824-1962*. Lloyds Register of Shipping, London.

Hope, R., 1990 *A new history of British shipping*. John Murray Publishers, London.

Hornell, J., 1938 *British Coracles and Irish Currachs*. Society for Nautical Research, London. (1946) *Water transport origins and early evolution*. Cambridge University Press. London.

Hourihane, C.P. and J.P., 1979 'The Kilnarune pillar stone, Bantry, Co. Cork' *JCHAS* **84**, (240), 65-73.

Hoving, A.J., 1995 'Seagoing ships of the Netherlands', in Gardiner, R., (ed.) *The*

Heyday of sail: the merchant sailing ship 1650-1830. Conway Maritime Press, London.

Hunt, J., 1994 *Irish medieval sculpture 1200-1600*, 2 vols. Irish University Press.

Hurley, M.F. and Scully, O.M.B., 1997 *Late Viking Age and Medieval Waterford: excavations 1986-1992*. Waterford Corporation.

Hutchison, G., 1997 *Medieval ships and shipping*. Leicester University Press.

Jeffris, R. and McDonald, K., 1967 *The wreck hunters*. Harrap, London.

Johnstone, P., 1980 *The Seacraft of prehistory. Routledge*, London.

Joyce, P.W., 1920 *A social history of ancient Ireland*. M.H. Gill, Dublin.

Kaul, F., 1995 'Ships on Bronzes', in Crumlin-Pederson, O. and Munch Thye, B. (eds.), *The ship as symbol in prehistoric and medieval Scandinavia*. Publications from the National Museum studies in archaeology and history vol. 1. Copenhagen.

Kelly, E.P., 1983 'Bronze sword hilt', in Ryan, M. (ed.) *Treasures of Ireland, Irish Art 3000BC-1500AD*. Royal Irish Academy, Dublin.

Kelly, F., 1988 *A guide to early Irish law*. Dublin Institute for Advanced Studies.
1997 *Early Irish Farming*. Dublin Institute for Advanced Studies.

Kelly, L., 1989 'History of the Port of Tralee', in Kelly, Lucid and O'Sullivan (ed.), *Blennerville: Gateway to Tralee's past*. Tralee, 199-305.

Kemp, P., 1978 *The history of ships*. Orbis publishing, London.
1988 *The Oxford companion to ships and the sea*. Oxford University Press.

Kerrigan, P.M., 1995 *Castles and Fortifications in Ireland 1485-1945*. Collins Press, Cork.

Kirkwaldy, A.W., 1914 *British Shipping, its History, Organisation and Importance*. Kegan Paul, Trench, Trübner, London.

Kirwan, S., 1994 'The Department of Arts, Culture and the *Gaeltacht* and Underwater Archaeology', in *The Future of Underwater Archaeology in Ireland* IUART and QUB Conference Papers.

Lanting, J.N. and Brindley, A.L., 1996 'Irish logboats and their European context' *Journal of Irish Archaeology*, **7**, 85-95.

Lavery, B., 1989 *Nelson's navy the ships men and organisation 1793-1815*. Conway Maritime Press, London.

Lenham, J., Bull, J., Dix, J., and Williams B., 1997 'Surveying submerged sites – remote sensing at Strangford Lough, Co. Down' *Archaeology Ireland*, **11**, (4), 18-20.

Little, G.A., 1945 *Brendan the navigator an interpretation*. M.H. Gill and Son Ltd., Dublin.
1957 *Dublin before the Vikings*. M.H. Gill and Son Ltd., Dublin.

Lucas, A.T., 1963 'The dugout canoe in Ireland the literary evidence' *Varbergs Museum Årsbok*, 57-68. Varberg, Sweden.
1966 'Irish-Norse relations – time for a reappraisal?' *JCHAS*, **71**, 62-75.

Lynn, C.J., (ed.) 1997 *Excavations at Navan Fort 1961-71* by D.M. Waterman. Northern Ireland Archaeological Monograph 3. DOE (NI) Belfast.

MacAirt, S. and MacNiocaill, G., 1983 *The Annals of Ulster* (to AD 1131). Dublin Institute for Advanced Studies.

MacAlister, R.A.S., 1926 'Miscellanea' *JRSAI*, **61**, 119-120.

MacGregor, D.R., 1983 (3rd edition) *The Tea Clippers: Their History and Development, 1833-1875*. Conway Maritime Press, London.

MacInnes, J., 1974 'West highland sea power in the Middle Ages' *Transactions of the Gaelic Society of Inverness*, **48**, 518-556.

MacPhilib, S., 2000 'Rush rafts in Ireland' *Ulster Folklife*, **46**, 1-8.

MacPolin, D., 1999 *The Drontheim forgotten sailing boat of the north Irish coast*. Playprint, Dublin.

MacAlister, R.A.S., 1943 'On graffiti representing ships, on the wall of Moyne Priory, Co. Mayo' *JRSAI*, **83**, 4, 107-117.

McCaughan, M., 1969/70 'The Lough Erne Cot' *Ulster Folk and Transport Museum Year Book*.
1988 'Double-Ended and Clinker-Built the Irish dimension of a European boat building tradition' in Gailey, A., (ed.) *The Use of Tradition*. Ulster Folk and Transport Museum, Belfast.
1991 'The enigma of carvel building traditions in Ireland', in Reinder, R. and Kees, P., (ed.) *Carvel Construction Techniques*. Oxbow Monograph 12. Oxford. 133-36.
1997 'Planked craft of Ireland', in Greenhill, B., (ed.) *Inshore Craft Traditional working vessels of the British Isles*. Chatham Publishing, England.

McCaughan, M. and Appleby, J., (eds.) 1989 *The Irish Sea: aspects of maritime history*. The Institute of Irish Studies, QUB and The Ulster Folk and Transport Museum, Belfast.

MacCullagh, R., 1992 *The Irish Currach Folk*. Wolfhound Press, Dublin.

McCormick, F., 1999 'Early evidence for wild animals in Ireland', in Benecke, N. (ed.) *The Holocene history of the European vertebrate fauna – modern aspects of research*. Verlag Marie Leidorf, Germany.

McCracken, E., 1970 *The Irish woods since Tudor times*. Institute of Irish Studies, QUB, Belfast

McErlean, T., McConkey, R., and McCooey, P., 1998 'A review of the archaeological resources of the Northern Ireland coastline' 2 vols. unpublished DoE (NI) report.

McErlean, T. and Crothers, N., (forthcoming) *Excavations at Nendrum tidal mill*. Northern Ireland Archaeological Monograph.

McGrail, S., 1978 *Logboats of England and Wales*. BAR British Series, **51**. Oxford.
1980 *The Sea-craft of Prehistory*. Routledge, London.
1987 *Ancient boats in North-West Europe*. Longman, London.
1993 *Medieval boat and ship timbers from Dublin*. Royal Irish Academy, Dublin.
1995 'Romano-Celtic boats and ships: characteristic features' *IJNA*, **24**, (2), 139-145.
1997 'The boat timbers', in Hurley M.F. and Scully O.M.B., *Late Viking Age and Medieval Waterford: excavations 1986-1992*. Waterford Corporation.

McKee, A., 1972 'The influence of British naval strategy on ship design: 1400-

1850', in Bass, G.F., (ed.) *History of seafaring*, 225-252. Thames and Hudson, London.

Mallory, J.P. and McNeill, T.E., 1991 *The Archaeology of Ulster from colonization to plantation*. Institute of Irish Studies, Belfast.

Marsden, P., 1972 'Ships of the Roman period and after in Britain' in Bass, G.F., (ed.) *History of seafaring,* 113-132. Thames and Hudson, London.
1994 *Ships of the port of London, first to eleventh centuries AD*. English Heritage, London.
1995 *Ships of the port of London, twelfth to seventeenth centuries AD*. English Heritage, London.
1997 *Ships and Shipwrecks*. English Heritage, London.

Martin, C., 1978 *Full fathom five: wrecks of the Spanish Armada*. London.
1979 'La Trindad Valencera: an armada invasion transport lost off Donegal: interim site report, 1971-76' *IJNA*, **8**, 13-38.
1989 'The Spanish Armada wreck La Trinidad Valencera in Kinnagoe Bay, Co. Donegal', in McCaughan, M. and Appebly, J., (eds.) *The Irish Sea*. Institute of Irish Studies, Queens University Belfast, 61-70.

Martin, C. and Parker, P., 1988 *The Spanish Armada*. Penguin, London.

Marquis of Landsdowne, 1937 *Glenarought and the Petty-Fitzmaurices*.

Meyer, K., 1994 (facsimile reprint) *The Voyage of Bran*. Llanerch Publishers, Felinfach.

Moloney, A., Jennings, D., Keane, M. and McDermott, C., 1993 *Excavations at Clonfinlough Co. Offaly*. Irish Archaeological Wetland Unit Transactions: vol. 2. University College Dublin.

Moore, M. J., 1996 *Archaeological Inventory of County Wexford*. Stationary Office, Dublin.

Moss, M.S., 1993 'Shipbuilding in Ireland in the nineteenth century', in Simon Ville, (ed.) *Research in maritime history*, 177-195. St. John's, Newfoundland.

Morrison, I., 1981 'Hieland gallayis, Scots and Scandinavian traditions' *IJNA*, **10**, (4), 275-6.

Movius, H.L., 1940 'An early post-glacial site at Cushendun, Co. Antrim' *PRIA*, 46C, 1-48.

Muckleroy, K., 1978 *Maritime Archaeology*. Cambridge.
(ed.) 1980 *Archaeology Under Water*. McGraw Hill, New York and London.

Mulvihill, E., 1995 'The Lusitania; a date with destiny' *SubSea*, **80**, 12-15.

Munday, J., 1998 *Naval Cannon*. Shire Album, 186. Buckinghamshire.

Murphy, D., 1896 *The Annals of Clonmacnoise, being Annals of Ireland from the earliest period to AD 1408*. University Press, Dublin.

Murphy, J.A., (ed.) 1997 *The French are in the bay: the expedition to Bantry Bay 1796*. Mercier. Cork.

Murphy, G., (ed.) 1998 *Early Irish lyrics*. Four Courts Press, Dublin.

Nayling, N., Maynard, D., and McGrail, S., 1994 'Barland's Farm, Magor, Gwent: a Romano-Celtic boat' *Antiquity*, **68**, 596-603.

O'Brien, W., 2000 *Ross Island and the mining heritage of Killarney*. NUI Galway.

Ó Corráin, D., 1997 'Ireland, Wales, Man, and the Hebrides', in Sawyer, P., (ed.) *The Oxford Illustrated history of the Vikings*, 83–109. Oxford University Press.

O'Donovan, J., (ed.) 1990 *The Four Masters: annals of the Kingdom of Ireland, from the earliest times to 1616*, 6 vols. De Burca Rare Books, Dublin.

Ó hEailidhe, P., 1992 'The monk's boat – a Roman-period relic from Lough Lene, Co. Westmeath, Eire' *IJNA*, **21**, (3), 185–190.

O'Flaherty, R., 1665 (Reprint 1793) *Ogygia*. Dublin.

O'Grady, S., 1633 (Reprint 1896) *Pacata Hibernia or a history of the wars in Ireland* vol. 2. London.

Ohlmeyer, J.H., 1988 'The Dunkirk of Ireland: Wexford privateers during the 1640s' Journal of the Wexford Historical Society, 12, 23–49.

O'Keeffe, P., 1958 'A map of Beare and Bantry, Co. Cork' in *JCHAS*, **63**, 26–31.

O'Kelly, M.J., 1958 'Church Island, near Valencia, Co. Kerry' in *PRIA*, 59C, 57–136.

Olsen, O. and Crumlin-Pedersen, O., 1967 'Skuldev Ships II' *Acta Archaeologica*, **38**, 73–174.

(1978) *Five Viking Ships from Roskilde Fjord*. The National Museum, Copenhagen.

O'Mahony, C. and Cadogan, T., 1988 'Shipwrecks on the Co. Cork coast up to 1810' *Harbour Lights, Journal of the Great Island Historical Society*, 1, 19–30.

O'Meara, J.J., 1982 *Gerald of Wales the history and topography of Ireland*. Penguin, Middlesex.

1994 *The voyage of St. Brendan*. Four Courts Press, Dublin.

O'Neill, T., 1987 *Merchants and Mariners in medieval Ireland*. Irish Academic Press, Dublin.

O'Rahilly, T.F., 1964 *Early Irish history and mythology*. Dublin Institute for advanced Studies.

O'Reilly, P.J., 1901 'The Christian sepulchral leacs and free-standing crosses of the Dublin half-barony of Rathdown, part III' *JRSAI*, **31**, 385–403.

Ó Ríordáin, S.P., 1947 'Roman material in Ireland' *PRIA*, **51**, 35–82.

Orpana Strand, K., 1997 *The Lore of Ships*. Tiger Books International Plc, Twickenham.

Oskamp, H.P.A., 1970 *The Voyage of Máel Dúin*. Wolters-Noordhoff Publishing, Groningen.

O'Sullivan, A., 1996 *Later Bronze Age intertidal discoveries on North Munster estuaries*. Discovery Programme Reports, **4**, 63–71.

2000 'Medieval boat and ships timbers' in Halpin, A., (ed.) *The Port of Medieval Dublin archaeological excavations at the civic offices*, Winetavern Street, Dublin, 1993. Four Courts Press, Dublin.

O'Sullivan, P., 1984 'The lost ships', *Bandon Historical Journal*, **1**, 10–17.

1988 'The English East India Company at Dundaniel' *Bandon Historical Journal*, **4**, 3–14.

1995a 'Light on air' *SubSea*, **80**, 16–18.

1995b 'The second explosion; was aluminium powder the cause?' *SubSea*, **80**, 25-26.

O'Sullivan, T., 1992 (Reprint 1996) *Bere Island*. Inisgragy Books, Cork.

Parfitt, K., 1993 'Dover Bronze Age Boat' *Current Archaeology*, **12**, 1.

P.M.O., 1834 'Ancient stone or flag' *Dublin Penny Journal*, **3** (128), December 13·

Pochin Mould, D., 2001 'The sailing-ships of ancient Ireland' *Archaeology Ireland*, **15** (1), 14-18.

Power, D., Byrne, E., Egan, U., Lane, S., and Sleeman, M., (eds.) 1992 *Archaeological Inventory of County Cork*. Volume 1: West Cork. Stationary Office, Dublin.

Quinn, R., Rooney, S., Barton, K., O'Hara, D. and Sheehan, K., 2001 'An integrated marine geophysical investigation of the *La Surveillante* wreck-site', in Breen, C., (ed.) *Integrated marine investigations on the historic shipwreck La Surveillante*. Centre for Maritime Archaeology monograph 1. University of Ulster.

Raftery, B., 1994 Pagan Celtic Ireland. Thames and Hudson. London.

Raymond, R.J., 1977 'Privateers and privateering off the Irish coast in the eighteenth century' *The Irish Sword*, **13**, (50), 60-69.

Reeves, W., (ed.) 1874 (Reprint 1988) *Life of Saint Columba*. Llanerch Enterprises, Lampeter.

Reynolds, C., 1995 'The Lusitania and the 90s' in *SubSea*, **80**, 22-24.

Riley, H.T., 1863 *The chronicles and memorials of Great Britain and Ireland during the Middle Ages*. HMSO.

Robinson, M.E., Shimwell, D.W. and Gribbin, G., 1999 'Re-assessing the logboat from Lurgan townland, Co. Galway, Ireland' *Antiquity*, **73**, (282), 903-8.

Roddie, A., 1976 'Jacob the Diver' *Mariners Mirror*, **62**, (3), 63-80.

Rodger, N.A.M, 1997 *The safeguard of the sea a naval history of Britain volume one 660-1649*. Harper Collins, London.

Roe, H., 1965 'Irish High Crosses – Morphology and Iconography' *JRSAI*, **95**, 213-226.

Rule, M., 1982 *The Mary Rose – the excavation and raising of Henry VIII's flagship*. Conway Maritime Press, Leicester.

Scammell, G.V., 1981 *The World encompassed: the first European maritime empires c.800-1650*. Methuen & Co., London.

Scott, R.J., 1996 (3rd ed.) *The Galway hookers*. Boyle, Co. Roscommon.

Severin, T., 1977 'The Voyage of Brendan' *National Geographic*, **152**, (6), 768-797. 1978 *The Brendan Voyage*. McGraw-Hill, New York.

Sharpe, R., 1991 *Medieval Irish saint's lives*. Clarendon Press, Oxford. (trans.) 1995 Adomnán of Iona *Life of St Columba*. Penguin Books, London.

Sheppard, T. 1901 'Notes on the ancient model of a boat and warrior crew found at Roos in Holderness' *Transactions of the East Riding Antiquarian Society*, **9**, 62-74. 1902 'Additional note on the Roos Carr images' *Transactions of the East Riding Antiquarian Society*, **10**, 76-79.

Sjøvold, T., 1979 *The Viking ships in Oslo*. Universitetets Oldsaksamling, Oslo.

Smith, C., 1746 (Reprint 1969) *The ancient and present state of the county and city of Waterford*. Mercier, Cork.

Spenser, B., 1988 'Pilgrim Souvenirs', in Wallace, P. (ed.), *Miscellanea 1 Medieval Dublin Excavations 1962-81*, Series B. **2**. Royal Irish Academy, Dublin. 33-48.

Spindler, K., 1931 (Reprint 1965) *The mystery of the Casement ship*. Anvil books, Tralee.

Steer, K.A. and Bannerman, J.W.M., 1977 *Late Medieval monumental sculpture in the west highlands*. The Royal Commission on the Ancient and Historical Monuments of Scotland. Edinburgh.

Stenuit, R., 1972 *Treasures of the Armada*. Newtown Abbot, London.

Stokes, W., 1890 (facsimile reprint 1995) *Lives of the Saints from the Book of Lismore*. Llanerch Publishers, Felinfach.
1893 'The voyage of Húi Corra' *Revue Celtique*, **14**, 22-69.

Stout, G., 1997 'Fishing at Brú na Bóinne' *Archaeology Ireland* **11**, (3), (supplement), 34-5.

Strickland, W.G., 1923 'Ancient official seals of the city of Dublin' *JRSAI*, **53**, 121 31.

Tapson, S., 1994 'Diving The Lusitania' *Diver*, **39**, (10), 22-25.

Tinniswood, J.T., 1949 'The English galleys, 1272-1377' *Mariners Mirror*, **35**, 276-315.

Troy, B.C., 1988 *Ballycotton wrecks and rescues*, vol. I 1800-1855, vol. II 1855-1900. No publisher supplied.

Tully, D., 1999 'Vernacular boats in Ireland'. Unpublished report for *Dúchas*, Dublin.

UNESCO, 1972 *Underwater archaeology: a nascent discipline*. UNESCO, Paris.

Unger, R., 1994 'Introduction', in Gardiner, R., (ed.) *Cogs, caravels and galleons: The sailing ship 1000-1650*. Conway Maritime Press, London.

Van Wijngaarden-Bakker, L.H., 1985 'Faunal remains and Irish Mesolithic', in Bonsall, C., (ed.) *The Mesolithic in Europe*. John Donald Publishers, Edinburgh.

Wakeman, W.F., 1872-3 'Proceedings' *JRSAI*, **12**, 74-6.

Wallace, J.N.A., 1941 'Carved Stone Pillar at Bantry, Co. Cork' *North Munster Antiquarian Journal*, **2**, (4), 153-5.

Wallace, P., 1985 'The archaeology of Anglo-Norman Dublin' in Clarke, H.B. and Simms, A., (eds.) *The comparative history of urban origins in non-Roman Europe: Ireland, Wales, Denmark, Germany, Poland and Russia from the ninth to the thirteenth century*. BAR **255**, (2), 379-410.

Walton, J.C., 1992 *The Royal Charters of Waterford*. Waterford Corporation.

Watkins, T., 1980 'A prehistoric coracle in Fife' *IJNA*, **9**, 277-286.

Ware, J., 1745 'The Antiquities of Ireland', in *The whole works of Sir James Ware concerning Ireland revised and improved vol. III*. Dublin.

Wardle, A.C., 1948 'The First Composite Ship' *Mariners Mirror*, **34**, 131.

Wheeler Cuffe, O., 1901 'The old gun found in R. Suir, January, 1900' *Journal of the Waterford and South East Ireland Archaeology Society*, **7**, 36-38.

White, E.W., 1950 *British fishing-boats and coastal craft*. HMSO, London.

White Marshall, J. and Walsh, C., 1994 'Illaunloughan: life and death of a small early monastic site' *Archaeology Ireland*, **8** (4), 24-28.

Wilde, W.R., 1857 *A descriptive catalogue of the antiquities of stone, earthen and vegetable materials, in the Museum of the Royal Irish Academy*. Dublin.

Wilkinson, D. and Williams, B., 1996 'The discovery of an early eighteenth-century boat in Lough Neagh' *IJNA*, **25**, (2), 95-103.

Williams, B., 1995 'Coastal zone heritage protection in Northern Ireland' in Dubsky, K., (ed.) *Coastal zone management: from needs to action*, 261-262. Trinity College, Dublin.

2001 'Commercial developments and their impact on maritime heritage: the Northern Ireland experience' *IJNA*, **30**, (1), 5-11.

Wilson, I., 1997 (3rd ed.) *Shipwrecks of the Ulster coast*. Impact Printing, Coleraine.

Wooding, J.M., 1996 *Communication and commerce along the western sealanes AD 400-800*. BAR International series, **654**.

(ed.) 2000 *The otherworld voyage in early Irish literature*. Four Courts Press, Dublin.

2001a 'St Brendan's boat: dead hides and the living sea in Columban and related hagiography', in Carey, J., Herbert, M., and Ó Rian, P., (eds.) *Studies in Irish hagiography: saints and scholars*. Four Courts Press, Dublin.

2001b 'Biblical narrative and local imagery on the Kilnaruane cross-shaft, Co. Cork', in Redknap, M., Edwards, N., Youngs, S., Lane, A., and Knight, J., (eds.) *Pattern and purpose in insular art*. Oxbow Books, Oxford.

Woodman, P.C., 1978 *The Mesolithic in Ireland*. BAR, **58**. Oxford.

1986 'Man's first appearance in Ireland and his importance in the colonization process', in Sleeman, D.P., Devoy, R.J. and Woodman, P.C., (eds.) *Proceedings of the Postglacial Colonization Conference*. Irish Biogeographical Society.

1985 *Excavations at Mount Sandel 1973-77*. Northern Ireland Archaeological Monographs 2.

1981 (reprint 1994) 'The post-glacial colonisation of Ireland: the human factors', in Ó Corráin, D., (ed.) *Irish Antiquity*. Four Courts Press. Dublin.

Woodman, P.C., Anderson, E. and Finlay, N., 1999 *Excavations at Ferriters Cove, 1983-95: last foragers, first farmers in the Dingle Peninsula*. Wordwell. Bray, Wicklow.

Woodmartin, W.G, 1886 *The Lake Dwellings of Ireland*. Hodges Figgis, Dublin.

Wright, E.V., 1976 *The North Ferriby boats. Maritime Monographs and Reports*, **23**. National Maritime Museum, Greenwich, London.

1990 *The Ferriby boats: seacraft of the Bronze Age*. Routledge, London.

Wright, E.V., Hedges, R.E.M., Bayliss, A. and Van De Noort, R., 2001 'New AMS radiocarbon dates for the North Ferriby boats – a contribution to dating prehistoric seafaring in northwestern Europe' *Antiquity*, **75**, 726-734.

INDEX

If you are interested in purchasing
other books published by Tempus, or in case you have
difficulty finding any Tempus books in your local bookshop,
you can also place orders directly through our website

www.tempus-publishing.com